CONSTRUCTING
EUROPE'S IDENTITY

CONSTRUCTING EUROPE'S IDENTITY

THE EXTERNAL DIMENSION

EDITED BY
LARS-ERIK CEDERMAN

LYNNE
RIENNER
PUBLISHERS

BOULDER
LONDON

Published in the United States of America in 2001 by
Lynne Rienner Publishers, Inc.
1800 30th Street, Boulder, Colorado 80301
www.rienner.com

and in the United Kingdom by
Lynne Rienner Publishers, Inc.
3 Henrietta Street, Covent Garden, London WC2E 8LU

Library of Congress Cataloging-in-Publication Data
Constructing Europe's identity : the external dimension / edited by Lars-Erik
Cederman.
    p. cm.
  Includes bibliographical references and index.
  ISBN 1-55587-872-5 (alk. paper)
    1. Political culture—Europe.   2. Europe—Intellectual life.   3. Europe—Politics and
government—1989–   4. Group identity—Europe.   5. Europe—Ethnic relations.
I. Cederman, Lars-Erik, 1963–

D1055.C59 2000
306'.094—dc21

                                                                      00-034208

British Cataloguing in Publication Data
A Cataloguing in Publication record for this book
is available from the British Library.

Printed and bound in the United States of America

⬁ The paper used in this publication meets the requirements
(∞) of the American National Standard for Permanence of
     Paper for Printed Library Materials Z39.48-1984.

  5 4 3 2 1

Contents

Part Three: Europe's External
Political Identity

Part Four: Europe's Civic Identity

Part Five: Conclusions for
Theory and Policy

Acknowledgments

If I had known what it meant to organize an international conference and edit a book based on it, I probably would never have embarked on these tasks. My inexperience makes me especially grateful, not just for the professional experience but also for the analytical and substantive insights about European integration that I have gained from working with a top-notch team of experts. Without their patience and encouragement, this project could never have been completed.

This project started as a conference, "Defining and Projecting Europe's Identity: Issues and Trade-Offs," held at the Graduate Institute of International Studies (IUHEI) in Geneva. It took many meetings with the director of the institute, Alexander Swoboda, before the main concept was fully articulated and the list of invitations drawn up. Claudine Schwab, also at the IUHEI, assisted in managing the conference and getting the project off the ground. Further advice from Jack Hayward and William Wallace, both at that time in Oxford, also helped pin down the analytical focus.

Throughout the long editorial process, which included commissioning new chapters as well as acquiring permission to reprint one article, I received sustained intellectual and moral support from my friends and colleagues Walter Carlsnaes, Simon Hug, and Iver Neumann. My work has also greatly benefited from the excellent working conditions at the University of California at Los Angeles and at the Robert Schuman Centre for Advanced Studies at the European University Institute. At the latter institution I had many stimulating discussions with Stefano Bartolini, Ron Jepperson, Anna Murphy, and Sidney Tarrow about the project. Their written comments are acknowledged in the chapters below. In addition, Jonathan Lipkin and Andrea Gates provided invaluable editorial assistance that went far beyond mere proofreading. Dan Eades and Leanne Anderson at Lynne Rienner Publishers were instrumental in bringing the project to a successful conclusion. Finally, I am grateful for the financial support from the IUHEI, the Center for German and European Studies at the University of California at Berkeley, and a Jean Monnet Fellowship granted by the Robert Schuman Centre.

Lars-Erik Cederman

1

Political Boundaries and Identity Trade-Offs

Lars-Erik Cederman

The Treaty on European Union, signed at Maastricht, put the question of Europe's identity firmly on the research and policy agendas. According to its first title, the European Union (EU) should strive "to assert its identity on the international scene." But the treaty is only one of several reasons for the current surge of interest in identity-related issues. The ratification crises following the signing of the treaty and the ongoing controversy about the EU's legitimacy have also highlighted the identity issue. In addition, the end of the Cold War has prompted a heated debate about the EU's eastern border, a discussion that is likely to continue for years to come.[1] As more authority is transferred to Brussels without a corresponding increase in the EU's popularity figures, a creeping malaise is undermining the legitimacy of the entire integration process.[2] The golden days of Jean Monnet's functional integration are definitely over.

Realizing this fundamental shift, we attempt in this volume to break new theoretical ground on which to base future theorizing of European integration and identity formation. This task involves reassessing and criticizing the conventional theories of integration, as well as applying theories and concepts drawn from related but hitherto comparatively neglected disciplines, including social theory, anthropology, and the literature on nationalism.

Despite its ostensibly self-evident quality, Europe belongs to the most elusive and contested entities in today's international system.[3] It is certainly not for lack of trying that Europe resists a commonly agreed-upon definition. In the 1960s the pioneering federalist Denis de Rougemont thought (perhaps somewhat prematurely) that he had found the Rosetta stone to European identity: "Here then is a measura-

1

ble fact which depends neither on pride nor our humility as Europeans, one which can be easily verified, the objective data for which can be read off our global atlases and economic maps pending the day when they are photographed by a man-made satellite: *Europe is actually the centre of the world.*"[4] Yet the launching of European satellites has done little to answer the identity question. This does not come as a surprise to William Wallace, who believes that "it is the task of the politician and the lawyer, more than of the geographer or the economist, to reduce . . . loosely defined spaces to precise and bounded territories. The boundaries of Europe are a matter of politics and of ideology."[5] If satellite technology fails to deliver the solution, it might thus be hoped that careful scrutiny of the legal instruments of the European Union would clarify the issue.

Such hopes also prove ill founded: Despite several references to a European identity, the Maastricht Treaty never formally defines the concept. The more recent Amsterdam Treaty adds little in the way of definition. Even though the EU is eager to project its power in world affairs, it remains unclear what the union stands for. Going back to the Treaty of Rome is no more helpful: Article 237 specifies that "any European country is eligible for membership to the EC" but fails to define what "Europeanness" stands for. Given the absence of an explicit legal definition and the plethora of competing identities, it is indeed hard to avoid the conclusion that Europe is an essentially contested concept.[6]

Why bother, then? Is it really necessary to engage in philosophical hair-splitting? As long as the European integration process advances, there appears to be little need to coordinate the notions of Europe that exist in people's minds. From this pragmatic standpoint, Michel Rochard admits to "being rather indifferent to the spurious controversy between the proponents of a federal Europe and those of an intergovernmentalist one. What we are constructing, in fact, has on the face of it no known precedent. . . . Thus let us refer to Europe and wait until it is created before defining it."[7]

As Paul Thibaud has argued, however, such a leap into the dark borders on irresponsibility rather than pragmatism, for while an explicit discussion of identity issues carries with it certain risks, so does its absence.[8] Silences and omissions in identity politics are often as eloquent as heated arguments.

Instead of relying on geographical eyeballing or legalistic inspection, this book adopts an interactive approach to the definitional puzzle. A firmer grasp of Europe's identity (or identities) can be obtained by studying how its boundaries emerge out of specific interactions with the EU's external environment. From this vantage point, the main question becomes how these interactive processes are regulated through inclusionary or exclusionary mechanisms and how such practices drive, and even constitute, the process of identity formation. More specifically, is there a trade-off between the exclusion of "non-European" goods, states, or people on the one hand and the strengthening of the EU's identity on the other hand?

By focusing on the external dimension, this collection of essays contributes to the literature on European identity formation. Although much has been written on the identity issue, so far there has been no book-length study of the EU's processes of boundary building.[9] Moreover, this book adopts a more critical stance with respect to identity formation than is common. Many integrationist politicians and scholars who study institution-building take the desirability of a common European external identity for granted: "Invariably defined in a positive way, [integration] implies the idea of relations transcending the nation-state as well as voluntary cooperation and peaceful change."[10]

This volume, by contrast, assesses not only the benefits but also the potential costs of attempts to assert Europe's identity. Those who try to forge a European identity and to put forward European ideals and values abroad need to consider not only the respective merits of "deepening" and "widening" but also the negative effects of "exclusion" and "dilution." On the one hand, defining too narrow an identity for Europe risks excluding foreign goods, immigrants, and entire countries. On the other hand, a wide and unfocused definition of "Europe" may dilute the very values that the European identity was intended to protect and project in the first place.

More specifically, the EU's structure suggests possible trade-offs associated with each of its three pillars. Since the first pillar, the European Communities, defines the economic core of the union, it is natural to consider the twin specters of trade protectionism and erosion of a European life-style in social and cultural terms. The second pillar, the Common Foreign and Security Policy, presupposes a political identity in external affairs. Will the inclusion of peripheral countries in the European Union undermine the EU's commitment to democracy and human rights and thwart the decisionmaking capacity required to project these values outside its borders? Finally, although the third pillar, pertaining to cooperation in the fields of Justice and Home Affairs, concerns mainly internal aspects of European integration, it also has important external repercussions. Here the possibility of a trade-off between exclusion and identity formation evokes the question of whether Europe's civic identity requires restrictions on the movement of people across EU borders and, if so, what the membership criteria should be.

Before turning to the empirical examples of interaction processes and their potential trade-offs, it is useful to consider the underlying logic connecting exchanges and identity formation. While this volume reinforces the need to disaggregate such processes according to the substantive issue at hand, the next three sections introduce the theoretical background of external identity formation in abstract terms. We start by exploring the notion of boundaries and how they are linked to identity trade-offs, followed by a survey of four ideal-type approaches to identity formation. Then the focus returns to the boundary logic in the light of the four theoretical schemes. Together these sections are meant to provide a general conceptual map before we break up the analysis according to the policy area under scrutiny. After the theoretical discussion, this chapter ends with two sections on the methodological assumptions and a preview of the individual contributions to this volume.

Theorizing Social Boundaries

Social boundaries are the key to interactive identity formation, for in regulating the flows going into and out of a group, these mechanisms shape the collectivity's notion of selfhood. Though using the language of independent and dependent variables can be deceptive given the inherent endogeneity of dynamic processes, it makes sense to think of Europe's identity as our main dependent variable and external interaction as the main independent one. Boundaries, then, mediate between a social organization's inside and outside. While some mechanisms operate inside such entities, there can be no general theory of identity formation without at least a rudimentary notion of boundaries.

How, more precisely, do boundaries shape identities? In order to reduce the complexity of this tricky question, I draw on one of the few political scientists who have analyzed boundary formation explicitly. Because of his interest in social communication, Karl Deutsch traced not only information exchanges but also the hurdles that lie in their way: "What really makes a *boundary* is a sharp drop in the frequency of some relevant transaction flow."[11] Observing that the density of transactions declines with distance, Deutsch studied the particular shape of density curves. While some "step-functions" exhibit a sudden fall in interactions, others, referred to as "threshold boundaries," are smoother.[12]

While replacing the behaviorist notion of interaction frequencies by a focus on an intersubjective measure of identity as the dependent variable, I draw inspiration from Deutsch's boundary curves.[13] Loosely modeled on Deutsch's graphical schemes, Figure 1.1 illustrates a stylized identity trade-off. The horizontal axis marks the openness of any interaction process ranging from exclusion to inclusion along some

Figure 1.1   A Boundary-Mediated Identity Trade-Off

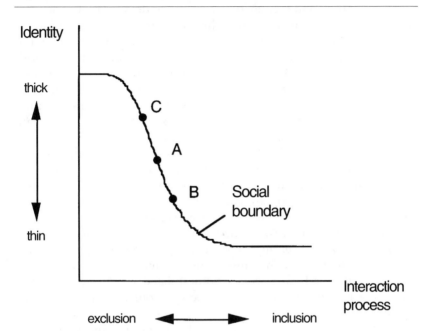

arbitrary dimension of exchange; the vertical one indicates the cultural "thickness" of the resulting identity.[14] Borrowing a dichotomy introduced by Michael Walzer, I define thick identities as those involving a comprehensive functional scope including many cultural aspects of private life. Their thin counterparts, in contrast, are limited to communication within the public sphere and thus to what is absolutely necessary to sustain political communication.[15]

To understand how this particular boundary definition creates an identity trade-off, let us assume that some arbitrary group can be described by the position A on the boundary curve. An attempt to expand the group's scope of interaction by moving to point B will reduce the identity's thickness. This effect captures the trade-off: Under the assumption that the boundary structurally constrains the possible interaction-identity combinations, inclusion can be had only at the price of dilution. Conversely, if the group seeks to "thicken" its identity in transition from A to C, exclusion will be the necessary side effect. In essence, inclusion and intensification of identities cannot be achieved at the same time. Whichever direction is chosen, the result is either dilution or exclusion.

if excl ↑ => thicker identity
if incl ↑ => thinner identity

It goes without saying that the shape of the boundary curve determines the nature, and even existence, of the trade-off. The sharper and more abrupt the boundary's drop, the more dramatic the loss of thickness beyond some level of inclusion. In the case of a vertical line, the boundary marks a razor-sharp, all-or-nothing limit. In contrast, a horizontal line represents the other extreme case. Here there is no boundary effect at all, and as a consequence no trade-off either. The interaction process runs orthogonally to the level of cultural identity formation, and inclusion can be embraced without any concern for cultural dilution.

It may seem that this bare-bones account lacks theoretical relevance, but this is far from the case. In fact, the idea that boundaries contribute to the crystallization of identities is not a new one. Sociologists, social psychologists, geographers, anthropologists, and indeed some political scientists have developed sophisticated conceptualizations along these lines. To start with the latter, no analytical review would be complete without a reference to Albert Hirschman's brilliant *Exit, Voice, and Loyalty,* which explicitly connects the internal structure with boundary mechanisms.[16] It is precisely the postulated negative relationship between "exit" and "voice" that connects a group's internal structure with its external dimension. Yet Hirschman's account is not directly applicable to our main puzzle, since his primary interest concerns movement out of the group rather than entry. In this respect, Stein Rokkan's application of Hirschman's logic to various cases of European state formation offers a more direct example of the exclusion-dilution dilemma. Breaking up his analysis along functional lines, Rokkan articulated mechanisms of boundary control operating according to an economic, cultural, power, or administrative logic. Like the contributors to this volume, he studied barriers to the flow of different units, such as goods, services, information, and people.[17]

To find earlier illustrations of explicit theorizing about boundaries, it is necessary to broaden our search from political science to sociology. Georg Simmel's famous conflict hypothesis offers perhaps the best-known and earliest example of a sociological theory connecting a group's inside with its outside.[18] According to this famous postulate, external conflict increases in-group cohesion. Translated to Figure 1.1, this hypothesis states that exclusion leads to a thicker group identity. Indeed, political scientists have used this idea to explain wars and other cases of political violence.[19] More seldom, however, they have reversed the causal arrows in order to explore the emergence of new and maintenance of already existing boundaries between the conflicting parties.[20] But Simmel's theory goes well beyond the simple but important conflict hypothesis. In fact, Simmel provides arguably the first full-fledged constructivist account of social boundary processes in time and space. To sum up his position using his own words, "The boundary is not a spatial fact with social implications, but rather a sociological fact that forms spatially."[21]

Following in the footsteps of Simmel and early social psychologists, such as George Herbert Mead, modern social theory has picked up the thread and continued to spin an often somewhat convoluted tale involving actors and their "others" interacting their way to selfhood.[22] Building on Pierre Bourdieu's conceptualization of habitus and identity, the German sociologist Bernhard Giesen has developed a theoretical framework for the study of nationalism that helps articulate the central logic of this volume.[23] To place identity into a truly historical perspective, Giesen proposes a process theory that traces boundary-forming practices and mechanisms:

> Boundaries separate and divide the actual multitude of interaction processes and social relations; they mark the distinction between inside and outside, between the foreign and the familiar, kin and alien, friend and foe, culture and nature, enlightenment and barbarism. Precisely because these boundaries are contingent social constructions that could have easily turned out differently, they require social justification and symbolic clarification.[24]

Rather than attempting to distill general principles of boundary formation, Giesen suggests that it is thus more fruitful to explore the "situational construction of difference." This strategy, which is the one informing the structure of this book, requires the analyst to focus on how the actors develop self-images to make sense of particular social environments. Such identities emerge from specific instances of symbolic interaction: "As a result of these communication processes, social structures form such as institutions, boundaries between social groups, etc. Collective identity is thus always a product of social communication processes."[25]

In order to understand the interactive logic of identity formation, then, the attention of the analyst should not be confined to the symbolic sources of internal unity but must be extended to the "ritual of inclusion and exclusion."[26] Whereas in the premodern world, this process boiled down to direct personal contacts, the long-standing trend leading to advances in communication technology has opened the door for abstract, symbolic codes.[27] Niklas Luhmann captures this historical transformation aptly: "Since the late Middle Ages and especially the early modern world, there is a growing trend toward politics of explicit exclusion (which is thus accessible through historical sources). Targeting abstractly defined groups rather than individuals, exclusion no longer remains under the control of households alone, but is part and parcel of the politics of professional organizations and territorial states."[28]

Inevitably, this trend toward abstraction leads to a "decoupling of code [i.e., identity] and process," with reification of collective identities the likely result.[29] It is the task of the critical social theorist to engage in reflection as an antidote to such reifying tendencies.[30] As will become clear, the constructivist approach guiding this book encourages problematization of objectified collective identities and mythical accounts of social boundaries.

Political geographers have also had a long-standing interest in boundaries.[31] The last few decades have seen a burgeoning literature on how competing and complementary spatiotemporal constructs are represented in the minds of both insiders and outsiders.[32] Taking his cue from social theory, the Finnish geographer Anssi Paasi introduces the notion of "spatial socialization" defined as "the process through which individual actors and collectivities are socialized as members of specific territorially bounded spatial entities and through which they more or less actively internalize collective territorial identities and shared traditions."[33] A focus on spatial socialization helps clarify the role of boundaries as "political manifestations of political processes" rather than static geographical compartmentalizations. From this standpoint, it is obvious that boundaries not only separate groups from each other but also allow for and regulate intergroup communication.

But it is perhaps in anthropology that we find the most explicit attempts to grapple with the interactive process of identity formation. Anthropologists routinely study interactions as a way to better understand identity formation and maintenance, though until recently mostly in premodern settings such as tribal communities and ethnic groups.[34] Even the briefest survey of anthropological perspectives on boundaries has to start with the classical volume *Ethnic Groups and Boundaries,* edited by the Norwegian anthropologist Fredrik Barth.[35] Whereas previous generations of anthropologists had been cataloguing ethnic groups according to their ostensibly objective cultural traits while holding their identities constant, Barth problematized boundaries as his conceptual starting point. In his view, "ethnic distinctions do not depend on an absence of social interaction and acceptance, but are quite to the contrary often the very foundations on which embracing social systems are built."[36] Here the original idea of interactive identity formation recurs in an especially lucid form.

Built on the (sometimes modified) foundations of Barth's interactive approach to boundary formation, contemporary anthropology conceives of social groups as socially constructed through social institutions and everyday practices. More recently, many anthropologists have attempted to liberate themselves from the professional norms of exoticism celebrating the hardship of fieldwork in the Third World by adding cultural phenomena of the developed world to their research agendas.[37]

In particular, Cris Shore's work on European identity formation anticipates more closely the analytical focus of the present volume. Combining fieldwork in Brussels with theoretically informed analysis of the European Commission's cultural policies, Shore adopts similar assumptions as those guiding the chapters that follow. In addition to being explicitly constructivist, his perspective also stresses the interactive nature of identity formation: "By emphasizing the 'imagined' and 'invented' character of collective identities, [anthropological approaches] alert us to the fact that all communities—European as well as nation—are culturally constructed. They also highlight the fact that identity-formation is an ambiguous and dualistic process involving the manipulation of boundaries and the mobilization of difference for strategies of inclusion and exclusion."[38] Agreeing with the conclusion that official EU sources fail to define Europe, the interactive approach to identities and boundaries offers crucial clues that help disentangle the definitional puzzle: "Evidence of a more coherent 'applied' definition can be seen emerging at the borders and boundaries of the new Europe, particularly in the spheres of immigration control and external customs barriers. In these areas the terms 'non-EC nationals,' 'third countries' and 'non-European' are being defined with increasing precision and thus, as if by default, an 'official' definition of European is being constructed."[39] Although the starting point is politics rather than culture, the structure of this volume reflects closely Shore's reference to identity formation in specific policy areas.

This brief multidisciplinary review of the literature has served to illustrate the importance of boundaries for the emergence of collective identities. Albeit applied to very diverse empirical settings, these analytical perspectives share the basic idea that groups categorize themselves by regulating the communicative flows between themselves and their respective environments. It is this fact that enables the analyst to adopt a pragmatic, interaction-oriented strategy of "revealed identities," to paraphrase the rational-choice equivalent.[40] →D VEDI SC POLIT.

Four Approaches to Identity Formation

The previous section's graphical depiction of social boundaries begs the question as to the curves' shape. The answer of course hinges on under-

Figure 1.2   The Essentialist Principle of Political Identity Formation

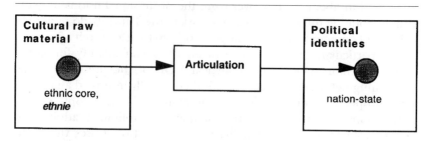

lying theoretical assumptions. To address this problem within the context of European integration, we will need to make a brief detour along two conceptual dimensions. Whereas the first dichotomy pits essentialism against constructivism, the second one separates theories that make optimistic predictions about supranational identity formation from those that are less sanguine in this respect.

As regards the first distinction, we use the terms *essentialism* and *constructivism* in a specific way. According to this classification, the main divide running through the literature pertains to the relationship between culture and politics: Essentialists argue that political identities flow more or less directly from the underlying cultural "raw material"; constructivists contend that the connection is much more tenuous.[41]

The essentialist approach to identity formation is driven primarily by cultural background variables. According to this logic, each ethnic core produces a political identity in a more or less direct fashion. To the extent that agency plays any important role at all, it is restricted to the articulation of a given cultural heritage. Thus, "primitive units" such as ethnic cores are presumed to exist, and the task of the nationalist entrepreneur is to "rediscover" and transform them into a politically operational identity.[42] While some strands of essentialism are primordialist in that they depict nations and other cultural units as naturally given, far from all of them are.[43] Others are less drastic in presupposing a large measure of historical continuity between ethnicity and political identification. Essentialist theories, then, require that there be a rough one-to-one correspondence between ethnic units and nation-states (see Figure 1.2).

Constructivism, by contrast, places more emphasis on politics.[44] In this view, the essentialist link between the cultural raw material and political identities is broken by an active process of identity formation entailing manipulation of cultural symbols.[45] Since cultural systems are inherently multidimensional, history does not deliver ready-made pack-

Figure 1.3   The Constructivist Principle of Political Identity Formation

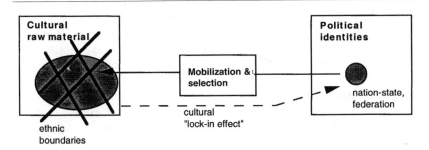

ages such as ethnic cores. Instead, it is up to the political activist to select the ethnic cleavages to be mobilized or suppressed.[46]

Instrumentalist constructivism lets the causal arrows run primarily "backward" from right to left (cf. Figure 1.3). Instead of assuming culture to be the starting point, instrumental constructivists begin with political identity formation, emphasizing the autonomy of political factors (typically driven by external material forces) and treating culture as a mere side effect of the process. Maximizing their influence, political leaders mobilize the population in question by carefully selecting out the cultural cleavages to be activated.

Yet other constructivist approaches adopt a less instrumental outlook, based on reciprocal interaction between culture and identity formation (see the dashed arrows in Figure 1.3). This interpretation allows for an "ecological" perspective on identity formation, limiting the freedom of choice of political entrepreneurs. Without ruling out agency, this perspective explains how identity formation is affected by the constantly changing availability of cultural raw material that acquires an autonomous role feeding back into the political process.[47] This process may also include an expressive or rule-following aspect that defies rationalistic explanation blocking or deflecting political initiatives.[48] In his recent introduction to nationalism, Craig Calhoun argues that "the development and spread of nationalist discourse is not reducible to state formation or political manipulation; it has autonomous significance, appears in cultural arenas not directly defined by state-making projects, and has often informed popular action to reform or resist patterns of state making."[49]

Regardless of their precise causal logic, constructivists reject the essentialist one-way street from cultural to political units. In other words, "we can assume no simple one-to-one relationship between ethnic units and cultural similarities and differences. The features that are taken into account are not the sum of 'objective' differences, but only those which the actors themselves regard as significant."[50]

The second distinction alluded to above pertains to the ease with which supranational identity shifts are expected to take place. The retention perspective emphasizes the staying power of the nation-state together with its ideational justification: nationalism, that is, the principle that requires cultural and political boundaries to coincide.[51] Those who believe in the viability of supersession, by contrast, expect that the nation-state will be transcended in one way or another. Obviously this can happen in many ways, which may result in dramatically divergent end points. The most important source of ambiguity is whether the transformation presupposes mere enlargement of existing nation-states into some type of "supernations" or whether it entails the transcendence of the nationality principle itself, thus leading to alternative ways of organizing politics.[52]

For the purpose of this volume, it can be assumed that the nation-state is superseded once an autonomous system of symbols on the supranational level has been established and is adhered to by most of the population in question. Note that this requires neither complete popular support nor a comprehensive political culture penetrating all realms of everyday life. Partial and "thin" political identities also have the potential to transcend the nation-state. The crucial question, however, is whether the old national identities lose their status as "trump" and whether the supranational locus of identification acquires at least some of this lost loyalty.[53]

Once this simple table has been introduced, the "straightforward" combinations can be identified as ethnonationalism and postnationalism, the first representing essentialists' assumption of the nation-state as the final equilibrium, and the second denoting constructivist integrationism (see Figure 1.4). In addition to those conventional positions, however, the table opens the door for supranational essentialism as well as for constructivist explanations of the nation-state. The first of these two "mixed" cases could be called pannationalism, since it argues for the existence of cultural entities greater than the nation-state, such as civilizations, grounded in culture. Finally, I label the opposite possibility bounded integration due to its emphasis of social closure characterizing political identities.

Equipped with this simple four-way taxonomy, we are ready to abridge the task of classifying the literature on nationalism according to its underlying assumptions about identity formation and expectations

Figure 1.4   Four Analytical Perspectives on Supranational Identity Formation

	Approach to identity formation beyond the nation-state	
Assumptions about identity formation	**Retention**	**Supersession**
Essentialism	Ethnonationalism	Pannationalism
Constructivism	Bounded integration	Postnationalism

about integration. We start by exploring the two "obvious" positions, then move on to the mixed, more counterintuitive combinations.

Ethnonationalism

Although some scholars use *ethnonationalism* interchangeably with *nationalism,* in this volume we reserve it for essentialist theories that highlight the nation-state as the prime locus of political identity.[54] Even so, the category comprises a wide range of theoretical propositions, from primordialist defenses of the nation-state as a holistic cultural entity to less normative depictions of culture's influence on politics. Common to them all, however, is the thought that nation-states can be "paired" with more primitive, premodern entities and that given these constraints, any attempt to transcend those underlying ethnic boundaries is doomed to fail. There are different views as to how these constraints manifest themselves, but most essentialist accounts refer to the emotional power and historical depth of long-standing traditions and memories, which together force people to think twice before they take the supranational plunge.

Essentialist scholars contend that instead of moving toward larger political units, the current trend consolidates, and in some cases even fragments, the existing nation-states. Anthony D. Smith is perhaps the most influential observer of this "ethnic revival."[55] He is also the essentialist theorist who has written most extensively about supranational integration.[56] Rejecting cosmopolitanism, Smith suggests that global culture "strikes no chord among the vast mass of peoples divided into their habitual communities of class, gender, region, religion and culture."[57]

According to this culture-driven interpretation, the nation acquires a life of its own regardless of the state: "It is the nation that must be nurtured, protected and rendered effective, and any framework that will afford such protection and bestow such efficacy is regarded as appropriate. The territorial state is the most obvious and best-placed candidate for such a protective role, but it is not the only one."[58] A cultural nation, then, is assumed to exist before the search for viable political identities can start. Multicultural constructions striving to transcend the nation-state, by contrast, lack historical depth and consequently fail to evoke mass emotions conducive to political loyalty.

The European Union is no exception to this rule. According to Anthony Smith, it is not even clear what a European cultural identity stands for. While acknowledging that there are shared political traditions such as "Roman law, political democracy, parliamentary institutions, and Judeo-Christian ethics" and cultural ones based on "Renaissance humanism and empiricism, and romanticism and classicism," Smith suggests that they add up not to "unity in diversity," but to "families of culture."[59] At best, "a European identity . . . would be likely to evolve through a slow, inchoate, often unplanned process, though selected aspects might be the objects of attempts at conscious planning."[60] Consistent with his essentialist outlook, Smith draws the conclusion that political change on the mass level can occur only incrementally through cultural evolution.[61]

Postnationalism

Whereas essentialist theories of ethnonationalism arrive at a negative conclusion regarding the chances of superseding nationalism, many constructivists conclude precisely the opposite. The underlying differences in philosophical and substantive assumptions between these two perspectives of course produce dramatically diverging expectations concerning the fate of the nation-state. To distinguish these thinkers from other constructivists who take a less sanguine view of supersession, we denote them postnationalists.

In opposition to the ethnonationalist emphasis on culture as the theoretical starting point, constructivists insist on the primacy of politics as a functional response to material conditions of production. Modern communications created the nation-state, but since technology continues to develop, political organization will keep up by increasing its own scale. Eventually this trend will break the politicocultural bond so dear to ethnonationalists. Depicting the latter as backward defenders of parochialism, postnationalists stress the desirability and ultimate irreversibility of political integration beyond the scale of the nation-state.

To illustrate this reasoning, we turn to a prominent scholar who attracts much attention in the following chapters. Basing his case on liberal principles of Kantian bent, Jürgen Habermas classifies nationalism as a "modern phenomenon of cultural integration" created through historiography and transmitted through "the channels of modern mass communications."[62] Stressing the historically contingent nature of nationalism as a political principle, he detaches politics from culture.[63] Habermas thus argues in favor of a thin political culture, as defined in the previous section, serving as a "common denominator for a constitutional patriotism which simultaneously sharpens an awareness of the multiplicity and integrity of the different forms of life which coexist in a multicultural society."[64] In case of clashes between these two organizing principles, politics will prevail, leading to a redefinition of culture to serve political functions, thus paving the way for integration. Using Switzerland as an example, Habermas does not view multilingualism as a serious obstacle to a European federation. True to the rationalist and individualist visions of the Enlightenment, he favors a procedural definition of democracy "that no longer hinges on the assumption of macro-subjects like the 'people' of 'the' community but on anonymously inter-linked discourses or flows of communication."[65]

Having considered the most obvious ways of connecting approaches to identity formation and historical outcomes, the analysis continues by considering two somewhat counterintuitive positions. As will soon be clear, the essentialist-constructivist divide does not always generate clear-cut approaches to supranational identity formation.

Pannationalism

Even though essentialists are usually associated with nationalism, there is no logical reason why a culture-driven approach could not be extended beyond the scale of the contemporary nation-states. Note that we are not talking about postnational units violating the politicocultural nexus, as described by the previous subsection on postnationalism. As opposed to the political manipulation that constructivist approach presupposes, the current one assumes culturally distinct entities formed as a result of long-term ethnogenesis.

Such a pannationalist approach tends to reify families of cultures in organic terms. Samuel Huntington's now famous "clash of civilizations" thesis offers the best-known recent example along these lines. Claiming that future conflict will follow civilizational rifts rather than national borders, this contentious proposition views civilizations as the "highest cultural grouping of people and the broadest level of identity people have short of that which distinguishes humans from other species."[66] In order to remove any doubts about the argument's essentialist, if not even primordialist, foundation, we observe that the Harvard political scientist clarifies that "differences among civilizations are not only real; they are basic. Civilizations are differentiated from each other by history, language, culture, tradition and, most important, religion."[67]

This strongly essentialist argument for supersession is reflected in Huntington's strictures about European integration: "The European Community rests on the shared foundations of European culture and Western Christianity."[68] Responding to his critics, Huntington does not hesitate to rally senior statesmen to his support: "In Europe, European Community President Jacques Delors explicitly endorsed [the] argument that 'future conflicts will be sparked by cultural factors rather than economics or ideology.'"[69]

Given the predominance of economics in European integration and the sparse evidence of such identities, it comes as no surprise that these essentialist views have never been held by more than a minority of analytical supranationalists.[70] But it is policymakers who are the most likely to make pannationalist assumptions at the European level. Indeed, much of the European Commission's cultural activism tacitly, and sometimes even explicitly, depends on a unified European culture.[71]

Bounded Integration

Many constructivist students of nationalism are much less optimistic about the prospects for erosion of the nation-state than are the postnationalists. They emphasize the staying power of nationalism, but for very different reasons than scholars subscribing to the ethnonationalist position. Instead of stressing cultural continuity as the key to nation formation, they argue that stable political identities may originate in and be upheld by conscious policies and mechanisms. If an institutional equilibrium of this type is reached, which may happen comparatively quickly, it usually proves very stable. Yet without ongoing processes of identity maintenance, identities often quickly dissipate. To the extent that the nation-state represents such an equilibrium, supersession becomes unlikely.

In practice, it is the state that plays the role as primary identity-carrying organizational "vessel." Political institutions in general, and the state in particular, stand for the reproduction and maintenance of political identities. As a result of a mutual convergence of culture and politics, the nation-state emerges as a functional solution.[72]

Contrary to the accusations of their ethnonationalist critics, not all constructivist theorists believe political identities to be inherently fickle. According to the bounded-integration perspective, the opposition between constructivist assumptions and ethnopolitical stability is a false one. Ernest Gellner, to take perhaps the most influential theorist belonging to this school of thought, interprets national identity as a functional response to the requirements of modernity. It is the state more than any other political institution that offers the prime means of cultural reproduction in the modern world. Though Gellner has rightly been criticized for his "demand-side" explanation of nationalism stressing the "needs" of modern industrial society, his account does point to specific institutional mechanisms on the "supply side," the most important of which is state-organized education: "At the base of the modern social order stands not the executioner but the professor. Not the guillotine, but the (aptly named) *doctorat d'état* is the main tool and symbol of state power. The monopoly of legitimate education is now more important, more central than the monopoly of legitimate violence."[73]

Once locked into their respective "power containers," national identities are unlikely to change drastically.[74] Whereas Gellner partially supports the postnationalist projections of cultural convergence as a result of the communication revolution, he parts company with this school's integrationist predictions, for, in his view, "it remains difficult to imagine two large, politically viable, interdependence-worthy cultures cohabiting under a single political roof, and trusting a single political centre to maintain and service both cultures with perfect or even adequate impartiality."[75] The reason for Gellner's skepticism stems from his belief in a strong, reciprocal link between politics and culture. The postnationalist effort to separate the two encounters difficulties since it fails to realize that "men are dependent on culture, and that culture requires standardization over quite wide areas, and needs to be maintained and serviced by centralized agencies."[76] The inevitable conclusion of this reasoning is that "the nationalist imperative of the congruence of political units and of culture will continue to apply. In that sense, one need not expect the age of nationalism to come to an end."[77]

A Derivation of Boundary Hypotheses

Having sketched four ideal-type positions, we can now articulate hypotheses about supranational identity formation. The first issue regards the very existence of such an identity at the European level. Second, if such a development does take place, what form would the identity take? To derive the hypothesis of each of the four ideal-type per-

**Figure 1.5   Four Approaches to European Boundary
                Formation**

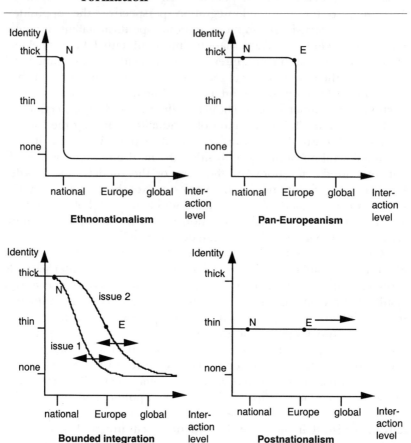

spectives, it is helpful to illustrate their respective approaches to boundary formation.

Figure 1.5 presents four boundary curves corresponding to the four theoretical perspectives. The basic outline of two axes is the same as in the previous graph, though the axes have been adapted to the particular historical context. Thus, the inclusion-exclusion spectrum is now mapped onto a national-European-global range. Likewise, in addition to thin and thick identities, there is also the theoretical possibility of no identity at all. This framework facilitates the pinpointing of the loci of identity formation at the national (N) and European (E) levels.

As would be expected, both essentialist positions feature a sharp fall of political identification beyond a certain level of interaction. In the case of ethnonationalism, this break point occurs already at the national level, which implies that there is room only for a national identity N. While intergovernmental cooperation is perfectly feasible at the European or even global level, identification is ruled out by assumption because of lacking cultural preconditions. The trade-off between diluted identity and exclusion could not be starker, because the latter would invariably imperil the entire existence of a national identity and lead to a complete identification void.

Within the European context, pannationalism could be called Pan-Europeanism. This approach extends the cultural plateau past the national locus of identity N all the way to a thick, Pan-European identity E. Beyond this point, however, the possibilities of identity formation dwindle quickly. While pannationalists deplore that national identity still holds sway at N, they advocate a quick shift to E. In this sense, they refuse to accept an identity trade-off at the national level, but their boundary curve tells them that such a trade-off starts to operate once the European scale of aggregation has been attained.

The two constructivist perspectives differ from their essentialist counterparts in their denial of fixed, exogenous trade-offs. Representing the most extreme position, postnationalists deny the very existence of culturally imposed trade-offs. Viewing national identification as revolving around a thin identity, their future scenarios include a swift outward shift of interactive scale from the national level at N, to Europe at E, and often even beyond that scale toward a fully global identity. If the integration process needs to slow down and stop at the European level, this is not for cultural reasons but rather a practical, infrastructural matter. In principle, Europe could be seen as a stepping-stone toward a globalizing trend that will ultimately create a world community. Postnationalists view any talk of exclusion-dilution trade-offs with great skepticism.

Parting company with this integrationist outlook, bounded-integration theory accepts the existence of trade-offs but maintains that the shape of the boundary profiles differs from issue area to issue area and insists that the curves themselves are subject to social (re)construction. The functionally specific difference in the boundaries' shape implies that European identity formation is unlikely to proceed uniformly across the board. It is possible that identification to E can proceed in one domain (e.g., issue 2), while others exhibit no supersessionist tendencies (e.g., issue 1). In addition, framing effects that may transform the slope of a curve not only differ between policy realms but may also vary as a function of the particular discourse that dominates a policy debate at any given time (thus the horizontal arrows).

Because of their ideal-typical status, these schemas should obviously be taken with a grain of salt. The difference between normative and analytical interpretations is important. For example, though the post-nationalist graph corresponds closely to the normative outlook of this school of thought, these analysts often recognize and deplore the existence of "thick" national identities. Their predictions about the viability of a European identity, however, leave no room for culturally driven identification processes. Similarly, the boundary curves drawn by state-nationalism do not always presuppose thick identities but may start out with thin identities. All the same, this perspective expects at least a slow fall of identity thickness as inclusion increases in most cases, though the gradient varies across the policy areas.

Another important caveat concerns other, internally generated sources of identity formation. The boundary graphs do tap one significant dimension of identification processes, but they do not exhaust all possibilities. Internally operating mechanisms, such as road building, education, language policies, media, and political parties, all contribute to the buildup of national loyalty.[78] Albeit very primitive at this point in history, similar mechanisms are at least theoretically possible at the European level.[79] Because we focus on boundaries, the task of assessing systematically the balance between internal and external sources of European identity formation goes beyond the scope of this book and must be put off for future research.[80]

A Note on Methodology

Before turning to the substantive processes of identity formation, a few remarks on methodology could help dispel potential misunderstandings. Given the multidisciplinary nature of this collection of essays, the authors' methodologies vary considerably. After all, this volume serves primarily a theoretical rather than a methodological purpose, and so its thematic coherence does not hinge upon any particular choice of methods.

In fact, together the contributions straddle the methodological divide between positivist and postpositivist analysis. Although it has been argued that the twain shall never meet, the concept of this book follows Alexander Wendt in exploring a methodological "via media."[81] Briefly put, this metatheoretical synthesis supports *both* traditional causal analysis *and* a postpositivist emphasis on constitutive effects of ideas and practices. Political boundary processes can be studied from both perspectives, and what is more, even if the two modes of analysis rely on mostly divergent methodologies, these could mutually support each other.

Thus, it would be a mistake to judge the contributions according to a strictly positivist standard, if by *positivism* we mean a commitment to methodological monism, naturalism, and a nomological model of causation.[82] Even if the volume's methodological pluralism rules out the two first criteria from the outset, the current approach to causation requires further comment. This book strives to analyze the formation of Europe's identity interpreted as a uniquely contextualized phenomenon in time and space rather than attempting to account for it in terms of putative covering laws.[83] Though many positivist analysts criticize as "unscientific" studies that home in on unique phenomena, there is reason to doubt that much headway can be made through mechanistic comparisons of the European integration process with other cases.[84] It is perfectly possible to engage in causal analysis of single, complex units if the explanatory effort concerns the uncovering of causal mechanisms instead of the subsumption of the explanandum under lawlike regularities.[85] The theoretical focus on interaction processes as the key to identity formation is compatible with such an outlook. Seen in this light, comparisons (such as the Swiss case analyzed in Chapter 3) become meaningful not primarily as mere observations of variable instances but as scenarios illustrating the unfolding of causal processes.

But even before such mechanisms can be found, it is necessary to describe social reality in such a way that causal analysis becomes possible. This is particularly important in cases featuring contested concepts and conceptualizations in flux. Consequently, most of the contributions rely on constitutive analysis of discursive practices. Such methods include the study of symbolic languages, intersubjective meanings, and discursive practices.[86] In contrast, mainstream positivist methodology tends to trivialize the task of description, but this is clearly a mistake, since observation is inherently "theory-laden," if not necessarily "theory-determined."[87]

Despite the utility of a constitutive focus in its own right since it answers "what" questions rather than "why" questions, in principle there is no reason to follow the postmodernists in abandoning the attempt to embed constitutive-discursive analysis in a causal framework.[88] In the end, failure to do so pushes us down a slippery slope of epistemological relativism. Not all ideas are viable in all situations, and causal effects relating to power often play a crucial role in selecting out the "winners."

To sum up, both causal and constitutive methodologies can and should be applied to the problem of European identity formation. This book does not precommit itself to any particular methodological position, but it does lean toward conceptual analysis, hypothesis generation, and discursive tracing. This emphasis reflects the need to conceptualize and describe the poorly understood interaction interfaces of the EU. Because the individual contributions outline their own methodologies, it is better to turn directly to a summary of the chapters.

A Preview of the Volume

In his exploration of the underlying historical roots and philosophical principles of identity, Craig Calhoun in Chapter 2 widens the scope to encompass normative issues animating current debates in political theory. He shows how "identity politics" differ from the conventional debates on economics and security. Once the topics of sovereignty and legitimacy have been abridged, the question about the "people's" identity becomes unavoidable. Though crying out for a solution, the dilemma of collective selfhood remains as tricky as ever but is by no means a novelty, as illustrated by the historical development of nationalism.

To mitigate the theoretical confusion, Calhoun discusses four dichotomies that have a tendency to recur in arguments about identity politics. These issues include the questions of self-equivalence, the opposition between essentialism and constructivism, the we-they dichotomy, and the difference between categorical and relational identities. These themes are leading threads throughout the whole volume. Adding a normative touch to his conceptual exposition, Calhoun ends his chapter by warning against emulation of closed national identities on the European level accompanied with an appeal for maximum pluralism.

Calhoun's discussion includes a reference to Switzerland, which figures as an important "existence proof" that pluralist, multilingual polities are not only theoretically possible but can also be eminently successful. To what extent are such arguments well founded? Attacking this question head-on, a team of Swiss political scientists, Pascal Sciarini, Simon Hug, and Cédric Dupont, devote Chapter 3 to a careful investigation of identity formation in three broad areas paralleling the pillar structure of the EU. Their consideration of Switzerland's participation in international cooperation as well as its trade and immigration policies reveals a more complex picture than that suggested by the adherents of multicultural rule. Identifying federalism, direct democracy, and neutrality as the crucial institutions on which the Swiss political system rests, they show that those institutions have a far from inclusionary influence on political identity formation. While strengthening local democracy, federalist decentralization and referenda create opportunities for exclusionary campaigns. In addition, neutrality rules out aggressive foreign policies and also promotes a fortress mentality. This does not mean that European pluralists have nothing to learn from the remarkable Swiss experience of multiculturalism. Yet, simple-minded extrapolation would be imprudent because Switzerland is as much an exception as it is an example to follow.

It is thus with utmost caution that we move the analysis up to the European level. The second part of the book considers the first of the EU's pillars. In Chapter 4 Philip Schlesinger provides a detailed analysis of the European Commission's cultural policies in the audiovisual and media sectors. Detecting a shift from "Hollywood bashing" to a more technocratic and instrumentalist orientation, Schlesinger finds that the EU's position has mellowed considerably in recent years, thus paving the way for a less conflictual climate in international trade negotiations. Rather than rejecting protectionist arguments offhand, Schlesinger scrutinizes the underlying logic of various exclusionary practices. Much hinges on whether one considers media trade a mere exchange of "cultural goods" or potentially explosive ideological "programming devices."

If the EU's official discourse has come to stress the former rather than the latter, it does not mean that there is a European communicative space. Schlesinger is careful to point out that despite high-minded rhetoric, political communication remains firmly rooted in its nationalist settings. Thus, in his view, Europe has a long way to go before it approximates the conditions of discursive democracy prescribed by postnationalist theoreticians, not to mention the more demanding standards of political participation.

Rounding out Schlesinger's exploration of Europe's potential cultural identity, Tobias Theiler in Chapter 5 investigates the reasons the EU's attempt to create an audiovisual "other" failed. Arguing that such an identity-building project requires an external boundary as well as an internal reification of the cultural identity, he shows that these conditions have to be complemented with a dissemination campaign making the identity constructs plausible in the eyes of both the governments and the national publics. In theory, this made the audiovisual area ideally suited as a candidate for a Pan-Europeanist process of reactive identity formation. Yet in practice things have proven to be more complicated. Theiler's chapter documents how the European Commission's aggressive efforts exhibited an anti-American rhetoric but also how these policy initiatives failed to resonate with Europe's television viewers and provoked strong resistance from many member states. Thus, "othering" is far from a foolproof strategy. Indeed, the EU's failure to strengthen Europe's cultural identity reveals some of the general conditions that have to be in place for such efforts to bear fruit.

The third part of the book considers issues related to the EU's external relations. In Chapter 6 Iver Neumann returns to the theme of reactive identity formation by applying it to the enlargement debates. Concerned that "othering" may be at play, Neumann explores how the Eastern and Central Europeans' bid for EU membership, as well as the

EU's admission criteria, affect not only the former's identity but also the definition of Europe itself. Given the political and economic gulf between Western and Eastern Europe, it is in the applicant states' interests to phrase their claims in cultural terms. In so doing, Neumann argues, the temptation is overwhelming to engage in exclusionary rhetoric depicting Russia as Europe's other.

Also examining the enlargement issue, Frank Schimmelfennig in contrast plays down the pannationalist temptation. Schimmelfennig contends in Chapter 7 that a "community perspective," as opposed to a rationalist one based on clubs, provides the key to understanding the eastern enlargement decisions that led to the EU's initiating accession talks with five states in Eastern and Central Europe. Although the EU's identity is a "thin" postnationalist one, enlargement does imply a trade-off between the risk of diluting its collective identity and disseminating its values and norms beyond its current borders.

The final pillar-related part of the book scrutinizes the identity issues related to the EU's third pillar. Though the legal definition of EU citizenship has found its way into the first pillar, and the Amsterdam Treaty envisages a further transfer of legislation in this area, most of the debate about political membership, internal security, and immigration has been conducted under the heading of Justice and Home Affairs within the third pillar.

Addressing the questions of Europe's civic identity empirically, Jef Huysmans uses Chapter 8 to study the actual evolution of membership criteria in the immigration debate. This takes him from the economistic, and thus liberal, interpretations of migration in the 1960s to the more recent securitization of the issue area. Huysmans thematizes this politicization according to the main goals justifying particular exclusionary practices, including references to public order, national identity, and welfare.

Extending the investigation of particular practices from migration in general to asylum policies in particular, Vera Gowlland-Debbas adopts a legal perspective in Chapter 9. In her view, the distinction between immigration and asylum policies is an important one since the latter evokes a different, more directly security-related imagery than the former. This observation puts the issue of asylum firmly within the context of "high politics," which is a connection that causes tensions between the apparent desire to protect either national or European identity and humanitarian norms.

The final chapter brings all the issues and levels of identity formation into the framework developed in the previous chapters. In Chapter 10 I take stock of the overall trends of inclusion and exclusion and compare interactions between issue areas and levels of integration. Here the focus is on possible interdependence and tensions between issues and levels. This concluding discussion leads to reassessment of several beliefs propagated by integration scholars.

Notes

I am indebted to Simon Hug, Ron Jepperson, Anna Murphy, Sidney Tarrow, and Tobias Theiler for their helpful comments.

1. See, e.g., Helen Wallace, "Whose Europe Is It Anyway?" *European Journal of Political Research* 35 (1999): 287–306; and Judy Batt, "The Long-Term Implications of EU Enlargement: The Nature of the New Border," Robert Schuman Centre for Advanced Studies, EUI, Final Report on the Reflection Group, Forward Studies Unit of the European Commission, 1999.

2. The sense of malaise appears to relate not only to the EU but more generally to the legitimacy of democratic institutions in the entire Western world. Cf., e.g., Fritz W. Scharpf, *Governing in Europe: Effective and Democratic?* (Oxford: Oxford University Press, 1999), 1. For an argument that the legitimacy issue in the EU context has been overdrawn, see Thomas Banschoff and Mitchell P. Smith, "Introduction: 'Conceptualizing Legitimacy in a Contested Polity,'" in Thomas Banschoff and Mitchell P. Smith, eds., *Legitimacy and the European Union: The Contested Polity* (London: Routledge, 1999).

3. Since the prime focus is on the European Union, this volume uses the term *Europe* synonymously with EU. Yet despite the widening of the EU to encompass most of the Continent, there are other organizations that can (or could) claim to represent Europe or large portions thereof, such as the Council of Europe, the Organization for Security and Cooperation in Europe, and the European Free Trade Area. Moreover, large parts of what has often been referred to as Europe in a wider, geographic sense remain outside the EU, including Turkey, the Balkans, as well as Russia and the neighboring regions in Eastern Europe.

4. Denis de Rougemont, *The Making of Europe* (New York: Stein and Day, 1965), 56.

5. William Wallace, *The Transformation of Western Europe* (London: Pinter, 1990), 8.

6. Ken Dyson quoted in Paul A. Chilton, *Security Metaphors: Cold War Discourse from Containment to Common House* (New York: Peter Lang, 1996), 25.

7. Quoted in Paul Thibaud, "L'Europe par les nations (et réciproquement)," in Pierre Rosanvallon, ed., *Discussion sur l'Europe* (Paris: Calmann-Lévy, 1992), 16 (my translation).

8. Thibaud, "L'Europe par les nations."

9. The literature on Europe's identity is constantly growing: Jacques Lenoble and Nicole Dewandre, eds., *L'Europe au soir du siècle: Identité et démocratie* (Paris: Éditions Esprit, 1992); Soledad García, ed., *European Identity and the Search for Legitimacy* (London: Pinter, 1993); Ole Wæver, Barry Buzan, Morten Kelstrup, and Pierre Lemaitre, eds., *Identity, Migration and the New Security Agenda in Europe* (London: Pinter, 1993); Klaus Dieter Wolf, ed., *Projekt Europa im Übergang? Probleme, Modelle und Strategien des Regierens in der Europäischen Union* (Baden-Baden: Nomos, 1997); Riva Kastoryano, ed., *Quelle identité pour l'Europe? Le multiculturalisme à l'épreuve* (Paris: Presses de Sciences Po, 1998); Reinhold

Viehoff and Rien T. Siegers, eds., *Kultur, Identität, Europa: Über die Schwierigkeiten und Möglichkeiten einer Konstruktion* (Frankfurt: Suhrkamp, 1999). See also the special issues of the *Journal of Common Market Studies* 34, 1 (Spring 1996) and *Journal of European Public Policy* 6, 4 (1999). Yet none of these works covers the problem of boundaries systematically. One of the few volumes that does, Philomena Murray and Leslie Holmes, eds., *Europe: Rethinking the Boundaries* (Aldershot, UK: Ashgate, 1998), analyzes the EU's borders according to geographic area rather than functionally.

10. Bertrand Badie and Marie-Claude Smouts in *Le Retournement du monde: Sociologie de la scène internationale* (Paris: Presses de la Fondation Nationale des Sciences Politiques, 1992), 187 (my translation).

11. Karl W. Deutsch, *Nationalism and Its Alternatives* (New York: Alfred A. Knopf, 1969), 97. See also Karl W. Deutsch, *Nationalism and Social Communication: An Inquiry into the Foundations of Nationality*, 2nd ed. (Cambridge: MIT Press, 1966).

12. Ibid., 98–99.

13. While constructivist scholars acknowledge Deutsch's contribution to the literature on nationalism, his work has often been criticized for having succumbed to behaviorist "bean counting." See, e.g., Emanuel Adler and Michael Barnett, eds., *Security Communities* (Cambridge: Cambridge University Press, 1998).

14. I use *exclusion* more generally than it has been employed in the debates about (mostly domestic) socioeconomic exclusion. For a conceptual overview applied to the European level, see Paul Spicker, "Exclusion," *Journal of Common Market Studies* 35 (1997): 133–143.

15. Michael Walzer, *Thick and Thin: Moral Argument at Home and Abroad* (Notre Dame, Ind.: University of Notre Dame Press, 1994). Cf. Scharpf, *Governing in Europe*, 10–13. This distinction has much in common with the historical-sociological dichotomy separating the German *Kulturnation* from the French *Staatsnation*. See, e.g., Friedrich Meinecke, *Cosmopolitanism and the National State* (Princeton: Princeton University Press, 1970); and Rogers Brubaker, *Citizenship and Nationhood in France and Germany* (Cambridge: Harvard University Press, 1992).

16. Albert O. Hirschman, *Exit, Voice, and Loyalty: Responses to Decline in Firms, Organizations, and States* (Cambridge: Harvard University Press, 1970).

17. Stein Rokkan, "Entries, Voices, Exits: Towards a Possible Generalization of the Hirschman Model," *Social Science Information* 13 (1974): 39–53. For a systematic and comprehensive introduction to Rokkan's lifetime work, see Peter Flora, ed., *State Formation, Nation-Building, and Mass Politics in Europe: The Theory of Stein Rokkan* (Oxford: Oxford University Press, 1999), especially ch. 3. Drawing on Hirschman and Rokkan, Stefano Bartolini has recently developed a theory of political representation that is of particular relevance: "Exit Options, Boundary Building, Political Structuring," Working Paper SPS No. 98/1, European University Institute, 1998.

18. Georg Simmel, *Conflict and the Web of Group-Affiliations* (New York: Free Press, 1955).

19. Arthur A. Stein, "Conflict and Cohesion: A Review of the Literature," *Journal of Conflict Resolution* 20 (1976): 143–172; and Jack S. Levy, "The Diversionary Theory of War," in M. I. Midlarsky, ed., *Handbook of War Studies* (Boston: Unwin Hyman, 1989).

20. David Sylvan and Barry Glassner, *A Rationalist Methodology for the Social Sciences* (Oxford: Blackwell, 1985); Andrew Abbott, "Things of Boundaries,"

Social Research 62 (1995): 857–882; Christopher Daase, *Kleine Kriege—Große Wirkung: Wie unkonventionelle Kriegführung die internationale Politik verändert* (Baden-Baden: Nomos, 1999); Lars-Erik Cederman and Christopher Daase, "Endogenizing Corporate Identities: A Sociational Theory of World Politics," European University Institute, 1999.

21. Georg Simmel, *Soziologie: Untersuchungen über die Formen der Vergesell-schaftung* (1908; reprint, Frankfurt: Suhrkamp, 1992), 697 (my translation).

22. George Herbert Mead, *Mind, Self, and Society* (Chicago: University of Chicago Press, 1962). For more recent examples, see William Connolly, *Identity/Difference: Democratic Negotiations of Political Paradox* (Ithaca: Cornell University Press, 1991); David Campbell, *Writing Security: United States Foreign Policy and the Politics of Identity* (Minneapolis: University of Minnesota Press, 1992). Alexander Wendt offers an often-cited application of Meadean identity theory to international relations in "Anarchy Is What States Make of It: The Social Construction of Power Politics," *International Organization* 46 (1992): 391–425. An excellent overview of the social theory literature can be found in Iver B. Neumann, *Uses of the Other: "The East" in European Identity Formation* (Minneapolis: University of Minnesota Press, 1999), ch. 1. As Neumann points out, social psychology has developed partly along a separate path from social theory, as shown, for example, by Michael A. Hogg and Dominic Abrams, *Social Identifications: A Social Psychology of Intergroup Relations and Group Processes* (London: Routledge, 1988). These authors focus on Tajfel's social identity theory, which has been adapted to international relations by Jonathan Mercer in "Anarchy and Identity," *International Organization* 49 (1995): 229–252.

23. Pierre Bourdieu, *Distinction: A Social Critique of the Judgment of Taste* (London: Routledge, 1984). See Craig Calhoun, *Critical Social Theory* (Oxford: Blackwell, 1995), ch. 5, for an introduction to Bourdieu's notion of habitus. Cf. also Stephen Mennell, "The Formation of We-Images: A Process Theory," in Craig Calhoun, ed., *Social Theory and the Politics of Identity* (Oxford: Blackwell, 1994), 177.

24. Bernhard Giesen, *Die Intellektuellen und die Nation: Eine deutsche Achsenzeit* (Frankfurt: Suhrkamp, 1993), 30 (my translation).

25. Ibid., 35.

26. Ibid., 43.

27. Ibid., 44. See also Craig Calhoun, "Indirect Relationships and Imagined Communities: Large-Scale Social Integration and the Transformation of Everyday Life," in Pierre Bourdieu and James S. Coleman, eds., *Social Theory for a Changing Society* (Boulder, Colo.: Westview, 1991) and Craig Calhoun, "Nationalism and Ethnicity," *Annual Review of Sociology* 19 (1993): 211–239.

28. Niklas Luhmann, "Inklusion und Exklusion," in Helmut Berding, ed., *Nationales Bewußtsein und kollektive Identität* (Frankfurt: Suhrkamp, 1994), 24 (my translation).

29. The notion of reification is defined and explained in Peter L. Berger and Thomas Luckmann, *The Social Construction of Reality: A Treatise in the Sociology of Knowledge* (Harmondsworth, UK: Penguin, 1966). For discussions of the concept in an international relations context, see also Wendt, "Anarchy Is What States Make of It," and Lars-Erik Cederman, *Emergent Actors in World Politics: How States and Nations Develop and Dissolve* (Princeton: Princeton University Press, 1997), ch. 2.

30. Giesen, *Die Intellektuellen*, 45.

31. J. R. V. Prescott, *Political Frontiers and Boundaries* (London: Unwin and Hyman, 1987) provides a good survey of geographical treatments of the boundary concept. In particular, he highlights the important distinction between borders and frontiers, the first being sharply demarcated boundaries and the latter more attenuated boundary zones. For an application to international relations, see Friedrich Kratochwil, "Of Systems, Boundaries and Territoriality," *World Politics* 34 (1986): 27–52.

32. For useful overviews of the literature, see Anthony Giddens, *The Constitution of Society* (Berkeley: University of California Press, 1984), ch. 3; and Guntram H. Herb, "National Identity and Territory," in David H. Kaplan and Guntram H. Herb, eds., *Nested Identities: Nationalism, Territory, and Scale* (Lanham, Md.: Rowman & Littlefield, 1999).

33. Anssi Paasi, *Territories, Boundaries and Consciousness: The Changing Geographies of the Finnish-Russian Border* (New York: Wiley, 1996), 8; see also Peter Sahlins, *Boundaries: The Making of France and Spain in the Pyrenees* (Berkeley: University of California Press, 1989).

34. See Neumann, *Uses of the Other*, 4–7, for a concise account of the "ethnographic path" and its link to reactive identity formation.

35. Fredrik Barth, introduction to Fredrik Barth, ed., *Ethnic Groups and Boundaries: The Social Organization of Culture Difference* (Boston: Little, Brown, 1969).

36. Ibid., 9. Cf. also Anthony Cohen, who states that "the boundary encapsulates the identity of the community and, like the identity of an individual, is called into being by the exigencies of social interaction." Anthony P. Cohen, *The Symbolic Construction of Community* (London: Routledge, 1985), 12.

37. See Thomas M. Wilson and M. Estellie Smith, eds., *Cultural Change and the New Europe: Perspectives on the European Community* (Boulder, Colo.: Westview, 1993); and Victoria A. Goddard, Josep R. Llobera, and Cris Shore, "Introduction: The Anthropology of Europe," in Victoria A. Goddard, Josep R. Llobera, and Cris Shore, eds., *The Anthropology of Europe: Identities and Boundaries in Question* (Oxford: Berg, 1994), 1–40.

38. Cris Shore, "Inventing the 'People's Europe': Critical Approaches to European Community 'Cultural Policy,'" *Man* 28 (1993): 781.

39. Ibid., 786.

40. On revealed preference theory, see Amartya Sen, *Choice, Welfare, and Measurement* (Oxford: Blackwell, 1982).

41. Amitai Etzioni, *Political Unification: A Comparative Study of Leaders and Forces* (New York: Holt, Rinehart and Winston, 1965) uses the term *identitive* assets instead of *cultural raw material.*

42. Anthony D. Smith, "Gastronomy or Geology? The Role of Nationalism in the Reconstruction of Nations," *Nations and Nationalism* 1 (March 1995): 3–23.

43. In "The Construction of Collective Identity," *Archives européennes de sociologie* 36 (1995): 72–104, Shmuel N. Eistenstadt and Bernhard Giesen refer to primordial identities as one of three ideal-types.

44. See also Chapter 2 of this volume for a discussion of constructivism.

45. Note that this definition differs somewhat from constructivism in international relations. Wendt, for example, defines constructivism as "a structural theory of the international system that makes the following core claims: (1) states are the principal units of analysis for international political theory; (2) the key structures in the states system are intersubjective, rather than material; and

(3) state identities and interests are in important part constructed by these social structures, rather than given exogenously to the system by human nature or domestic politics." Alexander Wendt, "Collective Identity Formation and the International State," *American Political Science Review* 88 (1994): 385. While this definition endogenizes "role identities" that make up security communities and threat complexes, the states' "corporate identities" are held constant, and thus also their outer boundaries. For a critique of this limitation, see Sujata Chakrabarti Pasic, "Culturing International Relations Theory: A Call for Extension," in Yosef Lapid and Friedrich Kratochwil, eds., *The Return of Culture and Identity in IR Theory* (Boulder, Colo.: Lynne Rienner, 1996); and Cederman and Daase, "Endogenizing Corporate Identities." Cogent introductions to international relations constructivism can be found in Alexander Wendt, *Social Theory of International Politics* (Cambridge: Cambridge University Press, 1999); Jeffrey T. Checkel, "The Constructivist Turn in International Relations Theory (A Review Essay)," *World Politics* 50 (1998): 324–348; John Gerald Ruggie, *Constructing the World Polity: Essays on International Institutionalization* (London: Routledge, 1998).

46. See, e.g., John Breuilly, *Nationalism and the State* (Chicago: University of Chicago Press, 1982); Paul Brass, *Ethnicity and Nationalism: Theory and Comparison* (Newbury Park, Calif.: Sage, 1991); Cederman, *Emergent Actors in World Politics*, chs. 6–8.

47. Michael T. Hannan, "The Dynamics of Ethnic Boundaries in Modern States," in John W. Meyer and Michael T. Hannan, eds., *National Development and the World System* (Chicago: University of Chicago Press, 1979).

48. John W. Meyer, John Boli, and George M. Thomas, "Ontology and Rationalization in the Western Cultural Account," in George M. Thomas, John W. Meyer, Francisco O. Ramirez, and John Boli, eds., *Institutional Structure: Constituting State, Society, and the Individual* (Newbury Park, Calif.: Sage, 1987).

49. Craig Calhoun, *Nationalism* (Minneapolis: University of Minnesota Press, 1997), 11.

50. Barth, "Introduction," 14.

51. Ernest Gellner, *Nations and Nationalism* (Ithaca: Cornell University Press, 1983), 1.

52. See Anthony D. Smith, "The Supersession of Nationalism?" *International Journal of Comparative Sociology* 31 (1990): 3. Multicultural federations, empires, feudal or "neomedieval" hierarchies and overlapping networks all break the link between culture and politics prescribed by nationalism. Another tricky issue is the status of subnational identities. This topic will not be elaborated further in this chapter, though see, e.g., Gary Marks, Liesbet Hooghe, and Kermit Blank, "European Integration from the 1980s: State-Centric v. Multi-level Governance," *Journal of Common Market Studies* 34 (September 1996): 341–378. Finally, it is also possible that national and supranational identities could start blending into each other to such an extent that they become inseparable.

53. Calhoun, "Nationalism and Ethnicity," 229.

54. Walker Connor, *Ethnonationalism: The Quest for Understanding* (Princeton: Princeton University Press, 1994), chs. 2 and 4.

55. See Anthony D. Smith, *The Ethnic Revival in the Modern World* (Cambridge: Cambridge University Press, 1981). Another authority on this topic, Walker Connor, has done much to dispel the assimilationist illusions propagated by liberal modernization and integration theorists. While emphasizing the "emotional" and "ethnic" aspects of nationalism, Connor distances

himself from the essentialist standpoint more clearly than does Smith. This can be inferred from the former's explicit emphasis on selection of cultural traits rather than "articulation" of preexisting cultural wholes. See Connor, *Ethnonationalism*, 75, 104–105. Still, Connor agrees with Smith's skeptical attitude toward a Pan-European identity: "No area of similar size has offered so drastic an illustration of divisiveness, reflecting strong national jealousies and rivalries. There is no reconciliation because a single European culture is a fiction, and a multiplicity of languages, dialects, religious denominations, and other cultural manifestations is the fact." Ibid., 134.

56. See also Liah Greenfeld's study of national traditions: *Nationalism: Five Roads to Modernity* (Cambridge: Harvard University Press, 1992). Though she agrees with constructivists that the nation is a modern invention, her reified "country focus" suffers from severe retrospective bias and thus fails to break loose from the tacit essentialist assumption of a direct link between the ethnic core and more recent political expressions of nationhood. Like other ethnonationalists, she takes a pessimistic view of the possibility of transcending the nation-state. Cf. Liah Greenfeld, "Transcending the Nation's Worth," *Dædalus* 122 (Summer 1993): 47–62.

57. Anthony D. Smith, *Nations and Nationalism in a Global Era* (Cambridge: Polity Press, 1995), 24. Elsewhere Smith follows the principles of this essentialist account, albeit with caveats: "Historically, the nation is a sub-variety and development of the *ethnie,* though we are not dealing with some evolutionary law of progression, nor with some necessary or irreversible sequence." He further weakens the link between *ethnie* and nation by remarking that the ethnic core, "however and whenever ethnogenesis took place, forms the essential building block of later national identities—even if that identity comes to include other *ethnies* or ethnic fragments than the core itself." It is clear, however, that those modifications do not detract from the existence of a premodern cultural core driving the entire process, thus the references to "other *ethnies*" and "the core itself." Anthony D. Smith, "A Europe of Nations—or the Nations of Europe," *Journal of Peace Research* 30 (1993): 130. See also Anthony D. Smith, "National Identity and the Idea of European Unity," *International Affairs* 68 (1992): 55–76.

58. Smith, *Nations and Nationalism in a Global Era*, 112.

59. Smith "National Identity," 70.

60. Smith, *Nations and Nationalism in a Global Era*, 125.

61. This is not to say that Smith entirely ignores education and other policy instruments as potential sources of identity formation. See, for example, especially "National Identity." Yet his most recent book, *Nations and Nationalism in a Global Era*, appears to downplay this theme. While putting the stress on more general phenomena such as "memories, myths and symbols," this work relegates "modern bureaucratic and cultural mechanisms" such as media and education to a merely reinforcing role of preexisting cultural communities (142). Exacerbating the circularity of this essentialist analysis, Smith goes on to say that "individual members [of nations] come to perceive the social formations of their dependence on the nation, including such collective needs as preservation of their community's irreplaceable culture values, the rediscovery of its authentic roots, the celebration and emulation of its exemplars of heroic virtue, the re-creation of feelings of fraternity and kinship and the mobilization of citizens for common goals" (155).

62. Jürgen Habermas, "Citizenship and National Identity: Some Reflections on the Future of Europe," *Praxis International* 12, 1 (1992): 3.

63. Brian Barry makes an impassioned appeal to separate politics from culture in "The Limits of Cultural Politics," *Review of International Studies* 24 (1998): 307–319.

64. Habermas, "Citizenship and National Identity," 6. See also Jo Shaw, "Postnational Constitutionalism in the European Union," *Journal of European Public Policy* 6 (1999): 579–597, and Jean-Marc Ferry, "Pertience du postnational" and "Identité et citoyenneté européennes," in Jacques Lenoble and Nicole Dewandre, eds., *L'Europe au soir du siècle: Identité et démocratie* (Paris: Éditions Esprit, 1992), 39–58, 177–188; and his more recent "L'Etat européen," in Riva Kastoryano, ed., *Quelle identité pour l'Europe? Le multiculturalisme à l'épreuve* (Paris: Presses de Sciences Po, 1998).

65. Habermas, "Citizenship and National Identity," 11.

66. Samuel P. Huntington, "The Clash of Civilizations?" *Foreign Affairs* 72 (1993): 24. For a book-length study, see Samuel P. Huntington, *The Clash of Civilizations and the Remaking of World Order* (New York: Simon and Schuster, 1996).

67. Ibid., 25.

68. Ibid., 27.

69. Samuel P. Huntington, "If Not Civilizations, What? Paradigms of the Post–Cold War World," *Foreign Affairs* 72 (November/December 1993): 194.

70. Richard N. Coudenhove-Kalgeri's Pan-Europa movement in the interwar period is a case in point. For a general discussion of pannationalism, see Louis Snyder, *Macro-Nationalisms: A History of the Pan-Movements* (Westport, Conn.: Greenwood Publishers, 1984). See also De Rougement, as cited above. More recently, Pan-Europeanist ideas have emerged in French right-wing circles, cf. Hervé Varenne, "The Question of European Nationalism," in Thomas M. Wilson and M. Estellie Smith, eds., *Cultural Change and the New Europe: Perspectives on the European Community* (Boulder, Colo.: Westview Press, 1993), 223–239.

71. For examples, see Shore, "Inventing the 'People's Europe.'"

72. Note that state-nationalism, as the term is used here, does not presuppose chronological priority of the state over the nation, nor a purely civic political identity based on voluntaristic and individualist principles. State-nationalism is not only compatible with the notion of the *Staatsnation* but also with the *Kulturnation* as long as the latter's constructedness is emphasized.

73. Gellner, *Nations and Nationalism*, 34.

74. In *The Nation-State and Violence*, vol. 2 of *A Contemporary Critique of Historical Materialism* (Berkeley: University of California Press, 1985), Anthony Giddens coined the notion of the state as a power container.

75. Gellner, *Nations and Nationalism*, 119.

76. Ibid., 121.

77. Ibid. For other prominent examples of retentionist analyses of nationalism, see Brubaker, *Citizenship and Nationhood in France and Germany* and Benedict Anderson, *Imagined Communities: Reflections on the Origin and Spread of Nationalism* (London: Verso, 1991)

men: *The Modernization of*

tenstaat als
" in Rudolf
91); Jürgen
keiten der

Entstehung einer europäischen Öffentlichkeit," *Zeitschrift für Soziologie* 22 (1993): 96–110; Tobias Theiler, "The European Union and the 'European Dimension' in Schools: Theory and Evidence," *Journal of European Integration* 21 (1998): 307–341.

80. Richard Münch, *Das Projekt Europa: Zwischen Nationalstaat, regionaler Autonomie und Weltgesellschaft* (Frankfurt: Suhrkamp, 1993), introduces the theoretical puzzle, but to my knowledge there does not exist any study that offers a solid empirical comparison of internal and external mechanisms.

81. Wendt, *Social Theory of International Politics*, ch. 2. For an argument denying this possibility, see Martin Hollis and Steve Smith, *Explaining and Understanding International Relations* (Oxford: Clarendon Press, 1990).

82. Naturalism believes that the social sciences should aspire to natural science methodology. The three criteria are elaborated in Georg Henrik von Wright, *Explanation and Understanding* (Ithaca: Cornell University Press, 1971).

83. The Hempelian idea of covering laws insists that all causal explanations have to be "covered" or "subsumed" by lawlike regularities. For a critique of such notions of causation in international relations, see, e.g., David Dessler, "Beyond Correlations: Toward a Causal Theory of War," *International Studies Quarterly* 35 (1991): 335–355; Cederman, *Emergent Actors in World Politics*, ch. 3. A passionate plea for the need to contextualize social theorizing in space and time is made by Andrew Abbott, "Of Time and Space: The Contemporary Relevance of the Chicago School," *Social Forces* 75 (1997): 1149–1182.

84. See, e.g., Andrew Moravcsik, "'Is Something Rotten in the State of Denmark?' Constructivism and European Integration," *Journal of European Public Policy* 6 (1999): 669–681. Elsewhere he has attempted to develop a "generalizable" theory of integration that allegedly applies to more than this case of integration; see Andrew Moravcsik, *The Choice for Europe: Social Purpose and State Power from Messina to Maastricht* (Ithaca: Cornell University Press, 1998). The problem with this approach is that in order to find comparable cases, Moravcsik is forced to equate integration with intergovernmental cooperation, thus ignoring the unique, supranational features of the European Union. An earlier attempt along these lines was made by Ernst B. Haas, "International Integration: The European and the Universal Process," *International Organization* 15 (1957): 366–392. On the "N = 1 problem," cf. also Simon Hix, "The Study of the European Union II: The 'New Governance' Agenda and Its Rival," *Journal of European Public Policy* 5, 1 (March 1998): 38–65.

85. Wendt, *Social Theory of International Politics*, labels this mode of causal analysis "inference to the best explanation," but it also is known as "abduction" or "retroduction" (62–63). In these cases causation entails finding the causal mechanisms that account for an empirical observation that may rely on a single case.

86. Albert S. Yee, "The Causal Effects of Ideas on Politics," *International Organization* 50 (1996): 69–108, provides a useful summary of such methods.

87. Wendt, *Social Theory of International Politics*, 62. For a typical treatment that privileges explanation over description, see Gary King, Robert O. Keohane, and Sidney Verba, *Designing Social Inquiry* (Princeton: Princeton University Press, 1994).

88. Ibid., ch. 2. Yee, "The Causal Effects of Ideas on Politics," 97–101, outlines a hybrid, "quasi-causal" position.

PART ONE

CONCEPTUAL AND HISTORICAL BACKGROUND

2

The Virtues of Inconsistency: Identity and Plurality in the Conceptualization of Europe

Craig Calhoun

When we speak of a European identity, we are not just asking whether there is a common image of the continent, the EU, or their people. European cars and clothes may have some stylistic similarities by contrast to American or Japanese, but this is at most tangentially related to the question of identity. That question, rather, concerns to what extent internal cultural similarity and external cultural distinction form the basis for European unity and produce a coherent and consistent European behavior from one context to the next.

We say that an individual has achieved a strong identity, thus, when she or he is able to maintain much the same way of thinking and the same sense of who she or he is when moving from family into public life, from one job to another, from work to leisure, or from a room full of friends to one full of strangers. We say people have a weak identity when their sense of personal autonomy is subordinated to others, as children's may be to parents'; when different contexts and external stimuli bring out very different versions of them; when it is unpredictable which of their conflicting internal impulses will come out on top.

Achieving a strong personal identity is generally considered a good thing. It is a desirable part, we usually think, of the individual maturation process. It is what gives each of us a sense of self in relation both to others and to our own biological needs and drives, our sensory experiences, and our impulses. It allows us to think of ourselves from the point of view of others, and as coherent and consistent enough to have biographies.

There are those who question whether this individualistic understanding of identity is altogether a good thing, who point to its costs in psychological stress and arguably loss of community. They point out that this kind of individual identity is especially valued within the modern European cultural traditions (with America perhaps an extreme case). They rightly suggest that "strength" can be taken too far and amount to rigidity, that when we understand strength as maintaining the same identity rather than achieving flexibility within a reasonable range of difference, we may wind up with brittleness instead of suppleness.

The questions may be multiplied at the collective level. Even if we accept the broad Western approach to individual identity, we must ask anew how much such identity is a good thing in large-scale political, economic, or cultural units; how it ought to be produced; and on what models it ought to be understood. Identity implies—indeed literally means—selfsameness. We should remember that even at the individual level we do not think this is an alloyed good. We worry, for example, that "a foolish consistency is the hobgoblin of little minds." At the large-scale, collective level, the pursuit of consistency, of strong cultural identity, of selfsameness may be a hobgoblin of another kind.

For most of its history, Western Europe has been characterized by a high level of local variation. In many ways villages differed from their neighbors; regions at the scale that eventually became counties and provinces commonly differed sharply from one another. Cities and towns differed dramatically from the surrounding countrysides. Artisans in the towns may have had more in common with members of the same crafts in relatively distant towns. Urban merchants may have had stronger links to their trading partners hundreds of miles away.

Gradually, as we know, this was changed in the era of absolutist monarchies and the formation of more powerful states. The major products were the units we now see as the primary bearers of large-scale collective identity: nations, or nation-states. As recently as the eighteenth and early nineteenth centuries, however, on matters as basic as fertility practices—the size of families, age at first birth—there was still more variation among counties and provinces within European countries than there was among those countries.[1] It was only with the spread of national communication systems, the development of national educational systems, that internal homogeneity in these practices came to coincide with the ever more strongly defended borders between countries. The countries, in other words, were not selfsame units, and neither was Europe as a whole.

The projects of making national identities have been very powerful and have been directed against many kinds of internal differences as well as external threats. In many cases international immigrants were more eager to assimilate to the new national identity than were "domestic" provincials.[2] Of course, national identity building required its infrastructure of roads, schools, administrative apparatus, citizen armies, and mass media. My point is not to trace its history so much as to point to its relative novelty.[3] We need to ask whether the attempt to achieve European identity is primarily a continuation of the same project. This project has been more attractive, to be sure, where coupled with high levels of political democracy, cultural freedom, and social self-organization in civil society. But the fact remains—shocking to modern ears—that by and large empires have been more tolerant of internal diversity than have nation-states.[4]

One relatively narrow definition of *Western* Europe might focus on the relative absence of empire, at least since Charlemagne's sons botched his effort at unification.[5] It was partly the history of empire that kept Iberia out of Western Europe despite geographic westernness. It was empires (and their aftermaths) as much as geography that defined "Central Europe" as something other than simply Europe. The less it recalled the Holy Roman Empire, for example, the more Germany joined the broad "Western" path of development. Habsburg Austria was famously ambivalent, but it was empire that distinguished it from Western Europe (as well as gave it much of its distinctive cosmopolitan cultural vitality, especially in the last half century of its existence). Western Europe has not had much history of the looser kind of large-scale integration brought by empires but quite a lot of nationalist history.

Is this a good thing or a problem to be solved? The cause of European identity has many attractions today. Some are material. But "identity" also figures as an approach to the legitimation of the European Union. The earliest and most successful framings of the basis of European unity were economic and political. Treaty-based cooperation after World War II was intended to bring prosperity and peace, and the second largely because of the first. Faced with challenges from national populations (and sometimes governments) resistant to greater unification, and with challenges from would-be members, the arguments for the EU, and for specific definitions of Europe and its boundaries, have become increasingly cultural. They turn, for example, on the declared common "civilization" of Europe.

But let us keep the picture complex. Europe has been internally diverse and sharply disunified for most of the last 1,000 years. It has resembled India more than China, but unlike South Asia it has never been successful at transforming imperial projects on the scale of the Mughals. Lacking imperial peacekeepers, Western Europeans have devoted a great deal of energy to killing each other and may have offered the world more innovations in the field of warfare than any other. This creativity has been closely linked to European development of the nation-state as a political institution and ideological project. But this disunified subcontinent (Western Europe) has also been creative in

other ways, inventing perhaps most notably capitalism and the democratic modern public sphere.

In this chapter I call attention to the virtues of inconsistency, the
advantages of being an internally heterogeneous and sometimes conflictual setting for creativity. I even maintain that this might be a good
thing for freedom. I argue for the project of conceptualizing Europe not
as a unitary, comprehensive, singular identity—not, certainly, a unity on
the model of the integral nation-state—but as an institutional arena
within which diversity and multiple connections among people and
organizations can flourish partly because they never add up to a single,
integrated whole. What is most important, in other words, is to build
institutions that encourage and protect multiple, discontinuous, sometimes conflicting public spaces and modes of public engagement rather
than to attempt to nurture or impose some unified European culture.
Since cultural creativity always produces cultural differences, I should
hate to see cultural unity assume primacy in the European project.

The Politics of Identity

It was long assumed that politics was largely about economic and
national security interests, and perhaps about power and its limits.
Recently, however, issues of identity have begun to claim a place in the
foreground of political theorists' attention. The issues are not altogether new, of course, and though the jargon is newly fashionable, it,
too, is of older provenance.

What is at stake in a "politics of identity"? To start with, sovereignty
and legitimacy. Much historical thought vested sovereignty in rulers, not
people, and approached the question of which ruler as a matter of identification: which king, determined by divine right and/or lineage.
Legitimacy flowed downward, from God or the ancestors. Increasingly
in the modern era, an idea of ascending legitimacy gained ground. The
notion was that ultimate authority was vested in the people, and so the
legitimate ruler (or system of rule) was that which (1) served the interests of the people or (2) better yet, received the consent of the people
or (3) best of all, was positively chosen or created by the people. All of
which raises the question, Who are the people?

The question is even thornier than might at first appear, because it
is not obvious that divided and plural opinions of various people will do
for such a question. At least on many theoretical interpretations, something more like Jean-Jacques Rousseau's general will is required. It is
necessary either that the people speak with one voice or that there be
some procedure available for determining how to represent the people

in a determinate, singular fashion. So in a sense, the question becomes the ungrammatical, Who is the people, the whole, the corporate body, as distinct from the heterogeneous and ill-bounded multitude? Now we see the question of identity.

Identity appeared in modern discussions simultaneously at two levels: individuals and nations. We are so accustomed today to distinguish the individual from the collective that we don't always grasp how closely connected the two are. But the early modern era saw an emancipation of individuals from restraints of family and pedigree, restrictions on mobility and economic opportunity, sumptuary laws, and especially, with Protestantism, from the need for intermediations between themselves and the word of God. All these helped to create the individual in such a way that he or she could be a unit of identity, separate and distinct from his or her fellows. Such identity required autonomy, according to many early modern thinkers. John Locke, for example, argued that someone who lacked the property to support himself and his family without relying on employment by another lacked full legal personality and accordingly lacked full political rights.

Such individuals no longer derived their basic identities in the same way from complex webs of social relations or fixed positions in a stable order. But they could constitute "the people" of an ascending claim to political legitimacy. They could appear as equivalent to each other not only in formal law and economic relations but as members of the nation—which emerged at about this time as the primary anchor to talk of legitimacy.[6] It is one of the distinctive and almost universal features of the rhetoric of national identity to treat each individual member as equivalently national and as directly and without mediation tied to the whole. National identity, as it were, is inscribed in the individual's body, not attached to the individual through membership in family, community, or other intermediate association.[7] While families had once been the basic unit of membership and had given people their distinctive sense of location in the world, now nations became basic. In place of the family home, increasingly lost to mobility if not expropriation, there was the national territory.[8]

The nation itself was conceptualized in ways very similar to the individual person. In the first place, it was a kind of "superperson" with a history that was conceived often in quasi-biographical terms as a kind of maturation. The problem with Germany, late-nineteenth-century nationalists thought, was not that it had to be created but that it had not achieved its maturity. This required that they become agents of its *Bildung*, cultivators of the national will as well as its culture. The problem with the image of maturation is that it implies not only prior existence as the same being but a foreordained path of development rather than an open and contingent process in which actual people make history and make the nation.

In the second place, the nation was "self-identical" and "indivisible" (as the American pledge of allegiance I recited in my youth put it). The nation, in other words, was literally "individual." It is no accident that the German philosopher Johann Fichte should have been a pioneer in both individualism and nationalism. Fichte's notion of self-recognition, of the person who seemingly confronts himself or herself in a mirror and says "I am I," is inextricably tied to the notion of the nation as itself an individual.[9] Just as persons are understood as unitary in prototypical modern thought, so are nations held to be integral. In general, each nation—or at least each nation that has succeeded in the process of individuation and become what Fichte called a "historical nation"—is understood as indivisible (individual) and as the bearer of a distinctive identity.

It is precisely in the context of and in response to this powerful modern account of identity vested in the twin individuals of person and nation that the "politics of identity" emerged. It emerged in contestation first over the definition and autonomy of nations and second in claims of various categories of people for public recognition, rights, and legitimacy. Although schoolbook histories of nations commonly present them as always already there, they are actually products of struggle. As Ernst Renan phrased it memorably: "Forgetting, I would even go so far as to say historical error, is a crucial factor in the creation of a nation, which is why progress in historical studies often constitutes a danger for [the principle of] nationality. Indeed, historical enquiry brings to light deeds of violence which took place at the origin of all political formations, even those whose consequences have been altogether beneficial. Unity is always effected by means of brutality."[10] Or as Benedict Anderson summarizes one English version: "English history textbooks offer the diverting spectacle of a great Founding Father whom every schoolchild is taught to call William the Conqueror. The same child is not informed that William spoke no English, indeed could not have done so, since the English language did not exist in his epoch; nor is he or she told 'Conqueror of what?'. For the only intelligible modern answer would have to be 'Conqueror of the English,' which would turn the old Norman predator into a more successful precursor of Napoleon and Hitler."[11]

Ironically, the writing of linear historical narratives of national development and the claim to primordial national identity often proceed hand in hand. It is no accident that nationalist history is generally written as though the nation were always already there. Indeed, the writing of national historical narratives is so embedded in the discourse of nationalism that it almost always depends rhetorically on the presumption of some kind of preexisting national identity in order to give the story a beginning. Atlantic crossings thus make English colonists into Americans *avant la lettre* when it comes to writing U.S. history books, whether or not they ever thought themselves part of an autonomous American nation. I saw a popular version of this in Sweden (just before the vote to enter the European Union). An extremely well attended museum exhibition presented Swedish history. It began with a display of fur-clad cave dwellers, whom, it confidently assured viewers, were Swedish cave-dwellers, in fact, the first Swedes.

It is common to suggest a sharp contrast between French and German nationalism, the former prototypically "civic," the latter "ethnic." There is something to this, of course, but it is easily exaggerated. The common contrast between France and Germany is at least in part between two different styles of invoking history and ethnicity, not radically between nonethnic and ethnic claims. French schoolchildren learn that their commonality is not merely ethnic but was achieved in the collective action of the revolution. Yet they learn also to claim as French a history stretching back 1,000 years before that revolution. French unity, after all, achieved the hexagonal shape that is etched into the minds of schoolchildren in the age of absolutist kings, not of Robespierre. It was forged by military conquest and administrative centralization before the revolution consecrated the product as the nation. French nationalist historians help schoolchildren "forget" that events like the massacre of Huguenots known as Saint-Barthélemy helped unify France even while they claim them as moments in French history. German nationalist historians, by contrast, put forward stronger claims for the primacy of common culture and ethnicity partly because their narratives must help schoolchildren "forget" that Germans spent most of their history as members of separate polities (often combative and not all uniform culturally), even while they celebrate the roles of Otto von Bismarck and others in unifying Germany. In France in 1991 Jacques Chirac found a brilliant rhetorical weapon against Jean-Marie Le Pen. When Le Pen appealed to "real Frenchmen" by pointing to the importance of being French by birth, Chirac neatly accused him of being "un-French" with all his "German" talk of a *nationalisme du sang.*

There is no need to belabor the extent to which the history of European nationalism has been conflict-laden. The 1848 "springtime of peoples" may have featured the Romantic belief that every nation could rise freely and take its rightful place in a peaceful community of nations, but by World War I it was clear that the ambitions of different nations crowded each other. It is rather surprising, then, that the idea that national identities are ancient and stable, even primordial, has survived with such force. It is clear that more potential nations have vanished or been subordinated into mere regions or ethnicities or stateless peoples than have flourished as hyphenated partners of states. Yet early in the Bosnian disaster, the U.S. secretary of state Warren Christopher could declare that the conflict was simply a reflection of ancient ethnic hatreds and there was nothing the rest of the world could do about it except ameliorate the suffering through the Red Cross and similar agencies. This kind of explanatory recourse to ancient hostility fails to make sense of the timing of the crisis and the ways in which it was actively shaped by state action under Habsburgs and Communists alike. Not least, it completely obscures the fact that the redeployment of nationalism in Yugoslavia came after years of economic crisis that sharply opposed the interests of Slovenia and Croatia to those of Serbia and other poorer parts of the country. It also conceals that Slovenia, Croatia, and Bosnia-Herzegovina had much brighter prospects in the Western camp than Serbia, which had been tied in trade as well as religion much more to the East. Finally, it makes it hard to see that it was the early and rapid departure of Slovenia and Croatia that first precipitated conflict (and Serb panic)—though the case for ancient ethnic hatred makes little sense for Slovenia.

The point of these brief remarks on nationalism and violence is to indicate that the violence is not simply fighting between clearly established, already neatly identified nations. It is, rather, a by-product of struggles to forge greater internal unity as well as to expand territory and weaken rivals. What we see today as the history of internal conflict involved in making France whole is only a retrospective view. That conflict did not always appear "internal" to protagonists—to the duke of Burgundy, for example, or to many a speaker of regional languages and dialects sacrificed in the pursuit of a standard national language. Nationalism, in other words, has always been a matter of "politics of identity." The famous Wilsonian edict about "self-determination" presumed that the identity of the selves in question was much more neutrally established than has ever been the case.

Indeed, the phrase politics of identity came to the fore in political and sociological discussions not with regard to issues of relations among states or nations but in response to mobilizations of women, gay men and lesbians, ethnic and regional groups, and a variety of other categories of citizens—vegetarians, environmentalists, youth—who claimed that their identities were not properly recognized and treated as legitimate *within* their nation-states. Retrospectively, we can see that class politics, too—the paradigmatic original social movement based on economic interests—was largely a matter of the politics of identity. Workers had to be persuaded to think of themselves as members of the working class and to put their class identity ahead of religion, region, and even nation when voting and ahead of craft, community, and company loyalties when deciding about economic struggles.[12] Contrary to Karl Marx's predictions, by no means all workers were so persuaded. Many continued for generations to find their primary large-scale identities not with other workers but with fellow speakers of regional dialects, fellow Catholics, or fellow masters of skilled crafts worried that the working class in general might swamp their trade and destroy their standard of living.

The long struggle for women's rights was a paradigmatic matter of identity politics. Women were, quite simply, subordinated to the identities of men—particular men rather than men in general. They were legally and politically placed under the authority and protection of first fathers and then husbands. Their rights to property and to public voice (e.g., voting) were restricted or denied largely on the original Lockean grounds that they lacked independent identity, independent legal personality. In some settings women could own property outright only if they were widows. As late as the 1980s, I heard a Swiss political scientist explain why women ought not to have full voting rights because they were already represented by their husbands. A gracious guest will not press the point.

This is not just a matter of ancient sexism, however, but of a distinctively modern construction of public rights. Women, for example, were excluded from the English Parliament and the French National Assembly in ways they had not been excluded from aristocratic salon culture and were not excluded from popular political discourse.[13] "Free" citizens of color had their political rights actually reduced in many European settings in the early nineteenth century as racial boundaries took on new significance.

All these sorts of "domestic" politics of identity have in common with issues of immigration and with nationalism the fact that they are about the rights of citizens and therefore about the identity of the "self" of national self-determination. The classical models of citizenship in European national states worked by treating citizens as presumptive equals, by making them equal before the law and equal in voting, even if they were manifestly unequal in wealth or other terms. The class and other differences of civil society were thus separated from the political realm by an account of identity not as difference but as equivalence. It is in this sense that all Belgians are equivalent to each other regardless of their linguistic or ethnic community and regardless of their class. But this model of citizenship came with two catches. First, it produced long struggles over the exclusionary rules that originally restricted full citizenship—especially the franchise—to segments of the population. Second, it tended to disqualify discourse over differences of identity among those fully enfranchised as citizens.

The issue of "democratic inclusiveness" is not just a quantitative matter of the scale of a public sphere or the proportion of the members of a political community who may speak within it. While it is clearly a matter of stratification and boundaries (e.g., openness to the property-less, the uneducated, women, or immigrants), it is also a matter of how the public sphere incorporates and recognizes the diversity of identities that people bring to it from their manifold involvements in civil society. It is a matter of whether in order to participate in such a public sphere, for example, women must act in ways previously characteristic of men and avoid addressing certain topics defined as appropriate to the private realm (the putatively more female sphere). Marx criticized the discourse of bourgeois citizenship for implying that it equally fitted everyone when in fact it tacitly presumed an understanding of citizens as property owners. The same sort of false universalism has presented citizens in gender-neutral or gender-symmetrical terms without in fact acknowledging highly gendered underlying conceptions.

All attempts to render authoritative a single public discourse privilege certain topics, certain forms of speech, certain ways of constructing and presenting identities, and certain speakers.[14] This is partly because of emphasis on the single, unitary whole—the discourse of all the citizens rather than of subsets—and partly because of the specific demarcations of public from private. If sexual harassment, for example, is seen as a concern to women but not men, it becomes a sectional issue rather than one for the public in general; if it is seen as a private matter, then by definition it is not a public concern. The same goes for a host of other topics of attention that are inhibited from reaching full recognition in a public sphere conceptualized as a single discourse about topics consensually determined to be of public significance.

The liberal model of the public sphere pursues discursive equality by disqualifying discourse about the differences among actors. These differences are treated as matters of private, but not public, interest. On Jürgen Habermas's account, the best version of the public sphere was based on "a kind of social intercourse that, far from presupposing the equality of status, disregarded status altogether."[15] It worked by a "mutual willingness to accept the given roles and simultaneously to suspend their reality."[16] This "bracketing" of difference as merely private and irrelevant to the public sphere was undertaken, Habermas argues, in order to defend the genuinely rational-critical notion that arguments must be decided on their merits rather than the identities of the arguers. This was, by the way, as important as fear of censors for the prominence of anonymous or pseudonymous authorship in the eighteenth-century public sphere.[17] Yet it has the effect of excluding some of the most important concerns of many members of any polity—both those whose existing identities are suppressed or devalued and those whose exploration of possible identities is truncated. In addition, this bracketing of differences also undermines the self-reflexive capacity of public discourse. If it is impossible to communicate seriously about basic differences among members of a public sphere, then it will be impossible also to address the difficulties of communication across such lines of basic difference. In more recent writings, Habermas has suggested a greater role for "identity" in public discourse, but only in the thin, lowest-common-denominator form of "constitutional patriotism."[18] By this he means above all attachment to certain procedural norms, a love of the conditions one's country provides for communicative action tolerant of differences, rather than of other, substantive manifestations of collective identity. Habermas somewhat surprisingly assumes the nation as the tacit locus of such constitutional patriotism. There is no intrinsic reason why "constitutional patriotism" could not work on the scale of Europe; a bigger question is how the concept helps to provide for the introduction into public space of other kinds of identities besides those that unify the polity as a whole. Habermas continues to presume that the cultural conditions of public life, including individual identity, are established prior to properly public discourse itself. It might be helpful to look at the public forging of diverse identities that fit together well enough to enable specific agreements about life together and collective action on multiple scales including (but not limited to) the nation-state or the European Union.

When protagonists of the so-called new social movements brought identity issues to the fore in the 1960s and after, they were protesting among other things the extent to which national unity and the norms of citizenship presupposed or called for a uniformity of personal identity. They were objecting to the notion that there was one right way to be a French man, for example, or to be an Italian woman. They were demanding that the rights and respect due citizens not be conditional on conforming to any set cultural ideal but instead be open to those who found in themselves or wished to forge different kinds of identities. These were movements of people who felt literally "alienated," made to feel like foreigners in their own countries.[19] It is worth remarking how very international these movements were.

Making Sense of Identity

All this is significant in the context of a discussion of European identity because a basic question is, How much internal commonality—or conformity—does political unity (or economic integration) require? I do not know the precise answer, nor do I propose to speculate. My goal is more to raise the issue, but I do want to comment on what is at stake in the very concept of identity. This will take the form more of a catalogue of different meanings than a serious and sustained discussion of the issues raised by each. We can gain an introductory purchase on the complex debates over identity by seeing several dimensions that focus different approaches and/or differences in understanding and constituting identities.

Self-Equivalence Versus Hegelian Non-Self-Identity

To start with, there is the Fichtean image I invoked above, of the man who looks in the mirror and recognizes with satisfaction, "I am I." As Marx and countless later sociologists have pointed out, this kind of solipsistic identity is not normal to human beings, who in fact recognize themselves primarily in the mirrors of their relations to other human beings and thereby see themselves as both linked and at the same time qualitatively distinct. The same is true of nations: The existence and self-recognition of a nation is never entirely an internal matter; it always presumes and depends on the existence of other nations. Which international mirror is most powerful makes an interesting question: The English seem mainly to see themselves as the not-French, the French as the not-German, and so forth. One of the spurs to European unity has been the protonational self-perception of Europeans as the not-Americans, though lately there have been some who perceive themselves in a multicontinental European civilization as the not-Asian.

It is crucial not to stop with Fichte. Hegel offered perhaps the key challenge early on by holding that the nature of creative, conscious human selfhood was precisely non-self-identity. This suggests, among other things, the possibility of wanting to be different than we are, wanting even, perhaps, to have different wants than those that drive us now.[20] It stresses the heterogeneous makeup of even the individual self, let alone any larger collectivity like Europe.

Essentialist/Constructivist, Determined/Chosen, Ascribed/Achieved

A basic issue in the politics of personal identity has been the question of whether there is some biological or other deep "essence" to any particular identity—say, gender identities—or whether these are socially constructed.[21] This has implications for how malleable such identities are understood to be. The analogous distinction in discussions of nationalism is between essentialist and constructivist theories of national identity. It seems clear that essentialists overstate their case if they do not recognize that all traditions and identities have to start somewhere and are subject to human action and manipulation. Conversely, constructivists too easily assume that once people are shown that their national identities are constructed, that their traditions are invented, then these will lose their force.[22] There is little evidence for this, and we might ask under what conditions historically constructed identities come to take on the sense of givenness and essential inevitability that fuels patriotic heroism and genocide alike.

Both essentialist and constructivist positions tend to emphasize the creation of identities by external determination, whether that of biology or of society. They accordingly downplay choice. Thus, while it has been a source of encouragement to some homosexuals, for example, that there is evidence that predispositions to homosexuality may be inborn, it has equally alarmed others who see dependence on such arguments as eroding the more basic liberal proposition that sexual orientation should be a matter of free choice.

The old sociological and anthropological distinction between ascribed and achieved identities captures a bit more of the dimension of self-making, while assuming that the alternative to choice is that which others will see in one regardless of one's own choice. The power of ascribed identities in politics is great and can easily act as a trump over personal choice. As Hannah Arendt, one of the most distinguished of the largely assimilated and secular Jews who were driven into exile from Germany in the 1930s, put it, when one is attacked as a Jew, one must respond as a Jew, "one can resist only in terms of the identity that is under attack."[23] One of the important features of the modern world is that a variety of ascribed identities hitherto treated as politically insignificant have become eminently and sometimes dangerously political (especially in the face of pressure for nationalist conformity).

We/They

In social psychological terms, one of the most basic questions is when and why people think sometimes in collective terms as "we" and sometimes in individual terms as "I." It appears that the capacity for "we-images" is an achievement, both historically and in terms of individual development.[24] We-images seem to be embedded deeply in individual personality, but people have a repertoire and can make use of different ones under different circumstances.[25] "We women" can give way to "we workers" or "we Irish" depending on the context and even the intention of the actor. These various collective identities may be more or less congruent; there is no sociological law indicating that they cannot be contradictory or in tension, and they often are. As the examples suggest, a

large part of the contextual basis for shifting from one collective identity to another is contraposition to other groups. This is equally true for
the experience of identity and its presentation or representation in
speech or other action. Like people who switch linguistic codes from
creole or pidgin to standard elite languages depending on who is lis-
tening, we all experience and even choose shifts in relevant identities
based on our situations. Much identity is always identification by contraposition. Whether "European" will be a meaningful identity depends
not just on internal cultural, political, or economic integration, in other
words, but on whether there are other identities of the same order to
which European can be counterposed. The possibility of discovering
such a similar collective identity was one of the forces driving the eager-
ness of European participation in the February 1996 Asian summit.

Categorical/Relational

Nationality is only one of a number of "categorical identities" that have
assumed central importance in the modern era. The discourse of nationalism thus shares much with those of race, class, gender, and other
appeals to cohesion based more on the similarity of individuals than on
their concrete webs of relationships.[26] In many traditional settings, kinship is the primary way of conceiving social identity; a specific person is a
member of the whole (which is often very fuzzy at its boundaries) and various intermediate groupings because he is related to others as brother,
cousin, and so on. Where categorical identities operate, individuals
become more autonomously the units of identity. Well before modern
nationalism, religious identities worked this way. One could thus become
a Christian by conversion, no matter who one's relatives were, and
Christians were understood to form a group—a very large group—
because of their common beliefs and practices, not because of any specific kinship of other relationships among them. While Christians did
have such relationships with each other, there were too many of them for
this to be the primary basis of their common identity; each could have
direct relationships with only a tiny minority of the whole. Conversely, the
Protestant Reformation (like many civil wars) divided many people with
close personal relationships against each other on the basis of categorical
identities (though also on bases of networks of allegiances).

While nations may have ideologies of common descent and shared
kinship, they are organized primarily as categories of individual members, identified on the basis of various cultural attributes: common language, religion, customs, names, and so on. Where the segmentary lineage system suggests "I against my brothers; I and my brothers against
my cousins; I, my brothers, and my cousins against the world," the discourse of nationalism suggests that membership in the category of the

whole nation is prior to, more basic than, any such web of relation-ships.[27] This suggests as well a different notion of moral commitment from previous modes of understanding existence. Advocates of nation-alism and other categorical identities are particularly likely to demand conformity, to treat membership in the category as a trump card to be played against all competing identities. Nationalist ideology thus offers the chilling example of children called to inform on their parents' infractions against the nation precisely because each individual is understood to derive his or her identity in such direct and basic ways from membership in the nation. This is sharply different from the dis-course of kinship and the ideology of honor of the lineage. There chil-dren derive their membership in the whole only through their rela-tionships to their parents.

Given the tendency to treat ethnicity as a matter of primordial tra-dition, it is worth noting that it is in some ways an intermediate forma-tion between the relational identities of kinship and more categorical identities, including nation. Ethnicity emerges primarily with the cre-ation of states, which draw people from remote regions into capitals and/or armies. In their local settings, kinship provides a highly specific sliding scale of relational identities. When, say, the Tallensi of Northern Ghana leave their FraFra region, however, and move as labor migrants to Accra, they discover a commonality with other Tallensi—including in the ascriptions of others—that does not depend on the internal specifi-cations of kinship that would make sense at home. Ethnicity is the cate-gorical construction of such common identity that organizes dealings with other groups or with the state.

Categorical identities require representation; they are not simply outgrowths of interaction but depend upon cultural labels and the pro-duction of ways of speaking about them. Their power reflects our aware-ness that the necessarily local relationships we may construct with con-crete others are incapable of managing the very large-scale modern world of states, capitalism, and global media and population movement. Nationalism draws its power and importance partly from this scale of social life. This is one reason why many forces that are held to spell the end of the nation-state, such as global economic integration, do not so readily do so. States respond most vigorously with nationalist ideology and policies precisely when threatened in this large-scale world.

What Is at Stake in
Talk of European Identity?

The first question has to be whether the identity of Europe is a being approached on the model of national identity. There is nothing fixed in advance about the appropriate scale of nations. They come as small as San Marino and Palau and as large as China. It would be an entirely plausible prospect for the amalgamation of European countries into a unified Europe to follow the path of the amalgamation of separate principalities, free cities, and other polities and cultural regions into the various national states. There might be greater or lesser respect for cultural difference and greater or lesser regional devolution of power in such a European state, just as there is in various current member states. But the logic would be that of the nation-state.

This is the model of seeking maximal internal coherence, partly as a support for maximally coherent foreign policy and maximally effective external economic competition. But it is not clear that such a model plays to Europe's strengths in all respects. One of the key questions any debate about identity needs to ask is in what realms coherence is really a positive good. The standardization that seems to me reasonable only with regard to electric circuitry, for example, may not be so appropriate with regard to intellectual life or even the organization of business institutions.

Take the latter as an example. Should it be a European goal to produce *a* single European business culture? To create a number of European superfirms that are largely similar to each other? Such a strategy would fly in the face of a great deal of current management theory (though I would not want to hold too much of a brief for the durability of any particular phase of that notoriously faddish field of knowledge). It would very likely stifle creativity. Whether the firms were public or private, they would be apt to behave all too much like Europe's existing, often nationalized behemoths. It seems to me that Europe's strength would more likely lie in creating an institutional framework that encouraged a diversity of business practices and organizational forms. This would be more likely to spur creativity. It would, indeed, be closer to the European approach that led the world in the nineteenth century.

Similarly, a great deal is made of the potential for European-wide media networks with the introduction of new technologies and partnerships among providers. But analysts tend to presume that the sole question is whether Europe will develop a single common media public or will be divided on national lines; they seldom consider the issue of subnational diversity and development of a multiplicity of specific cross-national media publics at a level much below that of Europe as a whole.[28] This is surprising given that the EU's facilitation of regional autonomy has been a major topic of discussion for years.

The arrival of common media may bring many commonalties, but we should be careful not to overestimate their impact. The enormous sharing of culture between the United States and Britain has kept the countries close, but (jokes in the era of Thatcher-Reagan friendship notwithstanding) links have stopped well short of political unity. If all Europeans watch Hollywood movies, this will add to their common frame of reference, but it will not produce a common European identity. That would be more likely to come, perhaps paradoxically, out of more heterogeneous cross-fertilizations of cultural *production* than from simple common media reception. If European policymakers are worried about Americanization by media, the answer is to produce, not restrict. In terms of the development of European political culture, surely a key issue is the development of the capacity for discourse, for engagement across lines of different opinions, not merely the representation of some putatively singular European field of political information. This, too, depends on diversity rather than singularity of models. It is worth noting, though, that while Europe has produced a substantially integrated economy and an increasingly integrated administrative framework, it has not produced an integrated public sphere. Political discussion—and the relevant media, like newspapers—is still organized overwhelmingly on national lines.

If Europe is not to be a large nation-state, the issue of European identity must also include the question to which I already alluded above, Identity as a member of what category of like units? In a world system of nation-states, how does the EU fit in? What status should it have in relationship to the UN? Should it push for a regionally structured complement to national membership?

One model for allegedly supranational unities is the idea of civilizations—proudly claimed by many Europeans who see the Continent on the model of Hellas or Christendom. Civilizations have sometimes formed the basis for empires, historically, but otherwise have not been bases for political units at all. Does the future lie with a division of the world into civilizational blocs? Would such blocs be constructed as empires or super-nation-states or federations? The thinking of the leading advocate of this view, Samuel P. Huntington, is actually very close to nationalism writ large.[29] We can thus ask about such blocs many of the same questions we ask about nations: Are these blocs really as internally homogenous as Huntington suggests? What level of conformity would be required as a price of integration (perhaps a bigger question in possibly neo-Confucian Asia but not insignificant for Europe)? Above all, does such a view radically underestimate the constructed character of these groupings, present them as much more historically continuous than they really are, as a base for overstating their likely unity? We may recall, for example, that at the time of those very European ventures the Crusades, Greece was decidedly a part of the non-Europe, the Christian East that crusaders set out to help but that turned out to have very different ideas from the West and not much interest in the help. The ancient Greeks were chosen by eighteenth- and nineteenth-century Western Europeans as their preferred ancestors. They are still idealized by many as the founders of European civilization and those who bequeathed it its characteristic love of freedom and democracy. But such assertions too easily forget not only that democracy has hardly been characteristic of all of European history but that today's chosen ancestors of European civilization were Byzantine "others" during much of European history. Claimed historical unities tend to be constructed on the basis of highly selective readings of history.

What is an alternative to selfsameness as a way of approaching large-scale collective identities? We can get one good idea from a point Ludwig Wittgenstein offered in a different connection: family resemblances. Why not think of Europe as a field of multiple, overlapping, and sometimes even conflicting identities? Europe is constructed out of both categorical similarities and relational ties, but no one set of these reaches all Europeans without joining a range of non-Europeans as well. Europeans derive their similarity not from a lowest common denominator nor from rigidly enforced boundaries but from characteristics that many Europeans hold in common without any being definitive of the whole. As some children have the family's characteristic eyes, others (for better or worse) its nose, and still others its immediately recognizable jaw, so some Europeans may share musical tastes but not politics; others may share trade union ties but resist cultural similarity; others may join European-wide political parties within which they form national or linguistic blocs; still others may develop close working ties in a European-wide business setting and spend their leisure time in enclave communities based on life-style choices. A family-resemblance view has the advantage of recognizing close connectedness without reducing it to the pursuit of simple sameness or consistency. It also has the virtue of approaching coherence—the sticking together of the Continent—on the basis of the multiple and diverse actual connections among people, mostly bottom-up rather than a top-down imposition of uniformity. Not least of all, it leaves room for continued cultural production, recognizing that a vital Europe will be the setting for a number of lively cultural fields, not simply a reflection of a single culture, already fixed in its essence. So, too, democratic politics must be a matter of difference, disagreement, and even conflict—peacefully pursued—not merely consensus.

We need to be wary of arguments that trade on illusions of homogeneity, of ancientness and natural or historical givenness. They forget violence. They forget that immigration is an old not a new phenomenon—and only sometimes a problem. Even France, after all, has long been a melting pot, as Gerard Noiriel has reminded us.[30] We forget this because France was for some time very good at assimilation, though not without considerable symbolic and sometimes quite physical violence, and because until recently the primary immigrants were other white Europeans. But Europe need not be simply a melting pot, *le creuset européen,* in which previous cultures are combined in a single new blend. This kind of consistency is not the only source of interconnection, of working together.

We might do well to remember, in praise of inconsistency and plurality, that the most creative loci of identity and individual action in much of European history were not nations, but cities. We should not let the dominance of nationalist ways of thinking over our intellectual categories too sharply dominate our ways of imagining European identity—or rather, imagining Europe as a place where institutional arrangements foster a plurality of identities.

Choosing inconsistency and a plurality of forms of social solidarity and collective identity does raise a hard challenge, which I can only raise here. To what extent are different kinds of groupings entitled to special status, or protected treatment of various sorts? Scholars are familiar with this less from European examples than from those of Quebec and aboriginal groups in Canada. Somewhat similar issues have arisen with regard to the Sami in the Nordic countries. There are two basic directions for approaching the issue. One is through the extension of special categories of rights and/or state services. The other is through some combination of federation and devolution of central state powers. The latter has much to recommend it, for it does not raise the issues of favoritism and corrosive jealousies as does the former. The former could be justified, as Charles Taylor has argued, when complete difference-blindness would in fact materially disadvantage a group—for example, by allowing urbanites of different ethnicities to buy up its ancestral lands for weekend homes—but it gives cause for worry.[31] First, it tends to make the state the guarantor of fixed lines of difference rather than allowing these to vary fluidly and overlap. Second, it encourages sharp distinctions among enclaves rather than development of lateral linkages among groups. Even while arguments for protected status commonly challenge nation-states in favor of smaller-scale or crosscutting groups, they often approach the issue of legitimate identity in terms deeply shaped by nationalist discourse—and indeed largely through ethnohistorical rather than civic claims as to what constitutes a group.

In short, differential claims on a central state that in general purports to treat its citizens equally raise problems that centralized protections for self-organizing group formation and maintenance of distinct identities do not. Beyond this I am not able to go in this chapter; I can note only that if Europeans choose the course of pluriform social organization—as I think they should and almost inevitably will—then they will be sailing in poorly charted waters and in need of serious theoretical work to make sure the taken-for-granted assumptions of nationalist discourse and its intellectual cousins do not close off attractive possibilities.

Notes

1. Susan Cott Watkins, *Provinces into Nations* (Princeton: Princeton University Press, 1992).

2. Recall Eugen Weber's point that it was only in the second half of the nineteenth century that most Frenchmen began to speak French as their primary language; *Peasants into Frenchmen: The Modernization of Rural France 1870–1914* (Stanford: Stanford University Press, 1976). See also Gerard Noiriel, *Le Creuset français* (Paris: Seuil, 1987); translated into English by Geoffroy de Laforcade as *The French Melting Pot* (Minneapolis: University of Minnesota Press, 1996).

3. I have considered these dimensions of nationalism (and reviewed much of the literature debating the issue of novelty) in Craig Calhoun, "Nationalism and Ethnicity," *Annual Review of Sociology* 19 (1993): 211–239; Craig Calhoun, "Nationalism and Civil Society," in Craig Calhoun, ed., *Social Theory and the Politics of Identity* (Oxford: Blackwell, 1993); and Craig Calhoun, *Nationalism* (Buckingham: Open University Press, 1997).

4. See discussion in Jeff Weintraub, "Introduction," and Craig Calhoun, "Nationalism and the Public Sphere," in Jeff Weintraub and Krishan Kumar, eds., *Public and Private in Thought and Practice* (Chicago: University of Chicago Press, 1996).

5. Obviously, I do not mean that Western Europeans were never imperialists. Far from it. The point is that for the most part they did not organize their political relations in Western Europe on the basis of empires.

6. See Calhoun, "Nationalism and the Public Sphere."

7. Swiss national identity constitutes Europe's most striking exception to this, insofar as it works very much in an "upward" direction emphasizing that individuals gain their Swiss nationality by being citizens of cantons, and Switzerland indeed exists as a confederation of these intermediate associations. They rather than the federal state are arguably primary, though for all the Swiss domestic emphasis on local distinction, Swiss identity is surprisingly cohesive and compact when projected outward and viewed from any distance. The Swiss model contrasts sharply with the categorical thinking (described later in the chapter) that makes the nation as a whole the primary collective identity, directly inscribed into individuals, who are from this point of view equivalent members of a set, tokens of a single type.

8. See Hannah Arendt's evocative discussion of this in *The Human Condition* (Chicago: University of Chicago Press, 1958), 257.

9. Schwarzmantel somewhat misleadingly portrays Fichte's idea of the nation as simply a domination and total absorption of the individual rather than seeing the sense in which Fichte sees self-recognition and self-realization as having noncontradictory individual and national moments. John J. Schwarzmantel, *Socialism and the Idea of a Nation* (London: Harvester, 1991), 37–40.

10. Ernst Renan, "What Is a Nation?" in Homi Bhabha, ed., *Nation and Narration* (London: Routledge, 1990), 11.

11. Benedict Anderson, *Imagined Communities*, rev. ed. (London: Verso, 1991), 201.

12. See Craig Calhoun, "'New Social Movements' of the Early 19th Century," *Social Science History* 17, 3 (1993): 385–427.

13. See Joan Landes, *Women and the Public Sphere* (Ithaca: Cornell University Press, 1989), and Geoff Eley, "Gender, Class and Nation," in Craig Calhoun, ed., *Habermas and the Public Sphere* (Cambridge: MIT Press, 1992).

14. In March 1996 *Le Figaro* ran an article asserting that "ultrafeminist" demands for abortion rights (and ultratraditionalist opposition) were simply failures to speak "the language of reason." In the same issue, Alain Peyrefitte wrote that this language was French—a language made for the expression of universal aspirations. Bernard Bonilauri, "Le Langage de la raison," and Alain Peyrefitte, "Le Contraire d'un ghetto," both in *Le Figaro*, 20 March 1996, 2, 1.

15. Jürgen Habermas, *Structural Transformation of the Public Sphere* (1962; reprint, Cambridge: MIT Press, 1989), 36.

16. Ibid., 131.

17. See Michael Warner, *Letters of the Republic* (Cambridge: Harvard University Press, 1992).

18. See Jürgen Habermas, "Citizenship and National Identity: Some Reflections on the Future of Europe," *Praxis International* 12, 1 (1992): 1–19 and Jürgen Habermas, "Struggles for Recognition in the Democratic Constitutional State," in Amy Gutman, ed., *Multiculturalism: Exploring the Politics of Recognition*, rev. ed. (Princeton: Princeton University Press, 1994).

19. See, among many, Alberto Melucci, *Nomads of the Present: Social Movements and Individual Needs in Contemporary Society* (Philadelphia: Temple University Press, 1989).

20. See Charles Taylor's helpful exposition and development of the Hegelian arguments in *Hegel* (Cambridge: Cambridge University Press, 1975) and *The Ethics of Authenticity* (Cambridge: Harvard University Press, 1991).

21. This is a central point of conflict in the debates over identity politics; I have reviewed many of the issues (but only a fraction of the literature) in Craig Calhoun, *Critical Social Theory* (Oxford: Blackwell, 1995), ch. 7.

22. This is the flaw in Eric Hobsbawm and Terence Ranger's otherwise helpful account in *The Invention of Tradition* (Cambridge: Cambridge University Press, 1983). The same notion that "invented" traditions (and therefore identities) are somehow less "real" is carried forward in Hobsbawm's influential survey, *Nations and Nationalism Since 1780: Programme, Myth, Reality* (Cambridge: Cambridge University Press, 1990).

23. Hannah Arendt, *Men in Dark Times* (New York: Harcourt Brace Jovanovich, 1968), 18.

24. See Norbert Elias, *The Society of Individuals* (Oxford: Blackwell, 1991) and Stephen Mennell, "The Formation of We-Images: A Process Theory," in Craig Calhoun, ed., *Social Theory and the Politics of Identity* (Oxford: Blackwell, 1993).

25. My emphasis is thus slightly different here from that of psychologists and political psychologists who study the relative propensity of different personalities for we- or I-images and language.

26. The distinction of categorical from relational identities was pioneered by social anthropologists, including especially Siegfried Nadel (*Theory of Social*

Structure [London: Cohen and West, 1957]), and brought into contemporary sociology by Harrison White (*Identity and Control* [Princeton: Princeton University Press, 1992]) and Charles Tilly (*From Mobilization to Revolution* [Reading, Mass.: Addison-Wesley, 1977]).

27. As Ekeh (1990) has noted, there has been a move to abandon the use of *tribe* in social anthropology and African studies and to replace it with *ethnic group*. But this has the effect of imposing a categorical notion—a collection of individuals marked by common ethnicity—in place of a relational one. Where the notion of tribe pointed to the centrality of kin relations (all the more central, Ekeh suggests, because of weak African states from whose point of view "tribalism" is criticized), the notion of ethnic group implies that detailed, serious analysis of kinship is more or less irrelevant. Peter P. Ekeh, "Social Anthropology and Two Contrasting Uses of Tribalism in Africa," *Comparative Studies in Society and History* 32, 4 (October 1990): 660–700.

28. Likewise, there is a great deal of discussion in contemporary Europe about subsidies for the arts and certain forms of media. The debate focuses heavily on the relationship between market logics and quality (however the latter is defined). Too little attention is paid in this discourse, however, to the issue of diversity itself. If maintaining diversity is considered at all, it is usually with regard to linguistic diversity and primarily to the reproduction of dominant national languages. But it might be appropriate to consider what kinds of actions both within markets and by governments encourage the production of a differentiated field of media options and different artistic style cultures (which are hard to rank on any single index of quality). Thus, tax codes might be modified to encourage both philanthropic foundations and venture capital investments in the arts, with the explicit goal of encouraging diversity in funding sources, production activities, and taste cultures. More attention might also be paid to the role of cities rather than nation-states as the key geographical loci of cultural production (and to some extent consumption). Cities and municipalities might be aided in entering into their own decentralized, hopefully divergent programs of support for and presentation of arts and media.

29. See Samuel P. Huntington, "The Clash of Civilizations?" *Foreign Affairs* 72 (1993): 22–49; see also the various criticisms in the following issue, especially that by Fouad Ajami, and Huntington's response, "If Not Civilizations, What? Paradigms of the Post–Cold War World," *Foreign Affairs* 72 (1993): 186–194.

30. See Noiriel, *Le Creuset français.*

31. "What Is the Meaning of Equal Citizenship?" paper presented to the Northwestern University conference "Citizenship Under Duress," 11–12 April 1997.

3

Example, Exception, or Both?
Swiss National Identity
in Perspective

Pascal Sciarini,
Simon Hug & Cédric Dupont

In Italy for thirty years under the Borgias they had warfare, terror, murder,
and bloodshed, but they produced Michelangelo, Leonardo da Vinci, and the
Renaissance. In Switzerland they had brotherly love—they had 500 years of
democracy and peace, and what did that produce? The cuckoo clock.
    —Harry Lime in *The Third Man,* by Orson Welles

The European Union is currently at a critical juncture: It not only faces
the challenges of enlargement and an expanding agenda but is also
simultaneously questioning its own destiny. A number of authors claim
that the European Union can face these challenges successfully only if
it gains the support of the European population for its current and
future projects. Instrumental to creating this support appears to be the
forging of some sort of commonly shared European identity, which,
according to most scholars, is largely lacking at the present time.
Although the absence of a European identity is not new, it has raised
increasing concern among observers. Notions like "common political
culture" and "social legitimization" reflect this quest for a more profound underpinning of the process of European integration.[1] It is necessary to ask, however, whether the construction of this kind of overarching identity is realistic. Is it possible to establish a feeling of belonging
among over 300 million citizens who speak different languages and
come from different cultural backgrounds? A significant part of the difficulty derives from the resilience of well-established national identities,
based on national cultural and political heritages. Given that these

anchors are not likely to vanish, the only way of proceeding is to super-impose a wider sense of belonging. Although it might be possible to find a minimal common cultural denominator for all the members of the European Union, this would clearly be too shallow to firmly ground the new identity. Any future European society will be multicultural, and thus its sense of common identity will have to be built upon noncultural factors. The problem, of course, is how to achieve such a task.

To help address this challenge, decisionmakers and scholars alike have started to look for blueprints in other similar processes of identity building within multicultural societies. Back in the mid-1960s, Amitai Etzioni took Canada, the Union of South Africa, Switzerland, Belgium, Nigeria, and India as good examples of this.[2] In a more recent contri-bution, Habermas explicitly cites the United States and Switzerland as multicultural societies that have achieved some sort of "constitutional patriotism," that is, an identification with constitutional principles and not with the state as such or with common cultural origins.[3] In such cases, he argues, "The political culture must serve as the common denominator for a constitutional patriotism which simultaneously sharpens an awareness of the multiplicity and integrity of the different forms of life which coexist in a multicultural society."[4]

He goes on to propose the United States and Switzerland as exam-ples for the construction of a European identity.[5] Is this a promising path to follow or, on the contrary, an illusory one? To answer this ques-tion, a detailed exploration needs to be made of already established cases of constitutional patriotism. This chapter addresses the Swiss expe-rience and its limited implications for the future of European identity. It does so by focusing on the relationship between exclusion and dilu-tion, the underlying theme of this volume.

The relevance of the Swiss experience for our understanding of identity formation in the EU seems indisputable. There are at least three strong parallels between the two cases. First, multiculturalism forms a part of this process. In Switzerland four linguistic regions and two major religions make it a truly multicultural society. Scattered over a small territory but geographically separated partially by mountain chains, different cultural traditions have formed and continue to this day. Similarly, the European Union comprises a large set of different lin-guistic traditions, religious faiths, and cultural backgrounds. Second, the hallmark of citizenship seems to be "harmony in diversity." Up to 1848 Switzerland consisted (with a short interruption during the Helvetic Republic) of a series of autonomous states (cantons) united in a confederation. Even after the foundation of the federal state, individ-uals continued to become citizens of Switzerland in an indirect way. Every Swiss person is recognized as being a citizen of a commune, which automatically confers to that individual the citizenship of the respective canton and, as a result, national citizenship. This process of becoming a citizen is similar to that created by the Maastricht Treaty. Article 8 of this treaty establishes the "citizenship of the Union" and stipulates that "every person holding the nationality of a Member State shall be a citizen of the Union." Third, one of the driving forces in the construction of the Swiss federal state was that of economic integration. Abolishing duties at the borders between cantons, setting up a common currency, and other economic measures were at the center in the building of the federal state. The parallel with the European Union is only too evident. Despite its undeniable underlying political aims, European integration proceeded by first forging economic coordination and integration.

Given these parallels, the emergence of a Swiss national identity in the second half of the nineteenth century and its persistence since then seem very encouraging for a future European identity. In this chapter we therefore carefully analyze the key institutional elements that lay behind the process of identity formation—the mix of federalism, direct democracy, and neutrality. Success came at a price, however. The considerable achievement of overcoming cultural differences and forming a national identity went together with exclusionary tendencies with respect to the outside world. We discuss these tendencies and attempt to determine whether they are inevitably linked to a national identity in a multicultural society. We go on to show that the balance between identity and exclusion is not easy to maintain under "constitutional patriotism." Since identity is so closely linked to the functioning of the institutions, perturbations in the latter can easily undermine the former, creating tensions and manifesting themselves in identity crises. The balance proves to be increasingly sensitive in a changing international environment, where outside pressure and influences are all the more pervasive.

How useful, then, is the Swiss experience in thinking of a future European identity? Should it be used as an example, as some argue? Whereas we do not dispute that Swiss national identity is a model of successful constitutional patriotism, we show that it offers a specific blueprint for identity formation, one marked by selected exclusionary tendencies toward the external world. The inclusion of different cultures inside the same polity has required a very cautious external policy in order to preserve the fragile domestic balance. Although some of the exclusion might have derived from historical and geographical contingencies, the Swiss case tends to reveal that the formation of collective identity inside multicultural societies is a delicate act of balancing inclusion and exclusion. Given this prudent assessment, we carefully derive some tentative implications for a future European identity.

Identity Formation in Switzerland

As in other countries, the emergence of a national identity in Switzerland is strongly linked to the creation of the nation-state in the nineteenth century. Up to the end of the eighteenth century, Switzerland consisted of a loose confederation of cantons. It was only during the military occupation by France and the establishment of the Helvetic Republic (1798–1802), followed by Napoleon's protectorate (1802–1813), that a unified state emerged. The new state did not survive the end of the protectorate, and the country reverted to a confederation of cantons, although larger and more diverse than the previous one. The entity comprised Catholic and Protestant cantons, with populations speaking French, German, Italian, and Romansch. Their common decisionmaking instrument was the *Diete*, which brought together the representatives of the cantons once a year. The main concerns of this body were to coordinate "foreign policy," which was still the responsibility of the cantons, and economic integration. In the latter domain, the reduction of duties leveled at the cantons' frontiers and other measures proved to be important steps toward the establishment of a common market. The completion of a unified economic market (suppression of trade barriers, introduction of a single currency, etc.) was later one of the prime achievements of the new federal state.

The loosely structured decisionmaking procedures of the confederation only weakly allowed for the emergence of a national identity. Nevertheless, signs of a common and persevering sense of belonging began to appear. Georges Andrey notes that three elements contributed strongly to this process.[6] First, the Swiss Confederation remained vulnerable to foreign involvement in its internal affairs. In particular, foreign powers exerted strong pressure on the asylum policy, forcing the cantons to adopt more restrictive measures. They argued that immigrants to Switzerland were engaged in subversive activities that threatened the security of these foreign powers. In addition, some foreign powers forced cantons to restrict the freedom of press to prevent the spread of political subversion. According to Andrey, these various types of intervention against the cantons' sovereignty stimulated the affirmation of a national identity. In fact, the resistance against foreign oppressors does not date back to that particular period but is a recurrent and central element of Swiss history that has had a strong impact on Swiss identity. The elite used the myth of the 1291 confederal pact among the three Alpine cantons and the long fight for independence of the old confederation to stimulate patriotism and national consciousness.[7] Focusing the Swiss inhabitants on a common enemy proved to be a successful strategy in raising a common sense of identity.

Second, a series of military, cultural, religious, scientific, and historical associations were created at the federal level in the 1820s and 1830s.[8] Composed of members from all cantons, irrespective of language or religion, these associations favored exchanges and various forms of collaboration across cantons and cultures. They played a significant role in the emergent feeling of belonging to some new entity.[9] Together with the liberal ideas of the time, they increasingly showed the need for more centralized institutions. The process of setting up these institutions and their specific design formed the third key element in the nascent national identity.

Questions regarding types of institutional structure and the distribution of powers between the federal level and the cantons in the 1830s and 1840s were controversial—so much so that they caused a short civil war in 1847 (the so-called *Sonderbund* war), which pitted radical Protestant cantons against conservative Catholic cantons. The former believed that Switzerland needed a political system with a common government that could impose identical policies on all cantons. Accordingly, they favored national centralization, or at least a federal government strong enough to further common interests. The conservative Catholic cantons, by contrast, were hostile to centralization and created an alliance, the *Sonderbund,* to oppose the creation of a central state. The radicals won the war but did not exclude the losers from the subsequent process of state-building. Thus, the creation of the Swiss federation reflected an institutional compromise: The radicals conceded to the Catholics a system that provided the cantons with a considerable level of autonomy.

Federalism made compatible two antagonistic principles, namely, unity and diversity.[10] Through the principle of subsidiarity, federalism leaves sufficient policy areas under the control of the cantonal authorities. In addition, any change in the distribution of competencies between the federal state and the cantons is subject to a dual ratification procedure. The introduction of any new jurisdiction at the federal level requires a constitutional amendment, which has to be approved by the double majority of people and cantons. Together the two factors explain why in 1848 even the losers of the civil war, the Catholic cantons, could identify with the newly created institutions. These institutions enabled the Catholic cantons to pursue a separate development without too many constraints from the federal level. By contrast, the other cantons were free to experiment with their more progressive ideas. The federalist structure thus defused the potential for conflict between cultural subgroups. Since this institutional arrangement allowed sufficient leeway for the different cultural entities to manage their internal affairs, it became a positive factor of integration and identity formation. Hence, while allowing different developments at the lower levels, it fostered at the same time a common sense of belonging.

The second main institution introduced in the 1848 constitution, that of direct democracy, also has historical roots, starting from the direct democratic or collective "self-government" of the local communities prevalent in the Middle Ages. In the nineteenth century, many cantons had already introduced into their jurisdictions semidirect democratic devices (popular initiatives and referendums that typically applied to amendments to the constitution), while others still relied on a "true" direct democracy (i.e., on popular assemblies, or *Landsgemeinden*). The development of direct democratic practices at the federal level occurred in three steps during the early years of the federal state. The mandatory referendum for constitutional changes was introduced immediately in the first constitution in 1848; the optional referendum was added in 1874, and the popular initiative in 1891.[11]

The instruments of direct democracy contributed to internal political stability and consequently fostered a stronger national identity. First, by giving citizens direct access to public affairs, they strengthened identification with decisions made at the national level. Second, the instruments of direct democracy strongly influenced the executive and the legislative branches. In the early years of the federal state (after 1874), they forced a monolithic government—formed exclusively of radicals—to respect the wishes of minority groups. Optional referendums, skillfully used by the Catholics, kept the government at bay. Their obstruction tactics proved successful, as the Catholic opposition was ultimately bought off by the radical majority and given a seat in the government. The opening of the executive sphere, coupled with the requirements of a collegial executive, resulted in greater consensual policymaking.[12] The threat of the optional referendum also forced the government and the elite in the parliament to cooperate more closely and to search for compromises well before the final stages of the legislation procedure.[13] Finally, by favoring the emergence of the citizens in the role of a potential opposition, the instruments of direct democracy heightened elites' attention to the different subcultures in Swiss society.

Although neutrality was not given a prominent place in the federal constitution, it nevertheless played a crucial role in setting up the institutions and in the successful formation of a national identity.[14] The defeat of Swiss troops by Francis I of France and his Venetian allies in Marignan in 1515 put an end to military involvement abroad and opened the era of neutrality—a foreign policy instrument with both internal and external functions. Internally, it was a factor of balance and peace between the different subcultures and cantons. Externally, the Congress of Vienna in 1815 recognized its role for peace and stability in

Europe.[15] At a time when militarized nation-states dominated Europe, this reliance on neutrality helped to create a perception of a special destiny and thus strengthened the identification of individuals with the nation. Facing expansionist-minded neighbors, the Swiss elite felt a strong need for internal strength in conjunction with the pursuit of neutrality in external affairs. In particular, the elite favored the development of a strong center that would be useful not only with regard to the military dimension but would also give more power for managing economic relationships with the external world.[16]

Neutrality was especially useful in crisis situations. During World War I, significant tensions appeared among the different linguistic regions, but these were reduced through the pursuit of a strict neutrality.[17] In World War II, neutrality played an even more important role as an integrative factor. At the same time, as on previous occasions, the country's neutrality allowed also for economic advantages by providing safe havens and a stable environment. This applied in times of war—trade was possible with both sides—and in cases of international economic sanctions against specific states (e.g., South Africa). In other words, neutrality gave Swiss companies a convenient excuse for picking up lucrative business opportunities abandoned by foreign competitors because of economic sanctions.

In the absence of a common culture, the three institutional cornerstones have made up an integrative framework that has allowed for the successful emergence of a national identity. The influence of political institutions has not only played a central role in this process but has helped to keep it stable ever since. The elite has always stressed the specificity of the Swiss federal democratic state, born out of a political will and in opposition to foreign powers, which has created the myth of Switzerland as a "nation of will" (*Willensnation*).

Exclusionary Tendencies

Neutrality, federalism, and direct democracy provided the ingredients for a peaceful, economically successful, and politically stable development of Swiss society. This success significantly enhanced the identification of the Swiss population with the institutional mix of its federal state. In this slow process, taking about 100 years from the foundation of the Swiss state, it was the Swiss institutions that became the rallying point of the national identity. The emergence of this identity was, however, partly premised on the existence of an ongoing succession of common enemies, as we showed above, starting with the Habsburg empire, continuing with Napoleon, and perhaps coming to an end with the fall of the Soviet empire. This dependence on common enemies points to an identity that is defensive in nature.[18]

How has this defensive behavior materialized? Has it simply remained present in the minds of Swiss citizens from the early glorious days of military battles against external powers? Or did it come into existence through the various exclusionary tendencies in different policy domains? In this section we seek to answer this question and focus on three policy domains: foreign involvement, trade, and immigration policy. These three areas are key interfaces between any sovereign entity and its external environment and as a consequence should be natural domains for the exercise, if there is any, of exclusionary practices.

Foreign Involvement

The prime example for such exclusions appears to stem from the hesitant involvement of Switzerland in affairs beyond its borders. Constitutional referendums held in Switzerland have recently attracted attention abroad for their surprising outcomes on several foreign affairs issues. In particular, the rejection by the Swiss people of the treaty on the European Economic Area (EEA) between the European Free Trade Association (EFTA) and European Community (EC) countries has largely contributed to an image of Switzerland as an isolated island in a European-wide movement toward economic and political unity. If one adds the fact that Switzerland is one of the few countries that is not a member of the United Nations, the overall impression is that it has been extremely exclusionary in terms of its foreign involvement. The commonly accepted argument states that these exclusionary tendencies can be explained by the mythical notion of neutrality, which is one of the cornerstones of Swiss identity. From this perspective, it is better to be Europe's odd man out and the world's archetype of a fearful actor in foreign affairs than to possibly endanger national identity. Whereas there is some truth in such a vision, it does not account for variation across time and issues in Switzerland's foreign involvement. Exclusion has not been systematic nor constant but selective and of variable geometry. We examine below how this variation is linked to considerations of national identity.

Before 1848, when the new constitution gave power to the federal state in this domain, there was virtually no Swiss foreign policy. Since then Switzerland's behavior has been driven by two key concerns. First and foremost, foreign involvement has been guided by the overarching goals of preserving and strengthening national sovereignty. Second, foreign involvement has traditionally been marked by a willingness to promote the economic development of the country. To achieve these goals,

Switzerland has mostly relied on the concept of neutrality, which has helped the country take advantage of the prevalent international environment while managing to avoid upsetting Switzerland's delicate internal cultural balance. Economic involvement and political restraint already characterized the first fifty years of Swiss foreign policy. Starting in the 1850s, Switzerland carefully refrained from participating in the unification movements occurring at its borders and retreated from any major political initiative. By contrast, economic involvement in both trade and monetary matters were quite important during that period.[19]

The outbreak of World War I signaled the onset of a difficult era for Swiss sovereignty and its internal stability. In terms of sovereignty, the suspension of normal trade flows severely restricted policy autonomy. External trade slipped largely out of the hands of the Federal Council and into those of the Swiss Society for Economic Surveillance, which was closely monitored by the Allies. With respect to internal stability, the different linguistic communities felt divergent attractions toward the warring factions. The Swiss Germans had more sympathy for the cause of the German empire, while the Swiss French tended to support the Allies. Neutrality could only partly prevent these internal conflicts, and unity clearly came under stress.

At the end of the war, the government attempted to increase its political involvement in world affairs, including participation in the nascent League of Nations. Given that there was no public willingness to abandon neutrality, however, the government had the difficult task of achieving more under the same domestic constraints. In practice, this consisted of becoming a member of the League of Nations while preserving neutrality. But the Swiss had to agree to participate in economic sanctions, which constituted a major break with the previous conception of full political independence.[20] In the context of the Versailles settlement, this change in the neutrality status caused deep domestic resentment in the German-speaking part of the country. For the most part, Swiss Germans felt that the economic conditions imposed by the Allies on Germany were unfair, and they resented participation in a system that would enforce them. Attitudes were different in the French-speaking areas, both because there was no sympathy for Germany and because there was a wider agreement over a more active involvement in world affairs. The ratification campaign reflected this deep cultural cleavage and strained internal integration and stability to a dangerous extent.[21] Hence, despite the ultimate success of the government in pushing the country into the League of Nations, the episode highlighted the limits of political activism at the external level. Subsequent behavior inside the league was therefore guided by as much restraint as possible: The idea was to participate while avoiding any political commitment. When this became impossible after the sanctions against Italy, Switzerland chose to leave the organization.

After the episode of the league, the pendulum of Swiss foreign involvement swung back to extreme restraint and a strict and comprehensive neutrality. Obviously, such an attitude was motivated by the unraveling of peace through Europe and the subsequent wave of violence and horror. Swiss neutrality revolved around the notion of the *réduit*, that is, of a retreat into the Alpine regions in the case of war. It was the cornerstone of Swiss domestic stability and external "survival" during World War II. The Swiss were willing to pay a very high price to preserve their unity and well-being. Policy implications ranged from strongly exclusionary behavior (such as the policy toward Jewish refugees) to the continuation of business as usual (for instance with respect to gold transfers from Nazi Germany, which have come to the forefront recently) to defusing outside pressure and keeping internal divisions at bay.[22]

Contrary to its conduct after World War I, Switzerland refrained from any active foreign involvement in the immediate aftermath of World War II and followed a rapid conception of neutrality. There were two reasons for this behavior. First, there was a general perception that neutrality, coupled with a strong military defense, had preserved the country from involvement in the conflict. Second, in contrast to the situation that prevailed during World War I, neutrality had helped to maintain Swiss internal unity successfully. In sum, neutrality had been a winning policy both externally and internally, and there was thus no reason for change. Accordingly, Switzerland did not take an active part in the institutional setup that took place in Bretton Woods and San Francisco.

The creation of the Organization for European Economic Cooperation (OEEC) in the wake of the Marshall Plan induced the Swiss to become more active on the external front. On the basis of the economic objectives of the newly created institution, Switzerland became a full member of the OEEC and as such a member of the European Payments Union (EPU). It actively pushed for trade and payments liberalization inside these frameworks, both because it suited powerful domestic economic groups and did not endanger neutrality. When a basic divergence on how to address the issue of tariffs with third countries ultimately led to the split into two camps within the OEEC, the Swiss sided against the six countries of the European Coal and Steel Community (ECSC). Any participation in the emerging European Communities was out of question, given the political commitment that this would have implied.[23] But Switzerland feared the economic implications of the new grouping, which included its two historically major trading partners, France and Germany. To help prevent discrimination, the Federal Council became an active supporter of British attempts to create a wide free trade zone among all the members of the OEEC.[24] When the talks finally collapsed in November 1958, Switzerland proposed a second-best alternative: a more limited free trade area among selected non-EC members. Endorsed by the British, the idea resulted in the creation of EFTA in January 1960.

The episode of the OEEC can be considered as the archetype of Swiss foreign involvement at both the regional and global levels since 1945. It features a kind of à la carte participation in economic institutions and strict avoidance of any participation in politically constraining organizations that might endanger its own fundamental institutions. Entry into the General Agreement on Tariffs and Trade (GATT) in the mid-1960s and policy regarding European economic and political integration both reflected this attitude. Regarding GATT, Switzerland considered joining the organization in the late 1950s after most European currencies returned to convertibility. But it remained a temporary member for almost ten years until it received a formal guarantee that its farm policy would be left untouched. Then the way was safe for participation, given both that the scope was limited to merchandise trade and that the GATT charter provided many loopholes and safeguard mechanisms that could be used where there might be some danger for its national sovereignty. On matters of European integration, the driving axiom was that of remaining economically as close to the EU as possible, while falling short of any actual political commitment.[25] This axiom prevented any major agreement with the EC until the 1972 signing of the free trade agreement on industrial goods, and it continued to influence the course of Swiss European policy throughout the 1970s and early 1980s.

A cautious and functional foreign involvement in external affairs enjoyed very high domestic political support. Entry into the GATT was not put to the popular ballot, and the free trade agreement with the EC was endorsed enthusiastically (approved by 72.5 percent of the voters). On the contrary, the Swiss people (73.5 percent of the voters) in 1986 massively rejected the government's only attempt to join the United Nations, which was perceived as a threat to neutrality, and they also turned down the EEA treaty in 1992 because they believed that it would ultimately mean full political and economic integration with the EC (as we will see below).

To sum up, the Swiss attitude on foreign involvement has since 1945 been significantly marked by political restraint and economic opportunism or, in other words, by selected exclusionary practices. This has proved to be an effective way of strengthening the political stability and enhancing economic prosperity for most of this period. Neutrality provided political elites with a useful and rallying guiding principle. Elites have repeatedly emphasized the considerable achievement of the policy of neutrality, even when this policy was either irrelevant or fared poorly.[26] To put it another way, Swiss elites have constantly overemphasized the achievement of neutrality and minimized its drawbacks. As a result, an attachment to and identification with neutrality has grown sharply among citizens.

Trade

The Swiss economy is commonly perceived as a liberal noninterventionist free market system. The term *liberal* mainly applies to three areas.[27] First, Switzerland is a model of "liberal evolution," which implies a low-profile economic policy on the part of the government.[28] In accordance with the subsidiarity principle, state intervention was called for only in cases of emergency, when civil society could not solve the problems itself. Second, the Swiss economy is liberal in its low tariffs for industrial goods. As a small economy with no raw materials, Switzerland has had no choice but to support free trade in international negotiations like the GATT. Foreign economic relations have been the main source of the country's prosperity, and the Swiss economy is still one of the most open with respect to many criteria.[29] Third, because of the absence of regulation of capital movements, Switzerland is an important financial center, and one-third of the earnings of Swiss banks is due to activities or services abroad. It is not surprising that Peter Katzenstein characterized Switzerland as the paradigmatic case of "liberal corporatist" adaptation to international economic changes.[30]

Katzenstein points out, however, that two different economic sectors have developed in Switzerland: one externally oriented and competitive, the other internally oriented and protected.[31] While the degree of economic openness is overall considerable in Switzerland, the internationalization of the economy has focused only on some branches of industry and services. In contrast, other sectors are oriented mainly toward the domestic economy, with high degrees of sheltering against international market forces.

The most conspicuous example of this protectionism is agriculture.[32] The history of Swiss agricultural policy has been strongly linked to and influenced by the policy of neutrality. In the strict conception of neutrality that has prevailed in Switzerland since the late 1930s, a neutral state should prepare for possible wars or import crises by securing a high degree of food self-sufficiency. Farm production has thus been stimulated (i.e., subsidized) and sheltered from international competition. The state has actively intervened to support every kind of farm product. Swiss farmers also benefited from a sophisticated system of import controls that function much like a protective dike. Without it, the domestic support regime would have been ineffective, and cheaper foreign products would have flooded the local market. Although Switzerland has obviously not been the only country shielding its agriculture from international competition, the level of protection has been very high compared to international standards.[33] Swiss farm policy is a special case even when compared to the highly subsidized and protectionist European agriculture under the Common Agricultural Policy (CAP).[34]

The willingness to protect agriculture has strongly influenced the government's behavior in world arenas. Switzerland has constantly been a strong advocate of free trade for industrial products, yet it has always insisted on leaving agriculture outside any liberalizing agreement, be it at the European or international level. Accordingly, Switzerland joined the GATT only after it gained special treatment for its agriculture and limited developments toward more integration within Europe to industrial products (and later services).

Direct democracy contributed largely to maintain, if not increase, these exclusionary practices. The threat of possible negative outcomes in referenda fostered the development of concertation in the early (preparliamentary) phase of the decisionmaking process. All major political and economic actors, that is, those who because of their ability to win a referendum campaign were able to endanger policymaking in agriculture, could voice their interests in this concertation phase. Until the mid-1980s, the farm lobby could thus use its quasi-veto power to block any attempt at reforming the system.[35] There was a broad consensus as well among Swiss citizens that agriculture should be supported, mostly because of the noneconomic functions it performed. In turn, the attachment to the rural way of life, traditions, and cultures became a significant part of the Swiss identity. Peasants saw themselves as the "heart of society."[36] This vision gained prominence during World War II. While the army defended Swiss independence at the frontier, the peasants waged a "plantation war" inside the country.[37]

Exclusionary practices have similarly applied to other sectors. Regulation either by the state or private contractual arrangements (cartels, price maintenance, and monopolies) to eliminate competition have ruled various areas of the secondary and tertiary domestic sectors, even though the situation has evolved to some extent over the last few years.[38] Switzerland thus represents a case of "selective liberalism."[39] As in agriculture, direct democracy has allowed interest groups of the domestic sector to oppose policy reforms favoring deregulation or liberalization. For instance, before the late 1990s powerful interest groups successfully opposed the adoption of a competition policy. The perverse effects of the third fundamental institution, namely, federalism, are also worth noting in this context. Federalism stimulated cantonal as well as communal protectionism, for instance, in public procurement in the construction sector. Because of "regional preference," access to public procurement was severely restricted for "nonlocal" firms, implying that mostly local firms gained contracts from the communes and cantons. These distortions to free market forces prevented the creation of a truly unified economic market. Moreover, federalism caused barriers to the free movement of persons, typically because of the limited recognition of educational diplomas.

A careful look at Swiss trade policy thus shows evidence of both economic openness and closure. Switzerland is not as liberal as might appear at first glance. As in foreign policy, exclusionary tendencies seem to be at work, here in the sense of a selective form of liberalism.

Immigration

Switzerland is often seen as a country with a strong tradition of humanitarian aid and open frontiers for refugees. This view is linked to the fact that several humanitarian organizations like the International Red Cross (founded by the Swiss Henry Dunand) and the High Commission for Refugees have their headquarters in Switzerland. In addition, the rather considerable share of foreigners in the resident population—around 25 percent—tends to suggest a relatively liberal immigration policy. This was true in the last century but has become increasingly less so.

The foreign population started to grow mostly at the end of the nineteenth century, as shown in Figure 3.1. During the religious wars in the sixteenth century, Switzerland accepted significant numbers of refugees.[40] Yet François De Capitani notes that in the eighteenth century the figures for immigration in Switzerland were rather low, the notable exception being the influx of Huguenots after the revocation of the Edict of Nantes.[41] At that time between 10,000 and 20,000 refugees sought protection in Switzerland.[42] In the nineteenth century the proportion of foreigners was still small (2.5 percent in 1837 and 3 percent in 1850), but they were heavily concentrated in certain regions: Basel and Geneva had 21.5 percent and 20.1 percent of foreigners on their territory.[43] According to Hans-Joachim Hoffmann-Nowotny, these low numbers were partly due to the rather limited economic attraction of Switzerland, but also to the stringent immigration policy adopted by most cantons and communes.[44]

With the foundation of the modern state in 1848, immigration policy shifted to the federal authority, which throughout the nineteenth

Figure 3.1   Foreigners' Share of the Total Swiss Population

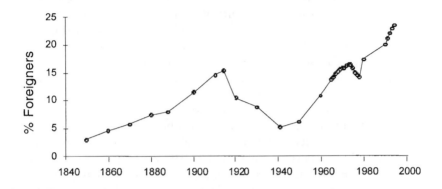

Source: Annuaire statistique de la suisse, 1987–1995. Bern: Office fédéral de statistique, 209.

century concluded treaties with other countries, leading to wide-open borders. Together with the demands from the economy, which was attempting to catch up on its late industrialization, this resulted in a sharp jump in the foreign population, reaching around 15 percent of the total population at the beginning of the twentieth century. The immediate postwar period and the economic crisis of the 1920s caused a significant drop in the numbers of foreign residents. Through World War II the share of foreign residents rose only slightly. This marginal increase through the war years might seem surprising, but Switzerland practiced a fairly restrictive refugee and immigration policy throughout those difficult years. An official report issued in 1957 by Karl Ludwig (a member of the cantonal government of Bâle) first broke the ice on this sensitive question. According to Ludwig, 10,000 Jewish refugees were rejected at the Swiss border between June 1942 and April 1945. This figure, however, considerably underestimates the true number. According to a recent study, Switzerland denied entry to 30,000 asylum seekers, a majority of them Jews.[45] Another study has also shed new light on the widespread anti-Semitism among Swiss high civil servants and officials.[46]

The economic recovery of the 1950s resulted in another increase in the foreign population. The large numbers of foreigners together with the economic crisis of the 1970s led to fears of overforeignization. Several popular initiatives attempted to limit drastically the number of foreigners admitted. One of these was almost passed and gave rise to a major "course correction" in the official immigration policy.

The legal foundation of the current immigration policy is a constitutional article adopted in 1925 and the derived law adopted in 1931.[47] The main instrument of this policy is the distribution of three types of permits: permits of abode, permits of permanent residence, and seasonal permits. Permits of abode are limited in time (but renewable) and allow foreigners to take up a particular job. Permits of permanent residence give similar status to foreigners as to the Swiss, except for political rights. Seasonal permits are granted to migrant workers in jobs such as construction and tourism and are limited to a maximum of nine months with a three-month leave requirement.

The distribution of permits was fairly liberal until the 1970s, especially for the permits of temporary residence (abode permits). The administration of permits depended mostly on the demands of the economy for additional workers. Regarding permits of abode, the main idea was to allow for some kind of rotation among foreign migrants. This policy failed, since most migrant workers decided to stay in Switzerland. Firms saw no reason to hire new migrant workers every year or so, and the migrant workers saw no reason to turn over their workplaces to fellow foreign workers. Permits of residence, and even more so citizenship through naturalization, were more difficult to obtain and submitted to important conditions on residence and employment. This allowed for a flexible influx (and also outflow in times of economic crisis) of migrant workers.[48]

In the 1970s, economic recession led to a falling demand for new permits and as a consequence to a decrease in the share of foreign residents.[49] At the same time, as a reaction to the fears of overforeignization and the popular initiative that was almost accepted, the government made it much more difficult to get permits of abode. Quotas based on the estimated demands of the economy were established and strictly respected. In contrast, obtaining permits of permanent residence became easier.[50]

Despite a relative openness in terms of admission policy, integration of foreigners in the society has not been strong. Switzerland has a "liberal" and largely decentralized policy of integration.[51] While immigration rules are largely an affair of the federal state, integration and especially naturalization occurs (or is supposed to occur) at the communal and cantonal levels. For the naturalization process, this division of competencies often adds another hurdle to the process, since each canton and commune is free to impose additional residence requirements. As a consequence, naturalization has remained low (1.5 percent of the foreign population in 1976, 1.8 percent in 1980, and 0.8 percent in 1990).[52]

Further evidence of the exclusionary effects of federalism can be found in the low level of expenditure for foreign migrants. Swiss public authorities (federal and cantonal) spent approximately 2 Fr ($1.40) per worker for vocational training in 1982. During the same time, the Dutch government spent an average of 80.5 Fl ($42) per worker.[53] Other consequences are the lack of civil rights, even at the local level (except in two cantons), and the little effort that is made in the school system to facilitate the integration of the children of migrant workers.[54]

Direct democracy has also tended to nurture exclusion. For instance, in some communes the local assembly of all the citizens has to vote on the attribution of Swiss citizenship.[55] Instruments of direct democracy have more generally been well suited to channel antiforeign expressions. They explain why resentment against foreigners emerged much earlier in Switzerland than in most other developed countries. Following the near adoption of a constitutional amendment to severely limit immigration in the late 1960s, direct democracy strongly influenced the change of course that occurred in the 1970s.

The relative closure of the borders for potential immigrants throughout World War II, in contrast, is closely linked to the third institutional cornerstone of Switzerland: Neutrality and the fear of being overrun by powerful neighbors resulted in a restrictive handling of refugees. As Figure 4.1 clearly shows, the share of the foreign population hardly increased during that time.

In short, the picture of Switzerland as a country with a strong humanitarian tradition describes accurately the situation of the nineteenth and early twentieth centuries. Since that time, however, Swiss immigration policy has become more restrictive. It is "liberal" not in the sense that it offers free access for immigrants or refugees but because it allows the private economy flexible management of the labor policy.

The Difficult Nexus Between Identity and Exclusion

In the previous section, we highlighted how exclusionary practices went together with the creation and the strengthening of Swiss national identity. The key to success was the continuous role of political institutions as identification magnets. Through selective exclusion and skillful redistribution, these institutions were able to absorb shocks from the external environment. Their task has, however, become more difficult since the late 1980s, and the first signs of failure have uncovered dangerous internal strains. In this section we turn to a discussion of these developments

Two major events have had far-reaching consequences for Swiss institutions and hence for Swiss identity: the collapse of the Soviet

Union and the globalization process. The former has strongly challenged the raison d'être of a policy of neutrality. Balancing behavior has become ill adapted to a less polarized world. The latter has highlighted both the limits and costs of exclusionary practices. Switzerland is largely integrated into an increasingly interdependent world characterized by multiple channels of interactions between and among domestic societies. Consequently, the maintenance of exclusionary practices faces an increasing number of obstacles.

Changes in the external environment require increased economic and political openness—in other words, lower levels of exclusion—notably in the three arenas discussed above: foreign involvement, trade, and immigration. External pressure is, however, not sufficient to ensure domestic change, especially given that the institutional setup was designed to privilege stability rather than innovation. The institutions provide powerful veto tools to those who oppose lowering the level of exclusion. As such, they have been seen as responsible for current difficulties by those who advocate change. The net result has been an erosion of the role played by the institutions in rallying the Swiss population around their national identity and thus a loosening of the feeling of belonging. Coupled with the impact of economic recession, these developments have led to a kind of identity crisis. We elaborate on these points and highlight how and why Swiss national identity is affected by external changes in the domains of foreign involvement, trade, and immigration.

Foreign Involvement (or the Difficulty to Include Oneself)

The collapse of the Berlin wall and the subsequent democratization process in Eastern Europe had deep repercussions for Swiss identity. First, these dramatic changes abruptly diluted a powerful cement, that is, a clearly identifiable external threat. The shock was all the more pronounced since the Swiss conception of the outside world and the policy implications of this notion had hardly changed since the 1930s.[56] External threats, among others the Habsburg empire, Napoleon, the Third Reich, and the Communist bloc, had been carefully cultivated by political and economic elites as a justification for both external behavior and internal cohesion. The sudden disappearance of the Soviet Union and its Communist satellites ruined decades of efforts to build the image of a common enemy and thus deprived the Swiss citizens of a significant part of their national identity. The absence of a common foe—an other that serves as a reference to which every member of the society can rapidly contrast his or her differences and thus recognize his or her equals—makes the process of collective self-definition much more problematic.

Second, the end of the East-West division in Europe was a blow to the external function of neutrality. In contrast to other neutral European states, definition of a new course of action has been more difficult in Switzerland given the important domestic function of neutrality. The government favors a more active involvement in foreign affairs and a loosening of the conception of neutrality.[57] This is based on the main idea that in the era of globalization a country like Switzerland can no longer defend its independence by a strategy of insulation from the outside world. Traditional sovereignty becomes an illusion because Switzerland is increasingly forced to adopt decisions made by others. International cooperation is the only route to defend national independence. From this perspective, the Swiss federal government envisions a definition of Swiss neutrality that would limit itself to its core elements—rights and obligations in time of war—but would leave room for maneuver under other circumstances, including economic sanctions.[58] From this perspective, neutrality would apply only to cases of "emergency"; in other situations priority would be given to solidarity with the international community and cooperation in supranational institutions.[59] The government has thus argued that Switzerland should join the United Nations and the European Union.[60] These proposals have found little support among the population: Swiss citizens still have a strong attachment to the traditional neutrality. Only a minority of these would be ready to admit that neutrality has lost its raison d'être.

The disagreement between the elite and the people on the reorientation of neutrality is only one aspect of a growing gap between definitions of foreign policy. Proposals from the elites that are subject to referendums have faced a higher risk of being rejected in this field than in other policy domain since the 1970s.[61] This is all the more problematic given that direct democratic institutions will play a significant role in future definitions of Swiss foreign policy—contrary to past practices. This change comes from two main factors: the increasing pervasion of domestic politics by international affairs through the process of globalization and the partial revision of the Swiss constitution in 1977 that greatly enlarged the scope of direct public scrutiny in foreign policy affairs.

The gap between the government's agenda and people's beliefs has also been striking on matters of European integration. The popular vote against the EEA in December 1992 constitutes a case in hand. This vote divided the Swiss electorate along a new dimension of the level of openness of the country.[62] Especially problematic for the country's unity was that the different linguistic regions held strongly opposing views, the French-speaking cantons supporting openness and the

German-speaking (in particular the small rural ones) and Italian-speaking cantons preferring insulation.[63] This division prompted several analysts to point to an identity crisis.

To improve relations among the linguistic communities, an official report issued by a group of committees of the Swiss parliament suggests relying on the leeway offered by federalism. Given the prior contributions of federalism in terms of "management of differences," this recommendation is hardly novel. In addition, it is unlikely to offer a convincing solution in the current era, characterized as it is by increased interdependence.[64] Solutions based on an autonomy of the cantons would seem to be inappropriate. Instead of relying on the federalist structure, it might be necessary to reconceptualize the role it is playing in current Swiss institutional arrangements.

Federalism has also created tensions in another guise. The requirement of double majority approval for constitutional amendments has increased frictions between the votes of the citizens and the votes of the cantons. This has particularly been the case on issues of involvement in European affairs. The requirement of the majority of cantons gives a strong blocking power to the conservative rural Swiss German cantons and thus impedes any change of course, despite the growing public support for such a move. The referendum on entry into the EEA reflected this worrying development. The popular vote was almost perfectly split, whereas the vote of the cantons was mainly against the proposal. Given that the core of small conservative cantons shows no sign of changing their stance, there is little prospect for a more open-minded attitude toward European integration in the next few years.[65] And the corollary will presumably be a further erosion of the identity cement.

Lowering the level of exclusion in foreign policy, especially toward the European Union, proves to be a source of conflict both between the elite and the people and among the citizens.[66] The three fundamental institutions are either the object of the struggle (especially neutrality but also federalism and direct democracy, due to the globalization process) or else act as channels for voicing any opposition to changes (especially direct democracy and federalism).

Trade

With respect to trade, strong pressures toward reducing exclusion arose from the international arena in the late 1980s. The rising international competition highlighted the need for internal structural adjustments that would improve the situation of the externally oriented sector. But these adjustments challenged the dual economic policy because they required the progressive deregulation of the internally oriented sector.

Thus, external opportunities for the export-oriented sector became threats for the internally oriented sector. This division applied both to regional developments—the road toward a single European market—and to global ones—the expanding agenda of the GATT.[67] The two cases have led to different results regarding the change in levels of exclusion.

The Uruguay round of talks in the GATT brought about a lowering of the barriers in Swiss agricultural policy. Thanks to external pressure, state actors were able to build a strong coalition with the export-oriented sector and overrode the opposition from the farm lobby.[68] Both external economic and political developments had weakened the position of farmers. A major blow for them was the diminishing relevance of a strict neutrality and of its requirement to maintain independence in food supply. In this particular case, direct democracy did not impede the reform process but instead stimulated it: The Swiss citizens' rejection on 12 March 1995 of a constitutional amendment in the field of agriculture, which was seen as not pushing sufficiently toward liberalization and ecology, led to a strengthening of the reform.[69] It paved the way for the adoption of a much more progressive constitutional article accepted by referendum in 1996.

The government has been less successful in bringing down economic barriers with regard to the European Community. When the EEA talks started, the Swiss wanted the four freedoms of movement (goods, capital, services, and persons) to apply wherever and whenever this would prove beneficial. More precisely, Switzerland demanded the exclusion of some sectors from liberalization efforts in order to protect them from European competition. The EU, however, opposed any permanent derogation to the *acquis communautaire* that would threaten the "homogeneity of the European space." The bargaining turned out to be a bitter experience for the Swiss government, which realized that there was no way it could negotiate à la carte participation.[70] A sense of defeat pervaded the general public and nurtured a strong movement against participation in European affairs and in favor of continued isolation. The end result was the public rejection of the EEA treaty in December 1992. Since then the government has adopted a low profile on matters of European integration, choosing to freeze the application for EU membership and instead bargaining on a bilateral basis for the abolition of barriers in some selected issue areas.[71]

Immigration

Like many other countries, Switzerland faces the challenge of increasing migration. This shift takes mainly two forms: There has been an increase of immigration from the Southern to the Northern Hemisphere, in particular of asylum seekers, and Switzerland has been repeatedly asked by the European Union to loosen its immigration policy, if not to actually take part in the completion of the free movement of workers on the Continent. This issue was at the heart of the EEA negotiations and was again the cornerstone of the bilateral talks between Switzerland and the EU from 1994 to 1998.

Access to the Swiss labor market has been a special concern for the EU's southern member states (Italy, Spain, and Portugal), the most important providers of the Swiss foreign workforce. In the initial phase of the EEA negotiations, Switzerland tried to escape from the implementation of the free movement of persons and asked for a permanent derogation to this rule. This request was not compatible with EU intransigence regarding the "homogeneity of the European space." Switzerland ultimately gained only a temporary derogation (seven years), during which barriers to the free movement of persons were to be progressively removed. Fear of an uncontrolled inflow of foreign workers that would threaten Swiss jobs was a major issue during the referendum campaign. After the rejection of the EEA agreement, the free mobility of persons again was in the spotlight during the bilateral talks with the EU. Whereas the EU insisted that the final agreement should include provisions for the complete freedom of movement for persons, the Swiss authorities argued that this goal would certainly lead to a rejection in a popular vote. The result was a kind of compromise: Switzerland agreed to complete freedom of movement after a long transition period but won an exit option after a trial period and a possible referendum on the issue.[72]

Besides being challenged by European demands, Swiss immigration policy is more generally at the center of the domestic political scene. Swiss attempts to control the inflow of foreign workers with the help of the system of permits and quotas is in fact a failure, since 80 percent of the immigrants are not concerned by the quotas and hence escape any control today.[73] In addition, the reunion of families has resulted in a significant increase of foreigners of the second and third generation. As a solution, the Swiss authorities have suggested providing them with a facilitated naturalization procedure. This proposal was, however, rejected in a popular vote in 1994.

Finally, in 1991 the Federal Council put forward a new proposal in the field of immigration, the so-called model of three circles.[74] According to this model, foreign workers would be divided into three categories: The interior circle would provide free access to the Swiss labor market to workers of the EEA space (EFTA and EU countries); the middle circle envisioned only a limited recruitment of workers from the

United States, Canada, and in the future possibly from Eastern Europe; the exterior circle, with no possibility of recruitment (apart from a few exceptions), would apply to the rest of the world. The Federal Council introduced some of these elements into executive ordinances, then backtracked on its decision and abandoned the model. A major factor in its reversal was the strong criticism by the parties of the left of the ethnic-cultural discrimination on which the model was based. In addition, there were very few foreign workers coming from countries of the second circle. Hence, the Federal Council recently proposed a new system of permits based on qualifications rather than nationality. But workers from the first circle will still experience privileged treatment. This seems to suggest that the difficulty of discriminating against workers from European countries has led to excluding workers from other geographical areas. In some sense this shift results in a redefinition of the other, which has become geographically more distant.

Conclusion

What are the main features of the process of national identity building in Switzerland? First and foremost, the cornerstones have been provided by the political institutions, in particular the triad consisting of federalism, direct democracy, and neutrality. The resulting institutional framework has gradually become the rallying point of collective feeling in belonging to Swiss society. Patriotism is thus primarily "constitutional,"[75] and the other is someone who does not share the public sphere delimited by these three key institutions. Second, the strengthening of collective identity has been compounded by exclusionary practices in the policy domains of foreign involvement, trade, and immigration. The policy of neutrality has accounted for the extreme restraint shown in international political affairs and has helped justify high levels of protection to several sectors, in particular agriculture, on the grounds of national independence and self-sufficiency, just as it also cultivated a restrictive refugee policy during the difficult times of the Third Reich. Immigration policy by itself appears very liberal, in that the search for adequate regulations has been largely left to economic actors. Yet neither direct democracy nor federalism, which generated a decentralized decisionmaking process in several domains, has favored an active incorporation policy.

Put together, these features imply that the process of identity formation in Switzerland has not escaped the trade-off between exclusion and dilution. As the Swiss case seems to suggest, even a national identity based on "constitutional patriotism" needs some barriers to protect

itself. The current problems that Switzerland is facing confirm this conclusion. Demands from the outside concerning exclusion levels—which
are closely linked to the main institutional features of Switzerland—
have upset the delicate balance inside the country. Changes in the institutional setup appear to be necessary, and these changes bring into
question the very bases of Swiss national identity. Gottfried Keller, a
Swiss author of the nineteenth century, envisioned the Swiss political
institutions as a bulwark against the authoritarian regimes surrounding
the country. He even considered that the Swiss institutions, and
Switzerland in itself, would become obsolete if the surrounding regimes
turned democratic.[76] This argument was echoed in the slogan "700
years are enough," which Swiss intellectuals created for the 700th
anniversary of Switzerland in 1991. Again, this seems to imply that the
exclusions that Switzerland has practiced over the period of its existence as a nation-state were intimately linked to the formation and
maintenance of a common multicultural identity.

Thus, the Swiss case would appear to indicate promising avenues
for the construction of a European identity, but at the same time it also
signals possible dangerous consequences. The main positive insight
appears to be that "constitutional patriotism" is not simply a theoretical
construct but has been successfully implemented. The Swiss case provides some support to those who argue that the drafting of a European
constitution and its popular ratification, leading to a social legitimization of the European Union, are a necessary step.[77] The view that
European citizens will acquiesce to being part of a new "nation" as soon
as the constitutional and political structure is put in place, however, is
too simplistic.[78] Contrary to Paul Marquardt, who seems to say that a
constitution matters irrespective of its content, the Swiss case shows that
the specific institutions chosen play a crucial role.[79] In Switzerland the
carefully managed principle of subsidiarity and direct avenues of influence for citizens have helped to build up a convergence of expectations
and ultimately resulted in a collective feeling of belonging. On the negative side, the Swiss experience shows how difficult it is to avoid exclusionary tendencies in the process of strengthening identification with
the collective. There seems to be a need for an other and for high levels of exclusion to preserve the multicultural balance.

What does this tell us for the future of a European identity? Can the
European Union pick out only the raisins of the Swiss cake, as some
scholars suggest? First, the Swiss case points to the necessity of designing central political institutions that can become the rallying point of a
collective identity. Constitutional patriotism cannot emerge without a
constitution and its structural apparatus. In Switzerland this has meant
moving from a loose confederation of cantons to a truly federal state

with a clear hierarchy of power and responsibilities. It is highly unlikely that the EU is ready to make such a move, at least in the short and medium terms. A widespread position is that the EU will remain a kind of unidentified political object, a mixture of confederation, federation, or even medieval forms of political organization. Without claiming that the specific institutional design elaborated in Switzerland is the only one that can serve as an anchor for a collective identity, the question remains whether an opaque political construction such as the EU (at the present or as it is likely to become in the future) will be able to achieve this goal.

Second, the Swiss experience casts doubt on the possibility of both widening and deepening efforts. The two can go together when widening does not extend to the existing other or at least goes together with a redefinition of the other.[80] The latter possibility implies that subsequent rounds of widening must allow for restive periods during which images of the other have to be reconstructed. In more concrete terms, internal consolidation seems to require external caution. Recent developments inside the EU tend to confirm this view. The Single European Act gave birth to the idea of a "Fortress Europe" where the common enemy was implicitly regarded as the competition from Southeast Asian countries (and the United States), although decisionmakers have tried to tone down this defensive posture in the meantime. Still on the issue of trade, active participation in world liberalizing trends has fostered internal strains, in particular regarding farm products. Aggressive behavior and the bitter row with the United States during the Uruguay round of talks ended in a division between France and its partners.[81] Similarly, expansion to the Central and Eastern European countries has been strongly opposed by those who consider the Common Agricultural Policy to be a cornerstone of the EU. From this perspective, the likely dismantling of the CAP that would follow an enlargement to the east would be a blow to the cement of the EU.

On foreign involvement, there have been few signs of any movement toward an active Common Foreign and Security Policy. More important, the few efforts that have been made in this direction have revealed dangerous strains. Germany's push for a common recognition of Slovenia and Croatia triggered a major crisis and has since relegated the EU to a secondary role in the Balkan crises, especially in Bosnia but also in Kosovo. Similarly, the EU has been reluctant to take the lead in designing new security arrangements for Central and Eastern Europe. It has also left participation in humanitarian actions to the discretion of individual members.

On immigration and internal security, the Schengen Agreement is the first example of the institutionalization of a multitiered EU with variable exclusion levels. More significant, the agreement reflects the need for exclusion, in particular with regard to Mediterranean neighbors. Finally, the case of the Economic and Monetary Union (EMU) reveals exclusion both externally and internally. On the one hand, decision-makers have gone back to the exclusionary message that was highly present in the late 1960s when the early plans for monetary integration emerged. A single European currency is supposed to upgrade the role of Europe vis-à-vis the United States in the conduct of international monetary affairs. The image of a common enemy is thus used to foster more integration and help people identify with the supranational collective. On the other hand, there was an intensive debate inside the EU on the limits of internal exclusion, debate that was finally resolved by the admission of most members that had stated their willingness to join.[82]

In sum, our analysis of the formation of Swiss national identity offers few easy recipes for the construction of a European identity. In particular, Switzerland appears to be both an example and an exception. It is an example of successful integration and identity creation in a multicultural society. But at the same time, it is an exception in the sense that this successful identity formation is not unrelated to the particular historical period in which it occurred. In addition, its association with exclusionary tendencies toward the external world makes it less popular for imitation. Thus, there seems to be little prospect of an easy road for the European Union toward the elusive emergence of a collective identity, as has been confirmed by some of its recent policy developments.

Notes

We wish to thank Lars-Erik Cederman, Ernst Haas, Malik Mazbouri, Lorena Parini, and Frederic Vandenberghe for their valuable comments on an earlier version of this chapter.
        1. Jürgen Habermas, "Citizenship and National Identity," *Praxis International* 12, 1 (1992): 17; Joseph H. Weiler, "After Maastricht: Community Legitimacy in Post-1992 Europe," in William James Adams, ed., *Singular Europe* (Ann Arbor: University of Michigan Press, 1992), 11–41.
        2. Amitai Etzioni, *Political Unification: A Comparative Study of Leaders and Forces* (New York: Holt, Rinehart and Winston, 1965), 22, 35. Etzioni is cited in Carol L. Schmid, *Conflict and Consensus in Switzerland* (Berkeley: University of California Press, 1981), 1. Today we would perhaps disagree with Etzioni in several of these cases, not least the case of Nigeria.
        3. Habermas, "Citizenship and National Identity." In the case of the United States, one might argue that the common language provided (at least to some degree) a common cultural denominator. This should not, however, obscure the fact that the cultural background of the immigrants in the United States has remained very diverse.

4. Habermas, "Citizenship and National Identity," 17.

5. See also Paul Howe, "A Community of Europeans: The Requisite Underpinnings," *Journal of Common Market Studies* 33, 1 (1995): 27–46.

6. Georges Andrey, "Auf der Suche nach dem neuen Staat (1798–1848)," in Comité pour une nouvelle histoire de la Suisse, ed., *Geschichte der Schweiz und der Schweizer* (Lausanne: Payot, 1986), 527–637.

7. In this pact the three founding cantons committed themselves to a defensive alliance against foreign oppressors. Yet the existence of the 1291 confederal pact was ignored until the late nineteenth century. The pact was first mentioned in 1887 by Johannes Dierauer in his book *History of the Swiss Confederation*. Moreover, the national holiday celebrating the 1291 pact (1 August) was not introduced by the Federal Council until 1891.

8. It is worth noting that despite the early market integration, federal economic associations appeared only much later in the nineteenth century.

9. Andrey, "Auf der Suche nach dem neuen Staat."

10. Federalism has often been considered the most typical element of the Swiss political system and political culture. See for instance, Jean-François Bergier, *Europe et les Suisses. Impertinences d'un historien* (Carouge-Genève: Editions Zoé, 1992), 160; Karl W. Deutsch, *Die Schweiz als ein paradigmatischer Fall politischer Integration* (Bern: Haupt, 1976); Wolf Linder, *Swiss Democracy: Possible Solutions to Conflict in Multicultural Societies* (London: Macmillan, 1994). Albeit a characteristic element of the Swiss institutional setup, federalism was a direct import from the United States. When drafting the constitution in 1847–1848, the founding fathers of the confederation drew inspiration from the U.S. Constitution, especially with respect to the federal elements, most visible in its bicameral legislature.

11. Under the mandatory referendum, any group may call for a final decision by the electorate on a bill adopted by parliament. In order for this to take place, the group has only to collect a certain number of signatures from citizens. The mandatory referendum takes place automatically, without popular impulsion. It applies, for instance, to any amendment to or revision of the constitution. By collecting a certain number of signatures, a group can place an issue on the political agenda and force the elite—and then the electorate—to vote on a constitutional amendment, whatever the subject.

12. Thomas Fleiner-Gerster, "Le Conseil fédéral: Directoire de la Confédération," *Pouvoirs* 43, 1 (1987): 49–63.

13. Leonard Neidhart, *Plebiszit und pluralitäre Demokratie. Eine Analyse der Funktionen des schweizerischen Gesetzesreferendum* (Bern: Francke, 1970).

14. Neutrality was referred to simply as a means of achieving independence.

15. Earlier, in 1648, the Wesphalia Treaty had recognized the confederation's sovereignty and declared its independence from the empire. The Congress of Vienna officially rooted a nationally chosen principle in international law.

16. Bergier, *Europe et les Suisses*, 120.

17. That one member of the Federal Council was forced to step down for an obvious breach of neutrality illustrates that this institution kept its integrative force even during these difficult times. See Hans Ulrich Jost, "Bedrohung und Enge (1914–1945)," in Comité pour une nouvelle histoire de la Suisse, ed., *Geschichte der Schweiz und der Schweizer* (Lausanne: Payot, 1986), 731–820.

18. Hanspeter Kriesi, *Le système politique suisse* (Paris: Economica, 1995).

19. With respect to economic issues, in 1864 Switzerland joined the Cobden-Chevallier bilateral network of trade liberalization and in 1865 the Latin Monetary Union, On the network of trade, see, for instance, Paul Bairoch, "European Trade Policy, 1815–1914," in *The Cambridge Economic History of Europe* (Cambridge: Cambridge University Press, 1989).

20. William Rappard, *L'Entrée de la Suisse dans la Société des Nations* (Geneva: Sonor, 1924); Cédric Dupont, "Succès avec la SDN, échec avec l'EEE? Résistances internes et négociation internationale," *Annuaire Suisse de Science Politique* 32 (1992): 249–272.

21. The vote for the League of Nations was exceptionally close, especially with respect to the vote of the cantons (56.3 percent of the citizens and half of twenty-three cantons accepted joining the league). The best accounts of the campaign can be found in Rappard, *L'Entrée de la Suisse dans la Société des Nations*.

22. The attitude of the Swiss government and the Swiss banking sector during and immediately after World War II have given the impetus to a newly created Independent Commission of Experts. See Jean-François Bergier, *Switzerland and the Nazi Gold* (Bern: Independent Commission of Experts, 1999).

23. This mostly amounted to the fear that such an endeavor would put limitations on neutrality, direct democracy, and federalism.

24. Annette Enz, "Die Schweiz und die Grosse Europäische Freihandelszone," *Studien und Quellen, Zeitschrift des Schweizerischen Bundesarchivs* 16/17 (1991): 157–261.

25. For a comprehensive treatment of the evolution of European integration policy in Switzerland from 1957 to 1999, see Pierre Allan, Cédric Dupont, Pascal Sciarini, and David Sylvan, *Cohérence d'élaboration et cohérence d'action: la politique suisse d'intégration européenne en perspective comparative* (Geneva: Rapport de synthèse PNR 42, 1999).

26. For instance, neutrality is essentially irrelevant to the decision to stay out of the Bretton Woods system. Sectoral economic interests are the main determinants of this decision. Caroline Baumann, Cédric Dupont, and Marcel Peter, "Forme et logique des engagements internationaux de la Suisse: quelques enseignements du cas des relations avec les institutions de Bretton Woods," *Revue suisse de science politique* 5, 3 (1999): 97–109.

27. Hans Rentsch, *Cartels and Wealth: A Paradox in the Swiss Economic System* (Zug: Forschungsinstitut für Wirtschafts- und Sozialpolitik, 1989).

28. Beat Hotz, *Politik zwischen Staat und Wirtschaft* (Diessenhofen: Rüegger, 1979).

29. In 1990 Switzerland was the fifth largest exporter of services in the world. Moreover, it has been a leading country in foreign direct investments since the beginning of the twentieth century. Paul Bairoch, "La Suisse dans le contexte international aux XIXe et XXe siècles," in Paul Bairoch and M. Körner, eds., *La Suisse dans l'économie mondiale* (Geneva: Droz, 1990), 103–140.

30. Peter J. Katzenstein, *Corporatism and Change: Austria, Switzerland, and the Politics of Industry* (Ithaca: Cornell University Press, 1984); Peter J. Katzenstein, *Small States in World Markets: Industrial Policy in Europe* (Ithaca: Cornell University Press, 1985). A discussion of Katzenstein's theoretical framework and its application to the Swiss case can be found in Pascal Sciarini, *La Suisse face à la Communauté européenne et au GATT. Le cas-test de la politique agricole* (Geneva: Georg, 1994).

31. Katzenstein, *Corporatism and Change*, 91, and Katzenstein, *Small States in World Markets*, 84.

32. Sciarini, *La Suisse face à la Communauté européenne et au GATT.*

33. In the late 1980s, studies by the Organization of Economic Cooperation and Development (OECD) showed that Swiss agriculture was the most heavily subsidized in the world. According to the OECD's production subsidy equivalent (PSE) measure, four-fifths of Swiss farm production relied on state support, with a total cost of 7 billion Fr per year. OECD, *Politiques nationales et échanges agricoles. Etude par pays: Suisse* (Paris: OECD, 1990).

34. Prices of Swiss farm products have usually been twice the price of those in EC countries.

35. In addition to its access to (and power in) the preparliamentary phase, the farm lobby could also count on the strong support of political parties in the parliamentary arena. See, e.g., Philip Halbherr and Alfred Müdespacher, *Agrarpolitik—Interessenpolitik?* (Bern: Haupt, 1985), 28–30; Erwin Rüegg, *Neokorporatismus in der Schweiz. Landwirtschaftspolitik* (Zurich: Forschungstelle für Politische Wissenschaft, 1987), 21.

36. Roland Ruffieux, "Die Schweiz des Freisinns (1848–1914)," in Comité pour une nouvelle histoire de la Suisse, ed., *Geschichte der Schweiz und der Schweizer* (Lausanne: Payot, 1986), 688.

37. Jost, "Bedrohung und Enge," 796.

38. E.g., Rentsch, *Cartels and Wealth.*

39. Jean-Pierre Danthine and Jean-Christian Lambelet, "The Swiss Recipe: Conservative Policies Ain't Enough," *Economic Policy* 5 (1987): 149–179. These authors argue that it is mainly the absence of an effective antitrust policy, which can in turn be considered an adverse effect of the Swiss laissez-faire, that has allowed all sorts of cartels to flourish.

40. Bergier, *Europe et les Suisses,* 60.

41. François De Capitani, "Beharren und Umsturz (1648–1815)," in Comité pour une nouvelle histoire de la Suisse, ed., *Geschichte der Schweiz und der Schweizer* (Lausanne: Payot, 1986), 450.

42. Hoffmann-Nowotny notes that "between 100,000 and 150,000 Huguenots rushed to Switzerland . . . , but only about one tenth remained there permanently." See Hans-Joachim Hoffmann-Nowotny, "Switzerland," in Tomas Hammar, ed., *European Immigration Policy: A Comparative Study* (Cambridge: Cambridge University Press, 1985), 206. This might be linked to the fact that most cities in that time adopted a very stringent immigration policy (see ibid. and Bergier, *Europe et les Suisses*). The size of the population exceeded 1 million in the course of the seventeenth century, 1.2 million at the beginning of the eighteenth century, and 1.7 million toward the end of the eighteenth century.

43. Hoffman-Nowotny, "Switzerland," 538.

44. Ibid., 206.

45. Ludwig's report cited in Guido Koller, "Entscheidungen über Leben und Tod. Die behördliche Praxis in der schweizerischen Flüchtlingspolitik während des Zweiten Weltkrieges," *Studien und Quellen* 22 (1996): 17–104. In addition, one should not forget that the J stamp in Jewish passports was the result of a demand by Swiss authorities. Conversely, 230,000 refugees were allowed to enter Switzerland (among them 22,000 Jews).

46. Heinz Roschewski, "Heinrich Rothmund in seinen persönlichen Akten: Zur Frage des Antisemitusmus in der Schweizerischen Flüchtlingspolitik, 1933–1945," *Studien und Quellen* 22 (1996): 107–134.

47. Lorena Parini, "Politica di immigrazione e politica di asilo in Svizzera: Due aspetti di una stessa logica," in Vittoria Cesari Lusso, Sandro Cattacin, and

Cristina Allemann-Ghionda, eds., *I come . . . identità, integrazione, interculturalità* (Zurich: Federazione delle Colonie Libere Italiane in Swizzera, 1996), 83–95.

48. See Russell King, "European International Migration 1945–1990: A Statistical and Geographical Overview," in Russell King, ed., *Mass Migration in Europe: The Legacy and the Future* (London: Belhaven, 1993), 19–39.

49. The outflow of migrant workers was also due to the fact that they were not covered by social security. Sandro Cattacin, "'Il federalismo integrativo.' Qualche considerazione sulle modalità di integrazione degli immigranti in Swizzera," in Vittoria Cesari Lusso, Sandro Cattacin, and Cristina Allemann-Ghionda, eds., *I come . . . identità, integrazione, interculturalità* (Zurich: Federazione delle Colonie Libere Italiane in Swizzera, 1996), 67–82.

50. Hoffmann-Nowotny, "Switzerland," 219, shows that in 1970 a majority of the foreign population had permits of abode, while from 1975 the majority had permits of permanent residence.

51. Yasemin N. Soysal, *Limits of Citizenship: Migrants and Postnational Membership in Europe* (Chicago: University of Chicago Press, 1994).

52. Ibid., 25.

53. Ibid., 56.

54. Cattacin, "'Il federalismo integrativo.'"

55. Hoffmann-Nowotny, "Switzerland."

56. Georg Kreis, "La Question de l'identité nationale," in Paul Hugger, ed., *Les Suisses. Modes de vie, traditions, mentalités*, vol. 2 (Lausane: Payot, 1992), 791.

57. See the Federal Council's report on Swiss foreign policy in the 1990s: Conseil fédéral, "Rapport sur la politique extérieure de la Suisse dans les années 1990," Bern, 1993.

58. This means a return to the "differential neutrality" of the period of Switzerland's participation in the League of Nations.

59. Jürg Martin Gabriel, "Neutralität für den Notfall: Der Bericht des Bundesrates zur Aussenpolitik der Schweiz in den 90er Jahren," *Schweizerische Zeitschrift für Politische Wissenschaft* 1, 2-3 (1995): 163–191.

60. Conseil fédéral, "Rapport sur la question d'une adhésion de la Suisse à la Communauté européenne," Bern, 1992; Conseil fédéral, "Rapport sur la politique extérieure de la Suisse dans les années 1990."

61. Yannis Papadopoulos, "Les votations fédérales comme indicateur de soutien aux autorités," in Yannis Papadopoulos, ed., *Elites politiques et peuple en Suisse. Analyse des votations fédérales: 1970–1987* (Lausanne: Réalités sociales, 1994), 113–160; Pascal Sciarini, "Opinion publique et politique extérieure," *Revue d'Allemagne* 28, 3 (1996): 337–352. Yet foreign policy is the field in which the optional referendum has been the least employed in the decades following World War II. Sciarini, "Opinion publique et politique extérieure"; Alexandre Trechsel, and Pascal Sciarini, "Direct Democracy in Switzerland: Do Elites Matter?" *European Journal of Political Research* 33, 1 (1998): 99–124.

62. Hanspeter Kriesi, Claude Longchamp, Florence Passy, and Pascal Sciarini, "Analyse de la votation fédérale du 6 décembre 1992 (EEE)," Département de science politique/GfS-Forschungsinstitut, Geneva and Bern, Analyse-Vox 47, 1993; Pascal Sciarini and Ola Listhaug, "Single Cases or a Unique Pair? The Swiss and Norwegian 'No' to Europe," *Journal of Common Market Studies* 35, 3 (1997): 407–438.

63. According to opinion polls, French-speaking citizens have felt more European than German-speaking citizens for several years (Kriesi et al., "Analyse de la votation fédérale," 11), and the priority given to European integration is sig-

nificantly higher among the former (Thomas Widmer, and Christophe Buri, "Brüssel oder Bern: schlägt das Herz der 'Romands' eher für Europa?" *Annuaire suisse de science politique* 32 [1992]: 367). One reason for this could be the fear of Germany. The French-speaking community might conceive of Europe as a way to "free" itself from the domination of the German-speaking cantons. More generally, a study of the linguistic cleavage in Switzerland shows that opposition between the French-speaking and German-speaking regions is stronger in issues of foreign policy than in most other fields. Hanspeter Kriesi, Boris Wernli, Pascal Sciarini, and Matteo Gianni, *Le Clivage linguistique: problèmes de compréhension entre les communautés linguistiques en Suisse* (Bern: Office fédéral de la statistique, 1996).

64. Kriesi et al., *Le Clivage linguistique.*

65. Accordingly, various proposals aimed at reforming the double-majority rule in the sense of a reduction of small cantons' veto power have been elaborated. For a summary and discussion of these proposals, see Adrian Vatter and Fritz Sager, "Föderalismusreform am Beispiel des Ständemehrs," in Simon Hug, and Pascal Sciarini, eds., *Staatsreform—La réforme des institutions—Institutional Reforms* (Zurich: Seismo, 1996) (special issue of the *Swiss Political Science Review* 2, 2 [1995]: 165–200).

66. Simon Hug and Pascal Sciarini, "Switzerland: Still a Paradigmatic Case?" in Gerald Schneider, Patricia A. Weitsman, and Thomas Bernauer, eds., *Towards a New Europe: Stops and Starts in Regional Integration* (Westport, Conn.: Praeger, 1995), 55–74.

67. According to an official study, the largest share of the expected 0.4 to 0.6 percent additional economic growth per year following integration into the common market would have been due to the liberalization of the formerly protected domestic sectors of the Swiss economy. Heinz Hauser, *Traité sur l'EEE. Adhésion à la CE. Course en solitaire. Conséquences économiques pour la Suisse* (Bern: Office fédéral des questions conjoncturelles, 1991), 48–52.

68. See Sciarini, *La Suisse face à la Communauté européenne et au GATT*; Pascal Sciarini, "Réseau politique interne et négociations internationales: le GATT, levier de la réforme agricole suisse," *Revue suisse de science politique* 1, 2-3 (1995): 225–252; Pascal Sciarini, "Elaboration of the Swiss Agricultural Policy for the GATT Negotiations: A Network Analysis," *Swiss Journal of Sociology* 22, 1 (1996): 85–115.

69. Pascal Sciarini, Lionel Marquis, and Boris Wernli, "Analyse-VOX des votations fédérales du 12 mars," GfS/Département de science politique, Zurich and Geneva, 1995; Conseil fédéral, "Politique agricole 2002," Berne, 1995.

70. Cédric Dupont, "Domestic Politics, Information and International Bargaining: Comparative Models of Strategic Behaviour in Non-Crisis Negotiations," Ph.D. dissertation, Graduate Institute of International Studies, Geneva, 1994; Pascal Sciarini, "La Suisse dans la négociation sur l'Espace économique européen: de la rupture à l'apprentissage," *Annuaire suisse de science politique* 32 (1992): 297–322.

71. Bilateral talks covered seven domains: public procurement policy, technical obstacles to trade, farm trade, air and road transportation policy, free movement of people, and research policy.

72. For a careful analysis of the bargaining process, see Cédric Dupont, Caroline Eggli, and Pascal Sciarini, "Entre cohérence et efficacité. Les négociations bilatérales Suisse—Union Européenne," paper presented to the Swiss Political Science Meetings, Balsthal, 1998.

73. Didier Chambovey, "Politique à l'égard des étrangers et contingente-ment de l'immigration. L'exemple de la Suisse," *Population INED* 2 (1995): 357–384.

74. Conseil fédéral, "Rapport du Conseil fédéral sur la politique à l'égard des étrangers et des réfugiés du 15 mai 1991," Bern, 1991.

75. Habermas, "Citizenship and National Identity."

76. Adolf Muschg, "Wieviel Identität braucht die Schweiz?" *Weltwoche Supplement*, April 1996, 22–27.

77. E.g., Weiler, "After Maastricht," and Paul D. Marquardt, "Deficit Reduction: Democracy, Technocracy, and Constitutionalism in the European Union," *Duke Journal of Comparative and International Law* 4, 2 (1994): 265–290.

78. Howe, "A Community of Europeans," 34.

79. Marquardt, "Deficit Reduction," 284.

80. Iver B. Neumann, "Self and Other in International Relations," *European Journal of International Relations* 2, 2 (1996): 139–174, and Chapter 6 of this volume.

81. Cédric Dupont, and Pascal Sciarini, "La Négociation agricole Etats-Unis—Communauté européenne au GATT: une difficile convergence," *Revue suisse de science politique* 1, 2-3 (1995): 305–352.

82. On this debate, see the special contributions in the *Swiss Political Science Review* 2, 1; 2, 3; 3, 1; and 3, 2.

PART TWO

EUROPE'S CULTURAL IDENTITY

4

From Cultural Protection to Political Culture? Media Policy and the European Union

Philip R. Schlesinger

The Cold War had a profound impact on how we categorized European culture. As we take our distance from its ending, we can see how much it shaped our thinking. The polar divisions between West and East—which constituted an organizing grand narrative about democracy and totalitarianism, capitalism and socialism, freedom and repression—disappeared with the collapse of the Soviet bloc. Such political designations were also cultural ones, in the sense that they constructed bounded social collectivities as different and symbolized distinctions between types of regime and of society. They marked, defined, and simplified, and in so doing distorted the complexities to be found on each side of the old iron curtain.

Today bloc no longer faces bloc. Instead, the transformed political geography of the Continent has left us with an incomplete architecture, whether this be thought of in political, economic, military, or cultural terms. In the case of ex-Yugoslavia and the former Soviet Union, political disintegration has been accompanied by the emergence of arenas of armed conflict and persisting instability in the Balkans and the Caucasus.

In this context the European Union's political trajectory remains uncertain. There is a long lineup of further would-be members, which implies added complexity in governance. The euro is still at an early stage of development. And progress toward coherence in foreign and defense policies will inevitably take time. The process of political and

A previous version of this chapter was published in *Media, Culture & Society* 19, 3 (July 1997): 369–390.

economic integration is far from unilinear in impact, in some respects evidently accentuating the sense of difference to be found in the European Union at the same time as it officially proclaims its supranationality. Even before the Maastricht Treaty of 1991 was signed, nationalist reactions to further integration were apparent in many member states, and below the level of the national state, autonomist claims have added to the complexity.[1] We might include xenophobic—sometimes neo-Nazi—reactions to the growth of multicultural diversity due to earlier or present migration into the EU space. There has also been a rise of "cultural fundamentalism," the postracist doctrine in which sacralized cultural difference replaces racial superiority as the ground for refusing pluralism.[2] Collective identity crises in Europe are thus vertical and lateral and occur at substate, state, and EU levels.

They are actually inherent in the transformative dynamics of Europeanization, which means that we cannot take as given "political structures and actors, boundaries and communities, collective identities and understandings, and distributions of resources and life chances"; consequently, the current European situation invites us to consider how "basic frameworks of political life might be changing."[3]

If we accept that invitation—and actually we cannot refuse—this still leaves the diagnosis of our times an open matter. We might well agree, for instance, that there has been a loss of economic sovereignty on the part of the national state and that dense networks of affiliation and communication now crisscross the European space, thereby modifying social relations and systems of representation. Yet we might still not be sure how we should theorize this. Are we entering a "postnational" era that demands a new politics and culture? Is Europe a kind of test bed today for arguments about the demise of the nation-state? There is a growing controversy on these questions, which need to be taken seriously, even if the debate can hardly be said to be settled.[4]

With such uncertainty about the kind of political formation that is emerging, the vagaries of a media policy that must negotiate different levels of political authority in an as yet unsettled framework need not surprise us. In what follows, I offer an interpretation of policy developments concerning audiovisual media in the EU as these came to symbolize the struggles over collective identity in the 1990s, most particularly against the threat of Americanization. This chapter is, therefore, not so much a policy analysis as a drawing out of the largely unstated underpinnings of policy debate. I wish to show how the assumptions underlying contemporary policies relate to conceptions of collective identity.

Both the GATT talks and post-GATT developments under the World Trade Organization (WTO) offer a useful way of addressing how

EU policymakers have thought about the Europeanization of culture in a global market. If federal state formation is where the EU will ultimately lead, then one of the prime objectives of media policy should be to help to achieve genuine pluralism and a widespread democratic commitment on the part of the European Union's peoples, present and future. As I demonstrate, the policy framework of the 1990s ran counter to this prospect or at best marginalized it. Dominated as it was by considerations of global industrial competition, media policy treated the task of building a democratic political culture in Europe as a subordinate issue.

The EU as an Emergent Cultural Actor?

During the GATT negotiations in 1993, the European Union took on the fleeting guise of a cultural collectivity. The EU had adopted a cultural protectionist stance based on a conception of a European collective identity largely modeled on that of a nation entitled to defend its own cultural space. National audiovisual production—something quite distinctive, rooted in a given heritage—was perceived as a source of authentic self-expression. It needed to be sustained so as to articulate a collective identity valued for itself. This set of ideas about the place of the audiovisual industries was drawn directly from the French response to the American challenge initiated during the first administration of President François Mitterrand. As a result of French persuasiveness, it became the "European" position in 1993 in the closing months of the Uruguay round.[5] Of course, its novelty lay in little other than its being represented as European, for there is a history of fear among European politicians and elites of the American cinematic invasion that goes back to World War I.

After the signing of the Maastricht Treaty in 1991, competence in cultural matters became a fully acknowledged part of the EU's remit.[6] During the GATT negotiations in late 1993, the EU operated as a single, sovereign cultural actor on the global stage, a distinctive departure from earlier practice. Although the lines between EU action in this domain and that of the member states remains a matter of contention, it seems reasonable to suppose that the more the EU begins to behave like a federal political formation, the more it will need to define a supranational cultural policy.

Before looking more closely at the details, however, we need to disentangle two distinct senses of culture commonly elided in contemporary discussion: (1) culture broadly understood as the way of life, broadly shared values, practices, and beliefs of a social group; and (2) culture narrowly understood as the production of artifacts that may become commodities traded in a marketplace.

In the European Union policy context, culture in the first sense is normally identified with national culture, namely, the body of values, practices, and identities deemed to make particular nations different from others. Culture in this sense may be thought of as thick, as dense, as exercising special demands on the affects and loyalties of those who live within it. Such national cultures have commonly been developed and sustained by states over extensive periods. Indeed, in the European Union the national state has been and remains the principal building block of political and economic integration. That said, stateless nations (such as the Catalans and the Scots) may also properly be said to have national cultures and to have institutionalized these in ways akin to states, adding both political complexity and another sense to the term *national*.

National cultures are not repositories of symbols, beliefs, and practices to which the entire population must stand in identical relation. Rather, as I have argued elsewhere, they may be thought of as sites of contestation in which competition over the very boundaries and nature of the national community routinely occurs.[7] The fault lines of power and inequality run through them. But at the same time, even if struggles occur within these national cultural spaces, they do remain crucial points of departure for thinking about community and belonging. It is this compelling and still resilient framework of national cultural reference that has to be both addressed and negotiated by the European Union.

Culture in the second, narrower sense, that of the production of artifacts, has traditionally been the object of debates about how such products may be classified and the kind of value they might be assigned, such as "high," "low," or "popular." In the current context, this particular framing of the argument is largely irrelevant to the main protagonists. While European audiovisual culture contains a vast range of output, running from the art-house movie via news and documentary to the soap opera, situation comedy, and popular cinema, it is not distinctions of genre, market appeal, or associated aesthetic value that have been relevant. Rather, it has been the defense of audiovisual culture only as an expression of collective identity that has been on the agenda. Nor, indeed, has it just been the expressive quality of the audiovisual domain that has been at issue. Instead, it has been the assumed impact of the production and consumption of audiovisual culture upon national (and European) culture as a way of life that has been central to the debate. Among those who make arguments for cultural defense, however, these two levels are not always kept distinct: Sustaining audiovisual production is commonly conflated with protecting (because it is believed to shape) a whole way of life.

Europeanization Versus Americanization

The process of European integration increasingly transcends traditional forms of international cooperation so that policymaking cuts across national boundaries.[8] This growth of complexity requires us to move away from the national level in terms of how we understand the policy context, policymaking processes, and policy outcomes. Europeanization involves increased complexity for political actors in pursuit of their strategies because there is greater heterogeneity in the political system.

In the context of global competition, audiovisual culture has become signally important. Articulated in different ways in different European states, current official worry about the Americanization of culture has long-standing roots among the national elites of a number of countries. Now, signaled as a "European" concern, it has an ideological function: It allows Europeanization to be presented as a kind of antidote to an external threat. There is also anxiety about competition in communication technologies from Japan, but to denounce the Japanization of culture is hardly a convincing rallying cry.

If official Europe is worried about America and Americanization, people's Europe most certainly is not, as witness its tastes in films, popular music, fast food, and casual clothes. Yet this does not mean that Europeans have all become identical any more than it means that—despite the globalization of a culture of consumption—there is a single, global culture. In fact, both Europe and the United States seem to be going through identity crises at present, exacerbated in many respects by the ending of the certainties of the system of Cold War blocs.

Americanization in a rather different sense is currently a preoccupation in the United States. For the liberal establishment, the traditional, hegemonic center of the culture is in question and the overarching political commitment of the population is perceived as under pressure. This is symptomized by concern about the position of English as the common language and reflected in the debates about political correctness, the curriculum, and multiculturalism.[9] Others, however, see the threat as an undelivered promise, a quest by the excluded, whether in terms of ethnicity, gender, or sexual orientation, to redefine the scope of the culture. Americanness is thus the object of discursive struggles based upon competing political agendas.[10] Opposed to the lament over the failure of assimilation, which is resolutely modernist, we find other voices that celebrate difference and indeed the decomposition of the nation-state form as a point of reference. Modern and postmodern, national and postnational visions jockey for position. How the national public space is to be constituted is in question; so, indeed, is whether it can be properly defined as national.[11]

The historical depth of the concern to define and redefine Americanness in the United States is not surprising in a state founded upon successive waves of immigration.[12] Present elite concerns about whether the assimilation process still works—now posed in terms of a crisis of national identity—are therefore nothing new.

Such matters are of no concern on the other side of the pond when official worries about importing American values are aired. Perhaps they should be, for this sketch suggests that we need to reconsider official fears of the Americanization of Europe with due skepticism. After all, we are not talking of one object confronting another. American diversity is such that whatever Europeans take from it is selective and is in any case integrated dynamically into Europe's wider national cultures.[13] Official worries about Americanization should tend to obscure a critical analysis of what is presently meant by the "Europeanization" of audiovisual culture.

The GATT and Cultural Exclusion

The economic stakes in the audiovisual sector are considerable. In 1995 the United States had a trade surplus of $6.3 billion with the European Union.[14] There has been a steady rise in the U.S.-EU trade gap over recent years. European cinema is widely recognized to be in crisis, characterized by a dual decline in cinema audiences and production coupled with Hollywood's increasing domination of the European box office.[15]

Audiovisual trade has been so important for the United States because of its particular success in international film and program sales compared to the performance of U.S. goods and services as a whole. This relative importance explains why the United States has repeatedly tried to remove barriers to trade in cultural products by negotiation. It has failed, most notably in the cases of the North American Free Trade Agreement (NAFTA) and the GATT. At the new round of WTO negotiations in 2000, the whole issue is being revisited.

If the U.S. market size is fundamental to its success, it is easy to account for EU policymakers' belief that the European single market may improve the global competitive position of the audiovisual industries.[16] Addressing one large audience would generate the high revenues necessary to enable higher production values to be used and significantly amortize the costs of production in the domestic market. But European diversity stands in the way of following a U.S.-style strategy. There are numerous linguistic and cultural barriers, based in the system of nation-states in EU Europe, that make such a solution inherently implausible. Strengthening production capacity at the level of the national state, therefore, does not obviously translate into a European capacity to compete with the United States.

If the causes of present U.S. dominance in audiovisual trade are predominantly economic and cultural, this has implications for the ultimate sustainability of protectionist positions: It implies that there are very long-term advantages in the global marketplace for U.S. audiovisual production that may not credibly be counteracted by using tariffs or subsidies.[17]

Just prior to the conclusion of the Uruguay round, more than 4,000 artists and producers from the twelve member states who then made up the EU signed an appeal for cultural works to be excluded from the GATT.[18] The scene for postulating cultural exclusion had been set earlier in July that year by a resolution of the European Parliament that identified the "cultural specificity" of cinema and television production and its need for preferential treatment.[19] The attack was spearheaded by the French, who have the clearest state policy on the question of cultural defense in Europe—and, not coincidentally, the greatest resistance to U.S. domination of the national box office.

The European Union succeeded in having audiovisual services excluded from the market liberalization package agreed with the United States (inspired in part by the success of the Canadian government in securing cultural exemption under NAFTA). The United States held to a position that goes right back to the origins of the GATT in the immediate post–World War II period.[20] It refused to accept the European Commission's wish to freeze television quotas and domestic film production support schemes. Although the United States moved to exclude the audiovisual sector, it is important to recognize that it did not accept the formal principle of cultural exclusion argued for by the French in particular. The United States insisted that there be bilateral negotiations between the EU and the United States in the future. These will take place under the auspices of the WTO. As the United States and the EU square off to negotiate the General Agreement on Trade in Services (GATS) in 2000, it looks as though once again the EU will try to maintain its defense of cultural exclusion. The U.S. position on free trade also remains unchanged.

Divergent Conceptions of Cultural Trade—and Collective Identity

The debate about cultural trade may be seen as a manifestation of U.S. cultural imperialism. What I find more interesting is how it expresses divergent conceptions of cultural identity. For the United States, audiovisual trade is just a business, whereas for Europeans it is both a business and (when convenient) a cultural matter. This emerged in the very language of debate. Mickey Kantor, the U.S. negotiator during the GATT talks, said: "We can best advance the interests of our artists, performers and producers—and the free flow of information around the world—by reserving all our legal rights to respond to policies that discriminate in these areas."[21] In a contrasting vein, the EU commissioner, Leon Brittan, talked of the EU's having a legitimate right to protect its culture (in the singular, note). More pointedly, the late François Mitterrand, then French president, invoked "the right of every country to create its own images. A society which abandons the means of depicting itself would soon be an enslaved society."[22]

Thus, whereas in the United States, the rhetoric is that of the market, business, and the freedom to communicate, in Europe, at least among producer and political interests, there is undoubtedly a tendency to use metaphors of cultural war and (when convenient) to represent Europe as though it had a singular national culture and identity. So behind the trade negotiations were far-reaching differences over how to conceive of the relationship between cultural products and collective identity.

We should note two points. First, the United States does not have a cultural policy as such for the audiovisual sector, which is one of its most successful businesses. Cultural industries are basically concerned with the provision of entertainment. Underpinning this is a commitment to free trade that accords no privilege to cultural goods and services, a line with historical roots that can be traced back to before World War I.[23]

Second, although the degree of interventionism varies considerably in Europe, generally there is a quite different conception of the relationship between culture and state from that of the United States. That is because the "European" view of audiovisual trade is in reality quintessentially French, marked by a long-standing preoccupation with the role of state intervention in shaping the national culture.[24] The United States position stems from a key unstated premise. As the ruling official conception of Americanness is a juridicopolitical image of the collectivity rather than a national cultural one, there is little official inclination to see mediated culture as an object of policy for conferring national identity.[25] The argument over cultural trade has therefore encapsulated two extremely simplified models of what counts in constituting national identities: The European conception of the collectivity is explicitly centered upon national culture in contrast to the U.S. constitutionalist conception of the polity.[26]

The European argument, moreover, has been characterized by two other features. First, at times it has a distinctly Third Worldist tone, driven by a sense of relative disadvantage to the dominance of Hollywood and therefore reiterating arguments about dependency that have appeared during earlier cultural debates, most notably over the New World Information and Communication Order back in the 1970s.[27] Second, it has rested on a simplistic counterposition between "American" and "European" culture, as though these were each homogeneous and also radically distinct, with no traffic between them.[28] In effect, the EU has pursued and continues to pursue an argument about national culture translated to the level of the union. But despite the rhetorical claims, the EU does not have a transcendent common culture and identity analogous to the national cultures and national identities of its component states.

The Shifting Ground of Policy

The 1990s also saw a shift to a new idiom—one more pronouncedly technicist and economistic—in which earlier talk of creating a "European audiovisual space" has been replaced by the call to institute a "European information area."[29]

In the latter part of the decade, beliefs about technological change have redefined above all the approach taken to media policy. It is assumed that the "convergence" of broadcasting, computing, and telecommunications will transform the postmillennial communications environment. Digital compression has profound implications for broadcasting capacity, with potential access for viewers of up to 500 channels. The demise of the analogue era has now been heralded in a number of countries. As distribution capacities outflank nation-states' systems of media and communications regulation, controlling content by means of quotas is increasingly impractical. The digital revolution has fed a technology-driven conception of the creation of a common communicative space in Union Europe. Furthermore, it has been accepted by policymakers that a new industrial strategy is required to develop a sufficiently large programming base in Europe to recapture a significant slice of the market.[30]

This approach has had profound implications for how culture and identity are thought about and for conceptions of pluralism and citizenship and their relations to the audiovisual media. From a policy point of view, a key shift in the debate in Europe was signaled by the European Commission's strategy options green paper of April 1994 along with the accompanying think tank report, submitted in March 1994.[31] These made the case for the Europeanization of a nationally fragmented audiovisual industry coupled with a shift from the microeconomic methods used so far in the MEDIA (for *mesures pour encourager le développement de l'industrie audiovisuelle,* or "measures to encourage the development of the audiovisual industry") program—the EU's main form of intervention in support of the audiovisual industries—to a more macroeconomic approach. Apart from the rhetoric of convergence and the invocation of the information superhighway, the employment considerations outlined in the December 1993 European Commission white paper also figured large.[32]

The diagnosis of the EU audiovisual industry could be summarized thus: In ten years European cinema had lost two-thirds of the audience; European films were largely confined to their national markets, with the European Single Market actually favoring U.S. productions backed up by effective distribution mechanisms; the European star system had collapsed as European productions did not attract investment from within the EU; the liberalization of television regulation and the growth of video distribution had strengthened the U.S. position. EU intervention (in the shape of funding and the Television Without Frontiers directive) had thus far been ineffective. Europe was mired in its national systems, with a low rate of transborder circulation of programs, weak production structures, and a shortage of marketable product.[33] Europeanization was needed to cure the ills of the European condition—notably, fragmentation into national markets—for otherwise the European Union could not compete in a transnationalizing economy.

This vision was substantially shared in the European Commission's industrial policy thinking. It was encapsulated in the report by industry commissioner Martin Bangemann's high-level group, published in May 1994.[34] Market mechanisms breaking through existing monopolistic and anticompetitive environments were hailed as providing the route to the "information society," central to which was liberalization of the telecommunications sector. Alongside this the group proposed comprehensive re-regulation on the European level, specifically in the field of cross-media ownership, privacy, encryption, and intellectual property rights. The report held out the possibility of a techno-utopia of meeting the demands of overcoming European cultural diversity through market forces alone: "Once products can be more easily accessible to consumers, there will be more opportunities for expression of the multiplicity of cultures and languages in which Europe abounds."[35]

Prolonging Uncertainty?

In the wake of the green paper on strategy options, Marcelino Oreja, then the EU's audiovisual commissioner, in April 1995 tried to set aside the 51 percent European quota provision in the Television Without Frontiers directive. He proposed scrapping the "where practicable" requirement for European broadcasters from the clause requiring at least 51 percent of airtime to be devoted to European programming. This was intended to please the French government, the most adamant supporter of quotas, by removing the vagueness and scope for evasion by television broadcasters. The trade-off for detractors, such as Germany and the UK, was to drop the quota over a period of ten years. The matter was temporarily resolved in December 1995, when it was decided to prolong the life of the existing European Union broadcasting rules and maintain the "where practicable" clause, despite its enforcement loopholes. Most European governments felt that quota enforcement was ultimately unworkable protectionism but came up against the resolute opposition of France.[36]

The issue came to the boil once again in February 1996 when the European Parliament voted substantially in favor of proposals to force European broadcasters to screen a 51 percent quota of European-made programs. Quotas were also to extend to new superhighway services. This decision pitted the majority of members of the European Parliament, backed by film trade unions and writers' organizations, against the Council of Ministers, the European Commission, and major media enterprises. At the close of the decade, it remained to be seen how divisions over the use of cultural protectionism would be overcome.[37]

A step in the direction of continued modest EU intervention in support of audiovisual production was taken in February 1995 as the European Commission decided to extend the expiring MEDIA 95 program to the year 2000. The allocation to MEDIA II was ECU 400 million (some $505 million), twice the previous budget. In an effort to bring greater focus to the project, three areas of intervention were identified: support for training, the development of programs with a "European dimension," and the "transnational distribution" of European programs. Inter alia, these measures were intended to address the key shortcoming of European audiovisual marketing at the preproduction and development stages and—crucially—to ensure that distribution improves.[38] MEDIA II will be extended beyond 2000, with some further reforms.

Economizing on Culture

Paradoxically, in EU policy circles cultural diversity and identity are seen both as obstacles to economic rationalization and at the same time as resources that might enable a particular kind of technically driven market growth to be effected. At one level, therefore, Union

Europe has the character of a market, a trading space. At another, it is filled with cultural content: It is linguistically and ethnically diverse, which, when looked at from an economic point of view, is a source of problems, an obstacle to uniform market growth and a source of increased transaction costs.[39] From the standpoint of such economism, culture can take on a positive value only when determined by a purely economic logic.

A central proposition of the ascendant argument is that the European Union needs to adapt to the emergent digitized, multichannel, multimedia, convergent information system. To this end, some protection and subsidy could be justified in terms of a logic of the market, provided that such intervention were to result in stimulating a virtuous circle of production and distribution. But this needs a move away from cultural defense to a "success and market-oriented approach" informed by an international vision alive to technological change.[40]

The European audiovisual heritage therefore needs to be turned into a program catalogue and intellectual property rights secured: The cultural patrimony is seen principally as a crucial economic asset that needs to be exploited, with technological trends potentially helping this along. The fragmentation of audiovisual markets emerging from the proliferation of border-transcending distribution systems and the relative decline of national systems of public service broadcasting, it is suggested, may result in cross-national niches that restructure European consumption patterns.[41] We are told: "'Mass communication' . . . is now a thing of the past. The current trend is now one of personalising the television supply and very individualised product mixes."[42]

This presumes a postnational—essentially a postmodern—conception of a television audience faced with generalized access to abundant information delivered by digital television technology. Personalized consumption moves center-stage, severed from its relationships to forms of collective action and identification, such as nation, region, class, ethnicity, language.

In recent policy discourse, the very cultural diversity that has been seen as an obstacle to the Europeanization of the market—"a negative factor"—has become a potential asset or resource: "Exploiting cultural diversity can be turned into an opportunity to be seized."[43] There seems to be a new magic formula: Digital compression plus Euroheterogeneity equals profitability, thus ensuring global competitiveness. And this thinking has evidently carried through into the most significant subsequent policy document, the European Commission's green paper on how to regulate the "convergence" of broadcasting, telephony, and information technology.[44] On one reading, this tends to favor economic and technological considerations and a liberalized market over the pursuit of social and cultural goals in the emergent European communications order.

Media and Pluralism

Alongside the debate about audiovisual policy, one increasingly dominated by technological "convergence," is the related matter of pluralism and media concentration in the single market. This has had a much lower profile, tending to take place in relative isolation from the audiovisual and information society arguments. Central to concern about pluralism in the media is the quality and quantity of information available to the citizen to enable political participation. There is also the matter of the ownership and control of media enterprises and the regulatory regimes intended to shape their actions.

The question of pluralism arises at a number of levels. First, there is the most obvious one of the national state, still the primary locus of political identification. Official, state-endorsed national identity is not going to fade away and will remain a dominant feature of Union Europe's plural character. To complicate the picture further, however, there are other levels and layers of collective identity that need to be taken into account, namely, nationality, language, and ethnicity.

The member states of the EU are not homogeneous. In several key instances there are fracture lines: distinctive national claims undercut or coexist with the overarching official identity claims of the state. Take the United Kingdom, for example, where the consequences of such diversity is institutionally embodied, as it is elsewhere. The national distinctiveness of the Scots and Welsh (and the complicated difference of Northern Ireland) has been reflected in special broadcasting provision.[45] Another example is that of Spain, where broadcasting in the autonomous communities of Catalonia, the Basque country, and Galicia has had to engage with politically charged linguistic differences based upon officially recognized "historical nationalities."[46]

Advocates of minority language and cultural rights have judged the EU's cultural countermeasures to the elaboration of the single market to be somewhat lacking. For instance, from this point of view, the political order (based in national states) and the linguistic order (rooted in ethnolinguistic communities not coterminous with existing political boundaries) are held to be in contradiction. One solution proposed is that all European linguistic communities be given constitutionally endorsed recognition of the "normal" status of their languages.[47] In a similar vein it has been argued that the small political, cultural, and linguistic communities have been largely ignored, the building of a transnational European audiovisual space being privileged over the actual regional diversity that pertains to the EU. The rationale of a countervailing "regional" communication policy is seen as lying in the encouragement of political participation through proximity, as reinforcing more localized "spaces" of cultural identity, as spreading economic opportunity, and as encouraging innovative uses of new communication technologies.[48] In light of the analysis offered above, it is unlikely that these claims are going to be perceived as other than highly marginal to the broader project of building the greater European audiovisual market.

Related but distinct is the question of "ethnicity," a term that in the EU context refers principally to non-European immigrants to EU states and their descendants, often (if not always) people of color. Members of non-Christian religions, Islam in particular, may also be bracketed as "ethnic minorities," however erroneously. As the European Union takes on a more fortresslike aspect and the control of inward migration becomes ever more central to the political agenda, critical voices have argued more volubly that those who do not belong to the hegemonic nationalities by descent are increasingly being marginalized as others, even though they may have the formal equality of citizenship.

Viewed from this standpoint, the EU's media policy, as outlined above, serves the interests of the dominant ethnic groups. Hence, it has been argued, positive policies are required to give minority groups fair representation in the media. The TV nation is a selective one, and since media may be seen as a significant vehicle for constructing a collectivity's sense of itself, the issue of appropriate access becomes crucially important.[49]

Of course, it is by no means the case that the politics of recognition will necessarily equally favor national states, nations without states, and linguistic or ethnic minorities. What these tensions do point us toward, however, is the acknowledgment that established conceptions of citizenship are increasingly under pressure. They also pose the question of how contemporary citizenship might relate to public communication, a normative question of the first importance for media policy.[50]

The issues of public access to information and the relations between media and the forms of representation in the public domain are central to current debate in the EU, as elsewhere, and have been forced onto the political agenda by changes of structure and organization. In recent years, for instance, there has been a pronounced trend toward the growth of transnational multimedia enterprises, in part fueled by a perceived potential advantage of size and vertical integration in meeting the challenges of new technology and expanding markets. The siren call of the so-called information superhighway has led to a rush by firms to bring together computing, telecommunications, and broadcasting. The expansion of distribution systems is putting an ever greater premium on the content to be distributed, spotlighting questions of intellectual property and copyright.

These trends have provoked a regulatory challenge for the EU. Not only are there competition concerns to do with the well-known tendency to oligopoly in media markets but also public interest concerns about safeguarding of pluralism and the role played by diversity in extending cultural and political enfranchisement among citizens.

The policy issues in this area were summed up in the European Commission's 1992 green paper on "pluralism and concentration in the internal market." The report discussed securing "pluralism" in terms of ensuring "diversity of information," and it singled out the question of who controls the media as a matter of paramount importance. The document noted "a complicated web of shareholding and media ownership networks centred around a few large national operators" and pointed to disparities among different member states' internal cross-media ownership rules that might represent obstacles to the proper functioning of the internal market.[51]

The Commission invited responses from member states and media industry participants as to which of the following options they would prefer regarding EU-level intervention: (1) no EU action on media ownership, (2), action to improve transparency (to facilitate the exchange of information among member states in the interests of transparency of media ownership), or (3) positive intervention, via a directive or a regulation, to harmonize national media ownership rules throughout the EU.

These options are still before the EU, and there are broad lines of division between those (principally among the major media companies) who favor greater flexibility on media ownership rules both at the national and the European level, the better to meet competition from the American and Japanese industries, and those (principally sections of the European Parliament) who support the implementation of a new directive on media ownership aimed at addressing the expansion of media conglomerates across European borders and cross-media ownership and the protection of pluralism.[52]

The position currently remains under review by the European Commission, with attempts to outline a viable approach for defining the concentration of media ownership through assessments of the share of the audience captured by any given media group. The Commission proposed "to set common standards across the EU on how many media operations a company or individual can own."[53] But the argument that it is essential to overcome the diversity of national rules in order to encourage cross-border investment in Europe's media industry has proved to be controversial within the Commission. Media interests remain intent on giving themselves maximum scope for expansion, and member states still wish to regulate their own media space under the principle of "subsidiarity."[54]

Whatever the level at which new rules of the game are eventually applied, the question of what ceiling to set for media ownership (and how to police it) remains open. Proposals exist for basing judgments on a combination of a company's audience share and the identification of the real "controller" behind an investment. The conundrum of how to balance the commercial interests of dominant EU media enterprises engaged in international competition against the consumer benefits of pluralism across the single market remains to be resolved. On one pessimistic (though plausible) reading, the EU's policy machinery is simply ill suited to address such concerns.[55] Moreover, it could plausibly be argued that in the era of convergence any realistic possibility of defending media pluralism is being increasingly circumvented by the growth of multimedia corporations that are concentrating ownership across formerly separate sectors in the pursuit of market advantage. Much will depend, therefore, on the countervailing efficacy of both member state and EU regulatory regimes.[56]

The Necessary Articulation of Culture and Economics

Does a vision of media dominated by technological and industrial considerations actually make sense for the Continent? It sidesteps the issue of what Europeans need to have in common in order to establish an eventual political community in the European Union, should this be desired. The dominant economic logic has to seek an accommodation with political and cultural logics—namely, to acknowledge resistances in the shape of national sovereignty and regional identity claims, embodied in the much-touted principle of subsidiarity. If, as argued above, the supranational drive is also producing resistance at other levels, it is indeed difficult to see how demands for subsidiarity can be effectively avoided.

A second point concerns the validity of the postmodern projection of cultural consumption. It would be convenient for a market-driven variant of Europeanization if nations were to disappear. It is by no means certain, however, that they will obligingly ride off into the sunset. Nationally based consumption patterns in Europe, crucially defined by linguistic differences, have been estimated to account for some 94 percent of total television viewing; this picture looks likely to continue for the foreseeable future.[57]

The reductive conception of European culture that has latterly emerged is the consequence of a consistent market logic and bypasses at least two main issues. First, there is a tendency to ignore the actually existing complexity of the relations among "Europeanness," national identity, and audiovisual culture. Cultural diversity is more than a set of consumption practices susceptible to rationalization by the policy process or by the market. It is the expression of historically produced differences, which in Europe are centrally focused upon the national state. This tendency is still vital; if we need to be reminded, we can simply consider the pattern of post-Communist state formation after 1989 and at the close of the 1990s, the tragedy of Kosovo. To the extent that audiovisual culture is conceived of merely as a vehicle for postmodern consumption, is purely marketized, it will necessarily play into existing differences rather than provide a basis for the building of commonality. There is therefore a case for rethinking the place of public service broadcasting not just in response to the commercialization of national markets but also in relation to the wider European project, which plainly needs a sustaining political culture.

Second, EU media and communication policy will need to articulate what is argued for the audiovisual domain and what is proposed in respect of cross-media ownership. It is precisely at this point that arguments about fostering cultural diversity link to those of democracy. At present there is a serious lacuna in an audiovisual policy governed by industrial and employment considerations and not at all (or hardly so that it shows) by political and democracy-building concerns.

The market plus technological innovation will not deliver pluralism. But as yet there are no clear institutional guarantees of how this might be achieved in the EU beyond the policy interest of member states in supporting national and other forms of identity and in regulating media ownership. Backing winners in Europe means encouraging the growth of Europe-based transnational multimedia groups and constitutes no guarantee that a plurality of voices will be heard. Although economic competitiveness in the global market is of major importance, it cannot be equated with meeting the key need of citizens for participation in the determination of political and cultural affairs.

Thus, it is time to engage in a comprehensive debate that embraces not only audiovisual and information policy but also the question of media pluralism. A report of the European Parliament has argued that under the Treaty on European Union "protection of cultural diversity and pluralism comes under the heading of cultural aspects."[58] The means by which this key objective is to be secured remain open to question.

The demand for a new articulation of culture and economics is likely to be unavoidable in the medium term, despite the current dominance of technological and market-led thinking. The present ascendancy of market-oriented individualism is not necessarily destined to endure, as it is dependent upon a specific balance of political forces. Consequently, although technology-driven consumption is offered as a solution to the problem of cultural identity, it is unable to address the underlying problem of how the collectivity can attain some measure of solidarity. Putting it differently, the question of how to fashion a cultural order and new collective identity for the EU will persistently reappear through the backdoor.

Back to Political Culture?

Perhaps we need to make the kind of normative leap Jürgen Habermas sketched out in his discussion of an emergent postnational European identity based on a new public. He states that "the political culture must serve as the common denominator for a constitutional patriotism which simultaneously sharpens an awareness of the multiplicity and integrity of the different forms of life which exist in a multicultural society."[59] In essence, Habermas proposes the reconstitution of the nation-state within a federal system with a political culture to match. The new community is linked not to deeply felt common symbols as the locus of identity but rather to the rule-governed matrix of a "constitutional patriotism."

What, therefore, might be the place of political culture in the European Union? This dimension of political life—one much broader than formal, institutionalized politics and indeed in part constitutive of it—is an important aspect of national culture in the sense delineated earlier. First and foremost (but by no means exclusively), political culture is located within the public space of the nation-state and significant in shaping conceptions of national identity. At the national level it is thick, dense, and compellingly imbricated in everyday life. For our purposes, however, it is also important to identify the emergent political culture of the European Union, which, detached from nationality, occupies a rather different space. It is located in what Keith Middlemas has termed a "unique political market-place" where elite participants drawn principally from the member states' political and business classes, together with a range of other lobbies, are involved in a long-term game in the framework of informal statehood.[60]

For insiders of the Europolitical process, the EU has taken on some of the complex affective pull of national sentiment and is seen as needing promotion as a desirable locus of collective identity.[61] However, because such engagement is hardly widespread, there remains a major lack of popular consent and support for the EU, widely known as the "democratic deficit."[62] By contrast with the density of national political cultures, the Europolitical culture is thin and broadly perceived as characterized by elite brokerage, bureaucratism, and legalism. For instance, the lack of EU-wide political parties and electoral campaigns and the still limited legislative role of the European Parliament together have ensured that there is no recognizable supranational center of popular legitimacy to European Union politics. This lack substantially defines the scope and nature of much media reporting of EU affairs. Moreover, the development of transnational information media in the EU (newspapers, magazines, television news) has worked to sustain a restricted, elite space of communication rather than to bring about generalized access to matters of public concern by European publics. In addition, the growth of EU-wide lobbying and public relations, which are largely undertaken for corporate or other sectional interests, has tended to reinforce the intense interactions that already occur within a relatively closed policy community. The present constitution of the EU's political and communicative space does not conduce, therefore, to the making of a European public and citizenry.[63]

The Maastricht Treaty's Article 8 instituted a category of European citizenship that arguably provides "the potential basis for the development of a varied and consequential 'Euro-citizenship' above and beyond the existing national citizenships guaranteed by member states."[64] But the exercise of these more than national rights is as yet embryonic, and it is too early to say how they might ultimately modify national political identities and cultures. Broad popular engagement in the emergent European polity is a necessary precondition for a significant shift of loyalty and sentiment to the European plane.

Habermas's vision of a European constitutional patriotism—par excellence a rationalistic model of political involvement and identification—has to be able to withstand the continual seductive pull of the national. This is no easy matter, as given the continuing potency of national identity, we must realistically appraise the difficulties of constructing acceptable rules of the game for a multiethnic and multicultural political community. Such difficulties, however, do not mean that we should neglect this focus. It counteracts the dominant economism and technicism. What this perspective implies is that apart from thinking about the rationality of a Europolitical culture, we also need to consider its affective dimension. The putative Eurocitizen is no dessicated calculating machine versed in the tropes of political philosophy, and the role of sentiments cannot be neglected.

Existing, state-bounded spaces of national culture, identity, and politics remain potent and crucially significant. Some, such as John Keane, argue that the national bindings have been substantially undone.[65] They cite developments in communications technologies, social movements, working life, and consumption patterns that have engendered new relations at levels below and beyond the nation-state. In a nutshell, the argument goes, cyberspace has reorganized political space by reconfiguring collectivities. Certainly, the transformative potential of new communicative practices should not be dismissed. The attraction of such techno-utopias, however, is apt to decenter the question of how political power is exercised and where it is ultimately located. This point is justly made by Nicholas Garnham, who emphasizes the continued importance of the national, state-bounded public space for the practice of democracy.[66] Yet Garnham's purist Habermasian rationalism does not provide a convincing framework for understanding what makes collectivities cohere. It quite underestimates the undoubted power of nonrationalistic elements of political and national culture that confer a wider, nondeliberative sense of solidarity and belonging. It is this hinterland of taken-for-granted presuppositions—akin to what Raymond Williams once called a "structure of feeling"—that first needs to be conquered politically for an ostensible constitutional patriotism to come into its own.[67] It also needs to be factored into any theoretical analysis.

If there are good grounds for believing in the persistence of national complexity and the continuing pull of national sentiment, it is the emergent supranational political culture that is likely to count most in shaping a new collective identity. Cultural and industrial defense, while important objectives, neglect the building of common political institutions and practices. They contribute little to the creation of those broader forms of solidarity that are necessary conditions for any conceivable European polity.

Notes

I wish to thank the UK Economic and Social Research Council for supporting research embodied in this chapter. The work in question was conducted for the Political Communication and Democracy project in the Media Economics and Media Culture Programme (ref. no. L126251022). Thanks, too, to the Research Council of Norway's Advanced Research on the Europeanization of the Nation-State (ARENA) program for supporting the project "Europeanisation, the Media and Democratic Communication." The present chapter revises an article originally published in *Media, Culture & Society* 19, 3 (July 1997): 369–390. My thanks to John Corner, Gillian Doyle, and Nancy Morris for their helpful advice at various times and to all those who commented on versions presented at the following meetings: the *Europaeum* conference, Geneva, March 1996; the Aspen Institute's working group "Principles and Paths for Democratic Media," Queenstown, Maryland, May 1996; the Norwegian Association of Media Research annual conference, Bergen, June 1996; the Euro-Conference "Symbolic Representations of Europe," Paris, July 1996; and the Flemish Communication Research annual conference, Brussels, October 1996.

1. See Philip Schlesinger, "'Europeanness'—a New Cultural Battlefield?" *Innovation in Social Sciences Research* 5, 2 (1992): 11–23.

2. See Verena Stolke, "Talking Culture: New Boundaries, New Rhetorics of Exclusion in Europe," *Current Anthropology* 36, 1 (1995): 1–24.

3. Johan P. Olsen, "Europeanization and Nation-State Dynamics," ARENA Working Paper 9, Oslo, March 1995, 3.

4. There is a growing debate on this. See, for instance, Philippe Schmitter, "If the Nation-State Were to Wither Away in Europe, What Might Replace It?" ARENA Working Paper 11, Oslo, April 1995, and the special issue of *Daedalus* 124, 2 (Spring 1995): *What Future for the State?* Also see Manuel Castells, *The Power of Identity* (Malden, Mass.: Blackwell, 1997).

5. See Armand Mattelart, "Excepción o especifidad cultural: los desafíos del GATT," *Telos: Cuadernos de comunicación, tecnología y sociedad* 42 (June-August 1995): 15–18; M. Palmer, "GATT and Culture: A View from France," in A. van Hemel, H. Mommaas, and C. Smithuijsen, eds., *Trading Culture: GATT, European Cultural Practices and the Transatlantic Market* (Amsterdam: Boekman Foundation, 1996), 29–38.

6. In fact, it was only in 1987 that media questions had begun to figure seriously on the European Community's agenda. See Paul Hainsworth, "Politics, Culture and Cinema in the New Europe," in John Hill, Martin McLoone, and Paul Hainsworth, eds., *Border Crossing: Film in Ireland, Britain and Europe* (Belfast: Institute of Irish Studies, Queen's University of Belfast, in association with the University of Ulster and the British Film Institute, 1994), 16.

7. These are themes that I have dealt with extensively in recent years. See, inter alia, Philip Schlesinger, *Media, State and Nation: Political Violence and Collective Identities* (London: Sage, 1991).

8. Svein S. Andersen and Kjell A Eliassen, eds., *Making Policy in Europe: The Europeification of National Policy-making* (London: Sage, 1993), 3, 11–14.

9. A symptomatic mandarin voice is Arthur M. Schlesinger Jr., *The Disuniting of America: Reflections on a Multicultural Society* (Knoxville, Tenn.: Whittle Direct Books, 1991).

10. A useful collection of otherwise engaged pieces is David Theo Goldberg, ed., *Multiculturalism: A Critical Reader* (Oxford: Blackwell, 1994).

11. See, for instance, Benedict Anderson, "Exodus," *Critical Inquiry* 20 (1994): 314–327; Arjun Appadurai, "Patriotism and Its Futures," *Public Culture* 5 (1993): 411–429.

12. See Orvar Löfgren, "Materialising the Nation in Sweden and America," *Ethnos* 58, 3-4 (1993): 173–174.

13. Richard Pells, "Resistance and Transformation: Europe's Response to American Mass Culture," in A. van Hemel, H. Mommaas, and C. Smithuijsen, eds., *Trading Culture: GATT, European Cultural Practices and the Transatlantic Market* (Amsterdam: Boekman Foundation, 1996), 49–66. Also see Richard Pells, *Not Like Us: How Europeans Have Loved, Hated, and Transformed American Culture Since World War II* (New York: Basic Books, 1997).

14. *Screen Finance,* 14 November 1996, 12–13.

15. Mattelart, "Excepción o especifidad cultural," 26; Hill et al., *Border Crossing,* 56.

16. Hill et al., *Border Crossing,* 60–61.

17. Steven S. Wildman, "Trade Liberalization and Policy for Media Industries: A Theoretical Examination of Media Flows," *Canadian Journal of Communication* 20 (1995): 367–388.

18. John Carvel, "Euroluvvies Cast Brittain as Hollywood Stooge," *Guardian,* 29 September 1993, 8.

19. Julian Nundy, "France Defends Its Heritage from *Rocky III,*" *Independent,* 22 November 1993.

20. Ian Jarvie, *Hollywood's Overseas Campaign: The North Atlantic Movie Trade, 1920–1950* (New York: Cambridge University Press, 1992), 251–252.

21. Cited in *New Media Markets,* 16 December 1993, 5.

22. Cited in Jeffrey Goodell, "The French Revolution," *Premiere,* May 1994, 26.

23. Jarvie, *Hollywood's Overseas Campaign,* 17.

24. During GATT it was rooted in the French audiovisual policy of Jack Lang (and his successors), which aimed to defend a French industry losing its share of the domestic market to the United States. See Susan Hayward, "State, Culture and the Cinema: Jack Lang's Strategies for the French Film Industry 1981–93," *Screen* 34, 4 (1993): 380–391.

25. See Marjorie Ferguson, "Invisible Divides: Communication and Identity in Canada and the US," *Journal of Communication* 43, 2 (1993): 51.

26. See Sheldon Wolin, *The Presence of the Past: Essays on the State and the Constitution* (Baltimore: Johns Hopkins University Press, 1988).

27. Philip Schlesinger and Nancy Morris, "Cultural Boundaries: Communication and Identity in Latin America," *Media Development* 54, 1 (1997): 5–17.

28. William Uricchio, "Displacing Culture: Transnational Culture, Regional Elites and the Challenge to National Cinema," in A. van Hemel, H. Mommaas, and C. Smithuijsen, eds., *Trading Culture: GATT, European Cultural Practices and the Transatlantic Market* (Amsterdam: Boekman Foundation, 1996), 67–80.

29. See European Commission, "Strategy Options to Strengthen the European Programme Industry in the Context of the Audiovisual Policy of the European Union," Brussels, April 1994, 17 and 35.

30. Michael Williams and Adam Dawtree, "GATT Spat Wake-up on Yank Market Muscle," *Variety,* 27 December 1993, 46 and 49.

31. European Commission, "Strategy Options"; Antonio-Pedro Vasconcelos, "Report by the Think Tank to the European Commissioner in charge of DG X," March 1994, 16.

32. European Commission, "White Paper on Growth Competitiveness and Employment—the Challenges and Ways Forward into the 21st Century," Brussels, 5 December 1993.

33. European Commission, "Strategy Options," ch. 2; Vasconcelos, "Report," ch. 2.

34. M. Bangemann, "Europe and the Global Information Society: Recommendations to the European Council," Brussels, 26 May 1994.

35. Ibid., 11.

36. Chris Fuller, "Commission Faces Fight in Toughening Directive," *Media Policy Review,* April 1995, 8; Miranda Watson, "Quota, Unquota," *Cable and*

Satellite Europe 143 (1995): 36–39; Emma Tucker, "EU's Ministers Finally in Tune on Broadcasting," *Financial Times*, 21 December 1995.

37. Stephen Bates, "TV Imports Battle Looms," *Guardian*, 14 February 1996, 17; Caroline Southey, "MEPs in Vote on TV Content," *Financial Times*, 15 February 1996, 2.

38. *Media Policy Review*, March 1995, 12.

39. Vasconcelos, "Report," 24.

40. Ibid., 57.

41. European Commission, "Strategy Options," 10; Vasconcelos, "Report," 64.

42. Vasconcelos, "Report," 64.

43. European Commission, "Strategy Options," 12.

44. European Commission, "Green Paper on the Convergence of the Telecommunications, Media and Information Technology Sectors, and the Implications for Regulation: Towards an Information Society Approach," COM(97) 623, Brussels, 3 December 1997.

45. See Sylvia Harvey and Kevin Robins, eds., *The Regions, the Nations and the BBC* (London: BFI, 1993); Mike Cormack, "Broadcasting and the Politics of Cultural Diversity: The Gaelic Television Debate in Scotland," *European Journal of Cultural Policy* 2, 1 (1995): 43–54.

46. Bernat López and Maria Corominas, "Spain: The Contradictions of the Autonomous Model," in Miquel de Morgas Spà and Carmelo Garitaonandía, eds., *Television in the Regions, Nationalities and Small Countries of the European Union* (London: John Libbey, 1995); Richard Maxwell, *The Spectacle of Democracy: Spanish Television, Nationalism, and Political Transition* (Minneapolis: University of Minnesota Press, 1995).

47. Josep Gifreu, "Linguistic Order and Spaces of Communication in Post-Maastricht Europe," *Media, Culture & Society* 18, 1 (1996): 127–139.

48. Miquel de Moragas Spà and Carmelo Garitaonandía, "Television in the Regions and the European Audiovisual Space," in Miquel de Morgas Spà and Carmelo Garitaonandía, eds., *Television in the Regions, Nationalities and Small Countries of the European Union* (London: John Libbey, 1995), 15–16.

49. Charles Husband, ed., *A Richer Vision: The Development of Ethnic Minority Media in Western Democracies* (London: John Libbey, 1995).

50. See Graham Murdock, "Citizens, Consumers and Public Culture," in Michael Skovmand and Kim Christian Schrøder, eds., *Media Cultures: Reappraising Transnational Media* (London: Routledge, 1992), 17–41.

51. European Commission, "Pluralism and Media Concentration in the Internal Market: An Assessment of the Need for Community Action," Commission Green Paper, COM(92) 480 final, Brussels, 23 December 1992, 18, 20–21, 27.

52. See European Commission, "Communication from the Commission to the Council and the European Parliament, Follow-up to the Consultation Process Relating to the Green Paper on 'Pluralism and Media Concentration in the Internal Market—An Assessment of the Need for Community Action," COM(94) 353 final, Brussels, 5 October 1994.

53. Emma Tucker, "Brussels to Revive Controversial Media Ownership Plans," *Financial Times*, 13 November 1995, 2.

54. C. Johnstone, "Monti Retunes Media Strategy," *European Voice*, 19 December–8 January 1996–1997, 1. "Subsidiarity" is the doctrine that no political issue should be decided at a level higher than is absolutely necessary. If it can be dealt with locally or nationally, then it should be left to the appropriate

authorities and the EU should act only where there is a clear-cut need for a supranational level of action.

55. Sophia Kaitatzi-Whitlock, "Pluralism and Media Concentration in Europe," *European Journal of Communication* 11, 4 (1996): 453–483.

56. Peter Humphreys, "Regulating for Pluralism in the Era of Digital Convergence: The Issues of Media Concentration Control and the Future of Public Service Broadcasting," paper presented to the European Consortium for Political Research (ECPR) Joint Research Sessions, workshop 24: "Regulating Communications in the Multimedia Age," Mannheim, Germany, 26–31 March 1999.

57. See Cathy Stewart and Julian Laird, *The European Media Industry: Fragmentation and Convergence in Broadcasting and Publishing* (London: Financial Times Business Information, 1994), 5.

58. Committee on Culture, Youth, Education and the Media, "Report on the Commission Green Paper 'Pluralism and Media Concentration in the Internal Market,'" COM(92) 0480–C3-0035/93, 5 January 1994, 8. The European Parliament has called for an anticoncentration directive and for European-level action to ensure freedom of information, professional ethics, and journalistic independence.

59. Jürgen Habermas, "Citizenship and National Identity," in Bart van Steenbergen, ed., *The Condition of Citizenship* (London: Sage, 1994), 22–23, 27.

60. Keith Middlemas, *Orchestrating Europe: The Informal Politics of the European Union, 1973–1995* (London: Fontana Press, 1995), 684–687.

61. Chris Shore, "Inventing the 'People's Europe': Critical Approaches to European Community 'Cultural Policy,'" *Man* 28, 4 (1993): 779–800; Howard Tumber, "Marketing Maastricht: The EU and News Management," *Media, Culture & Society* 17, 3 (1995): 511–519.

62. Philippe Schmitter, "Is It Really Possible to Democratize the Euro-Polity?" ARENA Working Paper 10, Oslo, 1996.

63. David Morgan, "British Media and European Union News: The Brussels News Beat and Its Problems," *European Journal of Communication* 10, 3 (1995): 321–343. On British media reporting, see also Peter J. Anderson and Anthony Weymouth, *Insulting the Public? The British Press and the European Union* (London: Longman, 1999), and Philip Schlesinger, Raymond Boyle, Gillian Doyle, and Vincent Campbell, *European Institute for the Media Project, "Building Bridges Between Cultures": UK Report* (Stirling: Stirling Media Research Institute, 1999). On the EU dimension, see Philip Schlesinger, "Changing Spaces of Political Communication: The Case of the European Union," *Political Communication* 16, 3 (July 1999): 263–279, and David Miller and Philip Schlesinger, "The Changing Shape of Public Relations in the European Union," in R. Heath, L. and G. M. Vasquez, eds., *The Handbook of Public Relations* (London: Sage, forthcoming).

64. Schmitter, "Is It Really Possible to Democratize the Euro-Polity?" 5.

65. John Keane, "Structural Transformations of the Public Sphere," *Communication Review* 1, 1 (1995): 19–20.

66. Nicholas Garnham, "Comments on John Keane's 'Structural Transformations of the Public Sphere,'" *Communication Review* 1, 1 (1995): 24.

67. Raymond Williams, *Marxism and Literature* (Oxford: Oxford University Press, 1977), 128–135.

5

Why the European Union Failed to Europeanize Its Audiovisual Policy

Tobias Theiler

As shown in the introduction to this volume, many commentators do not see the emergence of political identities as depending on a preexisting "cultural core." Instead, they hold that such identities are socially constructed. Their construction involves the drawing and reification of social boundaries through discursive framing, the manipulation of symbols, and various "othering" techniques. It also requires some control over identity-building tools such as school curricula, cultural policy, and the mass media.[1]

At first glance, such a constructivist perspective seems to augur well for the EU. If political identities can be built from cultural scratch, then the absence of a Pan-European "cultural core" (if one indeed believes it to be absent) would not preclude the potential emergence of a EU-wide political identity.

Yet as the introductory chapter also shows, some who argue in a firmly constructivist vein are nonetheless cautious regarding the feasibility of a European identity-building enterprise. Existing national loyalties and identifications may be deeply entrenched and therefore "sticky." Political symbols may be difficult to invent and manipulate in practice. Attempts to strengthen social boundaries through "othering" may lack credibility or even backfire, for instance, by being denounced as racist or xenophobic. What is more, for the EU to gain a foothold in policy areas with a high "identitive" potential, such as cultural policy and education, may prove difficult in the first place. Other observers, to be sure, are less skeptical. They contend that some kind of "postnational" EU-wide political identity is already in the making, though they disagree about the speed at which this is evolving and about the factors that propel this process.

In Chapter 4 of this volume, Philip Schlesinger shows that the anti-Americanization theme was an important rhetorical underpinning of EU-driven efforts to exclude "cultural goods and services" from world trade negotiations. The same theme also sustained (hitherto less successful) attempts to impose mandatory import quotas for non-European programs in the context of the Television Without Frontiers directive. The present chapter complements Schlesinger's account by focusing on a different category of audiovisual policy initiatives in the EU, namely, those which sought to Europeanize the audiovisual productions sector. It shows that from the early 1980s the European Commission and EP made a series of attempts to intervene directly in the audiovisual productions field by seeking to subsidize multinational coproductions. They hoped that a "mixing and mingling" of national audiovisual formats would over time lead to a partial cultural denationalization—or at least a kind of "compatibilization"—of those formats. This in turn would widen the market for European audiovisual producers and allow them to compete more successfully against their U.S. counterparts. In addition, the Commission and the EP hoped that Europeanized audiovisual content would help Europeanize political allegiances and foster a European identity in viewers. In trying to justify their audiovisual proposals, both bodies relied on a similarly mixed bag of arguments, whose central and recurring rhetorical fixation was the alleged need to curb Europe's reliance on audiovisual imports from the United States.

Yet despite being wrapped in the anti-Americanization argument, attempts to involve the EU in the audiovisual sector had achieved little by the end of the 1990s. Most had stumbled over resistance from within the ranks of the member states and a widespread lack of enthusiasm for the "European culture" and the anti-Americanization themes. And by the late 1990s, the Commission and the EP had given in to such resistance. They largely abandoned the cultural anti-Americanization rhetoric, along with references to "European culture." Moreover, their stated policy objectives no longer include the promotion of a Europeanized audiovisual format.

The story of the EU's largely unsuccessful attempts to Europeanize the audiovisual productions sector and to promote the anti-Americanization and "European culture" themes in the process carries some broader lessons. While in theory subtle discursive framing techniques and "othering" strategies may well be critical ingredients of political identity construction, they can be very hard to implement in practice. And it gives an indication of the powerful obstacles that could stand in the way of fostering a nation-transcending political identity in Europe.

Why the EU Became Involved
in Audiovisual Policy

Attempts to involve the European Union in the audiovisual productions sector from the early 1980s onward are often attributed to the economic and technical transformations that affected the broadcasting sector at the time. The end of public service monopolies in many member states, for one, brought broadcasting closer to the status of a commercial activity and thus nearer the EU's core economic remit. In addition, the proliferation of satellite and cable television increased the potential for broadcasting across borders and thus the perceived need for a regulatory framework at an EU level.[2]

Yet apart from such technical and economic developments, efforts to implicate the EU in audiovisual policy were also stimulated by two additional background conditions: first, by a tradition of cultural Americanization fears among elites in many European countries and, second, by apprehensions, mainly within the European Parliament and the European Commission, that popular support for integration was fragile and that audiovisual policy could be used as a tool to promote a European identity on a mass level. In conjunction with the economic and technological changes that affected the audiovisual sector at the time, those factors came to sustain a web of mutually reinforcing objectives and rhetorical justifications that sustained attempts to carve out an audiovisual role for the EU.

The Cultural Anti-Americanization Theme

Fears of an impending cultural Americanization have a relatively long history in many European countries. They go back at least as far as the rise of Hollywood as a dominant cultural producer and exporter. In particular, they have thrived on the appeal American cultural imports came to have for European working-class audiences. Long before World War II, many commentators in countries across Europe bemoaned the alleged vulgarity, brashness, and (bizarrely enough) effeminate and "feminizing" nature of American cultural imports, above all Hollywood-produced films and later television programs. In Britain, for instance, cultural elites from all parts of the political spectrum "were united by a fascinated loathing for modern architecture, holiday camps, advertising, fast food, plastics and, of course, chewing gum. . . . These were the images of the soft and enervating 'easy life' which threatened to smother British cultural identity [and of] the process through which authentic working-class life was being destroyed by the 'hollow brightness,' the 'shiny barbarism' and 'spiritual decay' of imported American culture."[3]

Sometimes such elite concerns for the survival of "authentic" national working-class culture led to more than rhetoric. For instance, the early BBC had as one of its core missions the maintenance of "national standards."[4] Other public service broadcasters (which, in many European countries, enjoyed a monopoly on television broadcasting until the early 1980s) maintained official or unofficial restrictions on foreign content, mainly directed against U.S. imports. Sometimes such quotas even applied to music played on the radio.[5]

It is hard to pin down the precise origins of such cultural resentment against the United States. Seen from a broadly Bourdieuan perspective, it owed much to fears by culturally dominant elites of seeing their dominance undermined by aesthetic influences beyond their control. In Britain and France in particular, more general misgivings about a declining global influence in relation to the United States may also have fueled cultural grudges after 1945.

Whatever their exact origins, fears of cultural Americanization in many European countries came to have a bearing on EU audiovisual policy in the 1980s and 1990s. As is shown below, they provided a background of lingering cultural resentment among national elites on which attempts by the EU to use the anti-Americanization theme to bolster its own audiovisual ambitions could seek to draw. All that was needed was a change in the definition of what, precisely, had to be protected from the United States. Instead of British, French, or Italian culture, it was "European culture" that became the EU's object of concern.

Concern for Public Support for Integration

A further factor that helped fuel the European Parliament's and Commission's attempts to involve themselves in the audiovisual sector was a growing concern for the EU's public standing. From the mid- to early 1970s onward, both bodies became concerned that popular support for European integration was weak and that this could undermine the EU's future development. Such fears stimulated various proposals for cultural and educational policies on an EU-wide scale. Their declared aim was to nurture a European identity on a mass level and thereby to improve the EU's popular appeal. This came to include proposals for a European lottery, "European rooms" in national museums, student and youth exchanges, the "correction" of history textbooks, a "European dimension" in national school curricula, and many similar measures. Important initial documents that proposed such measures were the Tindemans Report of 1975, a European Commission proposal in 1977

("Community Action in the Cultural Sector"), and in the education field the Commission's report "For a Community Policy in Education."[6]

Yet while the EP and the Commission depicted school textbooks, European memorial days, and cultural festivals as suitable instruments for European identity promotion, it was the audiovisual sector that soon attracted the greatest amount of attention, as reflected in a sheer, stream of EP and Commission reports devoted to audiovisual policy. For example, in 1982, the EP Committee on Youth, Culture, Education, and Sport presented a unanimously adopted report on "Radio and Television Broadcasting in the European Community." Calling for, among other things, the establishment of a Pan-European television channel, it argued that a "new dimension must be added to European unification to enable Europeans to identify with European union" and that "the instruments which serve to shape public opinion today are the media [of which] television . . . is the most important." Furthermore,

> European unification will only be achieved if Europeans want it. Europeans will only want it if there is such a thing as a European identity. A European identity will only develop if Europeans are adequately informed. At present, information via the mass media is controlled at [the] national level. The vast majority of journalists do not "think European" because their reporting role is defined in national or regional terms. Hence the predominance of negative reporting. Therefore, if European unification is to be encouraged, Europe must penetrate the media.[7]

According to the EP and the Commission, the potential of television to foster public support for integration was not limited to news programs, however. Instead, they advocated the infusion of a "European dimension" into the entire range of audiovisual productions, including fictional programs. Such Europeanized programs, "by appealing to a large audience . . . help develop a people's Europe through reinforcing a sense of belonging to a Community composed of countries which are different yet partake of a deep solidarity."[8] Moreover, it could "play an important part in developing and nurturing awareness of the rich variety of Europe's common cultural and historical heritage [and thus] do much to help the people of Europe to recognize the common destiny they share in many areas."[9]

At the same time, the EP's and the Commission's audiovisual pronouncements were characterized by a subtle but important ambiguity as to how, precisely, the aspired-for Europeanization of the audiovisual sector would manifest itself. In earlier pronouncements the declared objective was a measure of homogenization (or "compatibilization") of national audiovisual formats and styles. To this end the EP and the Commission sought to subsidize Pan-European television channels and multinational audiovisual coproductions. In later years this objective was superseded by the much more modest goal of making Europeans from different countries watch more of each other's domestic audiovisual material without at the same time encouraging a Europeanization of audiovisual content. This shift in policy objectives is further described below.

The factors just discussed—a tradition of latent cultural Americanization fears among national elites, the belief that television could be instrumentalized to promote popular support for European integration, and the changing technical and economic status of the audiovisual sector—provided the background to attempts by the EU to involve itself in the audiovisual productions sector from the early 1980s onward. The purported rationale for those attempts was partially economic, but in part it was also cultural, centering on the alleged need to use audiovisual policy as a tool to promote a European identity in viewers. And the one element featured throughout the European Commission's and the EP's rhetoric was a fixation on Europe's audiovisual position in relation to the United States.

The Cultural Americanization Theme
in EU Audiovisual Rhetoric

As I have shown, fears of a cultural Americanization have a relatively long tradition in some European countries. The European Union, by contrast, had long refrained from playing on such fears. Even though the EP and the Commission from the 1960s onward frequently alluded to the supposed necessity of bringing the "nonmaterial values" of integration to the fore and helping EU citizens "rediscover" or "affirm" their shared cultural roots, those pronouncements stayed at the level of "internal" framing; the EU did not try to make its "European culture" claim more credible by setting it up against foreigners.[10]

It was only in the early 1980s that the EU's discussion of "European culture" took on a strong external dimension, and this occurred in the context of attempts to involve the EU in audiovisual policy. In a plethora of declarations, which often accompanied concrete audiovisual policy proposals (as discussed in the next section), the EP and the European Commission began to depict "European culture" not merely as in need of being "rediscovered" and "reaffirmed" but, above all, as something that required urgent protection from erosion by films and television programs imported from the United States.

Yet even though, as we shall see, such warnings of an impending cultural takeover by the United States soon took on hysterical dimensions, it is important to understand they did not take place in an empirical vacuum. Instead, in issuing their Americanization warnings, the EP and the Commission could point to a range of more or less undisputed facts that appeared to lend those warnings a measure of underlying plausibility. These can briefly be summarized as follows: Since the end of World War II, most countries in Western Europe had maintained a considerable audiovisual trade deficit with the United States. The reasons for this trade imbalance were relatively obvious: U.S. audiovisual producers enjoy a large and linguistically more or less homogenized home audience. This offers them large economies of scale and has stimulated correspondingly high levels of audiovisual output and competitiveness in the world market. In the European Union, by contrast, cultural and linguistic barriers among the different member states are high, and the audiovisual market has thus remained fragmented. Most audiovisual producers are tied to their often very small home markets. As a result, they are deprived of sufficiently high economies of scale to bring the quantity and quality of their output up to a level where they could successfully compete against audiovisual producers from the United States, both inside the EU and worldwide. Add to this that among European audiences U.S. productions are typically much more popular than those from other European countries, leading some to argue that, ironically, the United States has come closer to developing a truly Pan-European audiovisual format than any European country.[11]

By the early 1980s there was much to suggest that the EU's reliance on audiovisual imports from the United States would grow. The end of public broadcast monopolies, coupled with the rise of cable and satellite distribution, was set to greatly increase the number of television channels. More channels would mean a greater demand for audiovisual material. Yet given their predicament described above, European producers would not be able to satisfy this demand in an economically viable manner. As a result, those new, mostly commercial channels would turn to the United States as a source of relatively cheap, plentiful, and popular programming input.

It was against the background of such empirical observations that beginning in the early 1980s the European Commission and the EP painted their "cultural defense" scenario in ever starker colors. In this scenario, American and European audiovisual producers were pitted against each other in a relentless struggle for market share, audiences, and cultural influence, with the former fighting for dominance and the latter for survival. And in the EP's and the Commission's rendering, what was at stake was not just the well-being of European audiovisual industries but, ultimately, the very survival of "European culture" and "European civilization."

In 1986, for example, the Commission warned that the "economic and cultural dimensions of communications cannot be separated. The gap between the proliferation of equipment and media and the stagnation of creative content production capacities is a major problem for the societies of Europe; it lays them open to domination by other powers with a better performance in the programming content industry."[12] Similarly, in 1988 it cautioned that "while satellites are getting ready to overwhelm us with hundreds of new television channels, Europe runs the risk of seeing its own industry squeezed out and its market taken over by American and Japanese industrialists and producers. [A] European response is required."[13] And Jacques Delors, in his first speech to the European Parliament after taking office as Commission president in 1985, proclaimed that

> the culture industry will tomorrow be one of the biggest industries, a creator of wealth and jobs. Under the terms of the Treaty [of Rome] we do not have the resources to implement a cultural policy; but we are trying to tackle it along economic lines. It is not simply a question of television programmes. We have to build a powerful European culture industry that will enable us to be in control of both the medium and its content, maintaining our standards of civilization.[14]

The European Parliament, for its part, was eager to join in the cultural anti-Americanization rhetoric to back its own calls for EU involvement in audiovisual policy. For instance, in 1985 the EP warned against "an increase in Community countries' cultural dependence" on the United States, and in 1983 it had already decried the "disastrous impact" of such a reliance "in social terms . . . as well as in cultural terms."[15]

Leaving aside the question of its factual merits, the Commission's and the EP's resort to the "cultural defense" argument as a rhetorical pillar of their successive audiovisual policy proposals was clever in many regards. First, as I have pointed out, to some extent their anti-Americanization warnings were rooted in hard economic facts that gave them a degree of plausibility. After all, there *was* an audiovisual trade deficit with the United States, this deficit *was* set to widen, and Europeans *did* spend a lot of time watching American films and television programs. Claims by the EP and the Commission that all this had a disastrous *cultural impact*, to be sure, can easily be dismissed as far-fetched or even absurd. Yet both bodies could not have made such claims with any kind of credibility in the first place had it not been for the underlying economic and statistical realities on which they were predicated.

The seeming plausibility of the "resistance to American cultural hegemony" theme was strengthened by a second factor. As we saw, this theme had a fairly long-standing tradition in many European countries, as had governmental attempts to counteract the supposed American cultural threat, for example, through content quotas and subsidy schemes for national audiovisual producers. And of particular importance in this context was the socialist government in France that came to power in the early 1980s. The EP's and the Commission's Americanization warnings started at precisely the moment when that very issue had evolved into a central plank of French cultural policy, and had also begun to resonate more strongly with some southern member states that had sided with French calls for protectionist quotas in the context of the Television Without Frontiers debate. France's commitment to the cause was epitomized by French culture minister Jack Lang's often-cited call for a crusade "against financial and intellectual imperialism that no longer grabs territory, or rarely, but grabs consciousness, ways of thinking, ways of living."[16] It was also evident in his ministerial colleague's denouncement of American "Coca-Cola satellites" undermining "our linguistic and cultural identity."[17] By turning that theme into a rhetorical pillar of their own audiovisual proposals, the Commission and the EP could at the very least hope to enhance their appeal to the French government. And as I show below, it was indeed France of all the member states that became the staunchest and most consistent backer of audiovisual involvement by the EU.

Finally, the EP's and the Commission's move to focus on Europe's audiovisual standing in relation to "other cultures" and "other civilizations" potentially carried a wider significance: It allowed them to try to remove the notions of "European culture" and "European civilization" from the realm of contested concepts into that of seemingly self-evident social and historical facts. This in turn reinforced a wider rhetorical trend at the time, as part of which "the notion of 'European identity' . . . became progressively transformed and reified, and then presented as a fixed, bounded and 'natural' category, through successive policy initiatives."[18] By the late 1980s, this had led to the frequent appearance in EU discourse of a shared European heritage, a European identity, and European values, accompanied by the claim that it was the EU's natural role to protect these against threats from foreigners.

Insofar as one holds that political identity formation requires discursive framing and the drawing of social boundaries, the EP's and the Commission's attempted reification of "European culture" and its setting up against the United States merits attention beyond the narrow confines of the audiovisual debate. But even as far as audiovisual policy was concerned, the "protection of European culture against Americanization" theme could have an impact. In particular, it might shift the terms of the audiovisual debate away from the question of European identity construction at the inside (too outspoken a commitment that risked leaving the EU vulnerable to accusations of wanting to "disseminate cultural propaganda," "flatten national identities," and overstep its constitutional prohibition from pursuing cultural policies) to that of Europe's position in relation to the outside world.[19] This was a less sensitive area: For one thing, the stated aim of "protecting European culture" could seem less contentious than one of wanting to "construct" it. For another, this "external" focus enabled the Commission and the EP to link the audiovisual sector to trade policy (where the EU enjoyed legal competences under its founding treaties) as well as to economic and technological competitiveness.

For all those reasons, then, the cultural anti-Americanization theme appeared to be an effective rhetorical pillar upon which the EP and the Commission could predicate their various audiovisual Europeanization proposals. Nonetheless, as I show below, the road to EU involvement in this field was littered with resistance and obstacles. And the kind of audiovisual policies the EU did eventually implement were a far cry from what the European Commission and the EP had originally advocated.

The Development of EU Audiovisual Policy

As far as its "software" aspects are concerned, the audiovisual sector falls mainly within the competences of the national ministers of culture. Owing in part to persistent pressure from the Commission, these had started to meet more or less regularly in an EU context from the early 1980s onward, even though prior to the Maastricht Treaty the EU lacked a cultural mandate.[20] And from the outset the European Commission worked hard to ensure that audiovisual policy, and potential ways of involving the EU in this field, would be on their agenda.

The basic argument the Commission put to the ministers in a succession of policy proposals, briefing papers, and expert reports echoed the logic outlined above: Because of Europe's cultural and linguistic fragmentation, most European producers suffered from low economies of scale that limited the quality and quantity of their output. This in turn caused a large inflow of audiovisual material from the United States, bound to increase further with the proliferation of commercial television channels. The remedy, according to the Commission, lay with a partial denationalization, or Europeanization, of the audiovisual productions sector in Europe through EU-led schemes to subsidize multinational coproductions.[21] Such coproductions were expected to have a denationalizing effect because they entail a "mixing and mingling" of national audiovisual formats. Moreover, they are produced from the outset for consumption in several national markets to which they must seek to appeal simultaneously. Over time, the Commission contended, this would lead to a partial cultural harmonization of different national programming formats, a corresponding "compatibilization" of viewing preferences, and thus a defragmentation of the European audiovisual market. European producers would enjoy greater economies of scale and be able to raise the quality and quantity of their output to a level where they could compete more successfully against their counterparts from the United States. The share of U.S. material on European television and cinema screens would ultimately fall, along with the threat to "European culture" that supposedly emanated from it.

While the "cultural defense" argument thus served as the Commission's primary justification for its proposed audiovisual subsidy schemes, it was not the only rationale. Echoing growing fears about a decline in the EU's popular standing as well as a faith in the ability of television to sway political identifications, most of the Commission's audiovisual policy proposals (as well as various EP declarations on the subject) expressed the hope that television, once furnished with a "European dimension," could make for an excellent tool with which to foster a European identity in viewers and thereby strengthen support for European integration. In this conception, audiovisual policy constituted a vehicle not only for European identity *protection* but also for European identity *construction*.

Yet despite such rhetorical underpinnings, the Commission's audiovisual proposals led to little in the way of tangible policies throughout the early 1980s. Whenever the Commission (backed by EP resolutions and from within the ranks of the member states, most staunchly and consistently France) managed to put concrete proposals on the ministers' table, they refused to adopt them.[22] For example, in April 1985 the Commission issued a proposal for a Council regulation on a "Community aid scheme for non-documentary cinema and television co-productions."[23] Accompanied by the habitual "metaphors of cultural war" against the United States, its declared aim was to "increase the number of mass-audience cinema and television co-productions involving nationals of more than one Member State."[24] To this end it would have created a system to aid such coproductions through grants and loans, covering production as well as distribution costs.

The Commission's proposal to aid coproductions, along with a similar proposal later in 1985, was vehemently opposed by several national governments, however.[25] And since the adoption of audiovisual policy proposals required the unanimous consent by all the member states, such opposition proved fatal. Germany, for one, objected that it was too expensive, yet German opposition was also driven by *Länder* hostility to the prospect of EU encroachment into their constitutional compe- tences, which include cultural policy in general and broadcasting in particular. The Danish government, traditionally the staunchest critic of the Commission's and the EP's cultural ambitions, rejected it on the grounds that the Treaty of Rome did not allow the EU to pursue cultural policies, audiovisual measures included. The Thatcher government in Britain, among the most fervent skeptics of both the European identity and anti-Americanization themes, rejected any EU intervention in the field. Instead, it "argued in favor of letting market forces have their way and of encouraging the television organizations [of the member states] to work together."[26]

The rejection of its initial coproduction and denationalization-ori- ented audiovisual initiatives prompted the Commission to subject its audiovisual wish list to a thorough revision and to come up with pro- posals that would stand a greater chance of being accepted by the member states. This it did in 1986, when it presented to the European Council for an "action programme for the European audio-visual media products industry."[27] It laid the foundation for the MEDIA program, which was passed later that same year.

The MEDIA Program

The MEDIA program was established, somewhat shakily, by Article 235 of the Treaty of Rome and started at the end of 1986.[28] It initially con- sisted of a range of pilot projects for which the EU provided seed money (generally up to 50 percent). This amount was to decrease over time as the projects would attain financial self-sufficiency.[29]

In contrast to the Commission's unsuccessful proposals in previous years, MEDIA's core ambition was to enhance the circulation of domestic, mononational audiovisual productions among the member states, not to encourage transnational coproductions. The Commission considered the program's top priority to be "the creation of a European film distribution system, which will make it easier for national productions to move more freely throughout the Community."[30] Concrete measures taken under the MEDIA umbrella included a European Film Distribution Office (EFDO) to give loans to low-cost European feature films that had to be distributed in at least three different member states and a scheme called BABEL (Broadcasting Across the Barriers of European Languages) to refine dub- bing and translation techniques. Also included were EURO-AIM, which offered assistance to independent producers in marketing their output, and an initiative to promote cartoon productions.

In 1990 MEDIA was finalized and renewed for a period of five years. Its funding rose to about ECU 40 million per annum on average, and it came to contain a range of additional measures, aimed, for instance, at boosting the production capacity of countries of small demographic or linguistic size.[31]

The MEDIA program calls for two main observations. First, MEDIA's funding remained very modest in relation to the generally high financial stakes involved in the audiovisual sector. On a per capita basis, it amounted to no more than ECU 0.13 (U.S.$0.117) per EU citizen per year. Second, as already suggested, MEDIA was almost exclusively geared toward boosting the circulation of audiovisual output throughout the EU. Measures to subsidize transnational coproductions, the centerpiece of the Commission's earlier audiovisual proposals that had been rejected by the member states, played only a relatively minor part in the MEDIA program. The same emphasis on strengthening domestic audiovisual production capabilities as opposed to Europeanizing them was also evident in that one of MEDIA's central aims was to promote the audiovisual potential of member countries with small demographic and/or linguistic size. What all this signified was that by the late 1980s "Community policy [had] shifted from emphasizing *unity* to emphasizing *diversity*"—a very different objective from what the Commission and the EP had initially envisioned.[32]

Audiovisual Policy in the Maastricht Treaty and After

If the 1980s were the formative stage of the EU's audiovisual policies, the 1990s saw little more than a change in rhetoric from the pattern established in the preceding decade. Actual policies remained unchanged by and large. Existing support schemes were renewed and in some instances expanded. Yet little was added that would have enabled the European Parliament and the European Commission to advance their audiovisual defragmentation agenda more successfully than they had hitherto been able.

On the constitutional front the most important development in that decade was the Maastricht Treaty. It was signed by the member governments in 1991 and came into force in 1993, after an arduous and crisis-prone ratification process. The Maastricht Treaty contained a new Article 128, which gave the EU, for the first time, a limited constitutional standing in the realm of cultural policy.[33] The audiovisual sector is explicitly mentioned as an area of possible EU activity. But according to the treaty the EU can act only upon the unanimous consent by national governments, and then only to take "incentive measures" or adopt "recommendations" (neither of which are legally binding) to promote what the treaty describes as the "flowering of the cultures of the Member States while respecting their national and regional diversity and at the same time bringing the common cultural heritage to the fore." This is deliberately ambiguous language, and it is not clear how precisely it circumscribes the types of measures that may be taken. In any event, it is of critical importance that the Maastricht Treaty subjects cultural policy to the unanimity requirement. It means that all audiovisual proposals remain vulnerable to veto by any single national government.[34]

All the while, supporters of the European Commission's demand for more aggressive measures to defragment the European audiovisual market found it easy to bolster their case with concrete figures. By the mid-1990s 94 percent of television consumption in Europe could still be accounted for by viewers watching their respective domestic channels with primarily domestic program scheduling.[35] Moreover, insofar as those domestic channels featured programs that were not of domestic origin, these often came from overseas (mainly of course from the United States) rather than from other European countries. Figures for film consumption in cinemas pointed in much the same direction.[36]

Yet despite the starkness of those figures and the intensity of its pleas, the Commission's and the EP's audiovisual policy achievements after Maastricht have remained modest. There were no qualitative leaps but merely a continuation and cautious expansion of existing programs. This became borne out by the subsequent version of the MEDIA program (called MEDIA II), which was passed in 1995 and extended into the year 2000.

MEDIA had its budget increased to ECU 310 million (U.S.$279 million) in total, and it featured a range of additional support measures. This included schemes to encourage the networking of audiovisual production companies, the showing of films in cinemas outside their country of origin (through "cooperation networks" among European film distributors, audiovisual festivals, promotional fairs, and the like), and the European-wide distribution of national television programs. At the same time, those measures suggest that MEDIA's primary objective is still that of stimulating an increase in nationally produced output and its circulation throughout the EU, not the Europeanization of audiovisual content by directly subsidizing multinational and multilingual coproductions or by other means. Demands by the European Parliament in its proposed amendment to the initial Commission proposal that the new MEDIA program should embrace measures to "develop the ability of professionals to understand the European cultural dimension to audiovisual works in order to develop their ability to address a European, rather than simply a national audience" failed to make their way into the final version of MEDIA II.[37]

Apart from securing the renewal of the MEDIA program, the Commission's and the EP's accomplishments in the content-related part of the audiovisual sector remained modest throughout the second part of the 1990s, though not for lack of trying. In 1995, for instance, the Commission issued a proposal for a European audiovisual guarantee fund.[38] It was to run parallel to the MEDIA II program and foster the development of fictional works "with considerable European and international market potential" by providing credit guarantees. The proposal was approved unanimously by the European Parliament and (not surprisingly) welcomed by the audiovisual industry with similar enthusiasm. Yet the member states have thus far refused to adopt it. Even some less costly ideas have shared a similar fate. For instance, the suggestion of having the EU sponsor annual "European Oscars," albeit a personal favorite of the former Commissioner in charge of cultural and audiovisual policy, has thus far not materialized.[39]

Against the background of such unabated resistance, the Commission's most recent audiovisual innovations have largely been confined to a discursive level. There it has come to treat audiovisual policy—in its technical as well as content-related aspects—as a subsector of what it refers to as the "multimedia" field, involving everything from the Internet to mobile telephones and digital broadcasting. What is more, in the Commission's rendering, "multimedia" in turn is but one dimension of the broader group of issues it bunches together under the vaguely defined heading of "information society." By the late 1990s, *multimedia, information society,* and *technological convergence,* along with ubiquitously invoked *networks* and *information gateways,* all had become buzzwords in official Commission rhetoric, featured in numerous reports, positions, discussions, and strategy papers.

Still on the level of Commission rhetoric, moreover, audiovisual policy became largely "deculturalized." On occasion the Commission continues to maintain that EU involvement in audiovisual policy should seek to foster "enhanced social solidarity" or help in the dissemination of "European cultural values."[40] But as those themes failed to make its audiovisual Europeanization agenda more palatable to many member states, the European Commission (and to a lesser degree also the European Parliament) gradually abandoned them. The Commission now treats audiovisual policy primarily under economic and technological rather than cultural guises, stressing the economic stakes involved in the audiovisual sector and the supposed link between its "software" and "hardware" aspects, the latter encompassing areas such as new distribution techniques (mainly the Internet), digital broadcasting, and high-definition television.

As for the cultural anti-Americanization theme, it, too, has lost much of its former standing in Commission rhetoric. The Commission still makes frequent reference to the United States. Rather than depicting the United States as a cultural menace, however, it now casts it in the role of a *technological* competitor, together with Japan and other Asian countries.

But just as the Commission's and the EP's embrace of the "European culture" and cultural anti-Americanization themes from the early 1980s onward did little to promote their aspirations for EU-led policies to Europeanize the audiovisual productions sector, so the growing abandonment of those themes has had little impact either. In the face of continued resistance by many member states and the weak audiovisual mandate the EU received in the Maastricht Treaty, potential future attempts by the Commission and the EP to push through audiovisual policies beyond those that seek to subsidize productions in minority languages and to encourage the wider circulation of domestically produced audiovisual output appear to stand minimal chance of success. And the Commission may well have started to bow to the limits of the politically possible: It has not, as of late, tried to submit a new and farther-reaching audiovisual policy initiative to the member states, along the lines of its ill-fated proposals to support transnational coproductions in the 1980s.

In sum, judged by the EU's policy record to date, the Europeanization and defragmentation of the audiovisual productions sector is not a project that is in the process of building up momentum. To the contrary: efforts to implement relevant policies may well turn out to have been no more than a sustained but largely inconsequential episode that began in the early 1980s but started to run out of steam some two decades later. And so, too, did pleas for the protection of "European culture" against the United States.

Conclusion

There remains the question raised at the beginning of this chapter: What can the EU's record in audiovisual policy tell us about the prospects for political identity construction in the EU? And what does it say about the obstacles that may stand in the way of such a project?

One important point to consider at the outset is that the EU's relatively poor audiovisual policy record is not an isolated case. Instead, throughout the 1980s and 1990s attempts by the EP and the Commission to pursue European identity-building policies in areas beyond the audiovisual sector shared much the same fate. Plans to set up a Pan-European lottery and "European showrooms" in museums, to insert "European content" into the school curricula of the member states, and many similar initiatives were also vehemently rejected by some national governments. Like the Commission's and the EP's audiovisual initiatives, they led to the implementation of few concrete measures.[41]

Against this background, the fate of audiovisual policy in the EU seems one more indication of what many observers of the integrative process in Europe have long argued, namely that a conception of European unification in a social, cultural, and "identitive" sense as a state-transcending undertaking is not ultimately one that is widely shared beyond the confines of the European Parliament and the European Commission. It is not, most significantly, shared by political elites in many member states that continue to bear the main responsibility for policy outcomes in the EU.[42] Many national governments remain unwilling to give the EU the tools necessary for political identity construction at the supranational level precisely because they do not subscribe to such a project in the first place. And this leaves the project's feasibility in doubt.

Beyond this, the story of the EU's largely unsuccessful attempts to Europeanize the audiovisual sector also points to some of the difficulties linked to discursive framing, both as a technique to advance particular policy initiatives and, more generally, to establish and reify the EU's social and cultural boundaries.

As I have shown, on the face of it the EP's and the Commission's resort to the cultural anti-Americanization theme appeared to have genuine potential because of the empirical backup it enjoyed: There *was* a large audiovisual trade deficit with the United States, and Europeans *did* watch many American films and television programs. What is more, on an elite level fears of a cultural Americanization had a long tradition in many member states. Yet while the Commission's and the EP's warnings against an impending cultural Americanization found some resonance in France and certain southern member states, many others remained thoroughly unconvinced. In countries ranging from Denmark and Germany to Ireland, the Netherlands, and the UK, cultural Americanization fears of the kind articulated by the EP and the Commission appeared grossly exaggerated, if not downright weird. And for a wider public across the EU the anti-Americanization argument was bound to be even less convincing, given that it was this very public that was an avid *consumer* of American films and television programs. But the commitment even by the French government to the Commission's and the EP's audiovisual rhetoric was relatively soft. While broad sections of the French elite (far beyond the socialist government of the day) were receptive to the notion of "resistance to American cultural imperialism," their primary concern was for *French* culture and the *French* language, not for European culture, however defined. French cultural and language policy at the time clearly bore this out. In sum, the anti-Americanization theme was granted *some* legitimacy in *some* member states, yet to serve as a viable rhetorical foundation for ambitious and culturally intrusive audiovisual policy initiatives by the EU, it was simply not considered plausible enough.

Much the same applied to the "European culture" theme. It, as we saw, was the discursive flip side of the anti-Americanization coin. But it, too, enjoyed only limited credibility. Indeed, in many member states the EP's and the Commission's insistence on "European culture" could only be grist for the rhetorical mill of EU opponents. These were often quick to try to use it in support of their depiction of the EU as an intrusive and manipulative entity, determined to erode national identities and homogenize national cultures. Against this background, the EP and the Commission were wise to drop gradually the "European culture" theme in the 1990s, especially after the Maastricht debate had given rise to widespread fears about the effect of European integration on national identities.[43]

If the anti-Americanization and "European culture" themes have largely failed to advance the Commission's and the EP's audiovisual policy agenda, could alternative rhetorical frames be more effective? Developments in the coming years will cast more light on this. For as we saw, the European Commission and the EP have started to modify their audiovisual rhetoric. Though to some extent still focused on the United States, they now highlight the economic rather than the cultural stakes involved in the audiovisual sector. Moreover, they claim that Europe's performance in the audiovisual "software" field is crucially linked to its future success in its "hardware" parts (such as the development of new transmission technologies). To many national governments and mass publics alike, the focus on economic and technological objectives may well be less alienating than the idea of protecting "European culture." But at the same time, it suffers from a potential plausibility problem: India, Brazil, and Egypt are countries whose audiovisual "software" capacity is impressive yet whose "hardware" performance seems to have benefited little from this. In any event, as I have noted, the EP's and the Commission's stated audiovisual ambitions have become more modest. Their central objective is to boost the output of domestically produced and mononational films and television programs and their circulation throughout the EU, not the Europeanization of audiovisual content through coproductions or other means.

The Commission's and the EP's difficulties in finding an effective frame for their audiovisual initiatives also hint at a broader dilemma. For a given rhetorical frame to be effective in promoting a policy agenda (especially one that requires the unanimous consent of all the member states), it must have an EU-wide appeal. This, however, requires a compatibility of reception and responsiveness that does not exist in EU Europe, owing to the EU's social and cultural fragmentation and the diverse historical experiences of the different member states. Thus, the cultural Americanization theme could find some resonance in France and a few other member states, but in others it was doomed to lack such appeal from the outset. And this is where the Union's dilemma lies: The aim of its cultural and educational policy aspirations is precisely to create a minimum level of shared values and reference points among Europeans. But the very *absence* of such shared values and reference points means that the EU finds it hard to come up with discursive frames with a sufficiently broad appeal to sustain such policies in the first place.

The account of the EU's attempted involvement in the audiovisual sector raises many more questions this chapter has not addressed. For instance, even if the EU *had* succeeded in launching major initiatives to support transnational coproductions, their impact would have been far from clear. The European Commission's and the EP's claim that multinational coproductions would inevitably lead to a cultural denationalization of national audiovisual formats seems questionable, not least because it pays little attention to prevailing linguistic differences, which are not apt to be easily "denationalized." The notion that a Europeanization of audiovisual content would inevitably lead to a Europeanization of political allegiances calls for similar skepticism. The Commission's and the EP's confidence in this regard smacked of the kind of "hypodermic needle" and "remote control" conceptions of media impact to which few contemporary students of mass communications subscribe.[44]

Because the Commission's and the EP's audiovisual Europeanization proposals were never implemented, it is hard to gain much clarity on their likely impact. If the account in this chapter permits one clearly supported inference, it is thus mainly the following: For the EU to construct a supranational political identity may well be possible in theory, but the story of the hitherto largely unsuccessful attempts to involve the EU in the audiovisual sector suggests just how hard it might turn out to be in practice.

Notes

Parts from the last section of this chapter previously appeared in Tobias Theiler, "Viewers into Europeans? How the European Union Tried to Europeanize the Audiovisual Sector and Why It Failed," *Canadian Journal of Communication* 24, 4 (1999): 557–587. Thanks to Lars-Erik Cederman, Anne Deighton, Jennifer Jackson Preece, and Ron Jepperson for their helpful comments and suggestions.

1. For a good theoretical discussion, see Pierre Bourdieu, "L'Identité et la représentation: éléments pour une réflexion critique sur l'idée de région," *Actes de la recherche en sciences sociales* 35 (1980): 63–72. See also Rogers Brubaker, *Nationalism Reframed: Nationhood and the National Question in the New Europe* (Cambridge: Cambridge University Press, 1996), esp. ch. 1.

2. For a comparative perspective on the evolution of broadcasting throughout Europe, see Eli Noam, *Television in Europe* (New York: Oxford University Press, 1991). On the technical and economic factors that militated toward EU involvement in the audiovisual sector, see George Wedell, "The Establishment of the Common Market for Broadcasting in Western Europe," *International Political Science Review* 7, 3 (1986): 281–297; Ralph Negrine and Stylianos Papathanassopoulous, *The Internationalization of Television* (London: Pinter, 1990).

3. David Morley and Kevin Robins, "Spaces of Identity: Communications Technologies and the Reconfiguration of Europe," *Screen* 30, 4 (1989): 19.

4. See ibid.

5. Especially in France, such fears also revolved around the position of the national in relation to the English language. The desire to bolster the use of French, both inside France and globally, as well as to protect it from contamination with English words and idioms, led to a barrage of language policies by successive French governments. See, for example, William Safran, *The French Polity*, 2nd ed. (White Plains, N.Y.: Longman, 1985), 260–263.

6. "Report on European Union," *Bulletin of the EC*, Supplement 1, 1976; Commission of the EC, "Community Action in the Cultural Sector (Commission Communication to the Council Submitted on 22 November 1977)," *Bulletin of the EC*, Supplement 6, 1977; Commission of the EC, "For a Community Policy in Education," *Bulletin of the EC*, Supplement 10, 1973.

7. European Parliament, "Report Drawn up on Behalf of the Committee on Youth, Culture, Education, Information and Sport on Radio and Television Broadcasting in the European Community," EP Doc. 1-1013/81 8, 1982.

8. Commission of the EC, "Towards a Large European Audio-Visual Market," *European File*, April 1988, 4.

9. Quoted in Morley and Robins, "Spaces of Identity," 12.

10. Commission of the EC, "Declaration by the European Commission on the Occasion of the Achievement of the Customs Union on 1 July 1968," in Michael Hodges, ed., *European Integration* (Harmondsworth, UK: Penguin, 1972), 69.

11. For possible explanations for this, see Colin Hoskins and Rolf Mirus, "Reasons for the US Dominance of the International Trade in Television Programmes," *Media, Culture & Society* 10, 4 (1988): 499–515.

12. Commission of the EC, "Action Programme for the European Audiovisual Media Products Industry," COM(86) 255 final, 4.

13. Commission of the EC, "The European Community and Culture," *European File,* October 1988, 5–6.

14. Quoted in Richard Collins, "Unity in Diversity? The European Single Market in Broadcasting and Audiovisual," *Journal of Common Market Studies* 32, 1 (1994): 90.

15. European Parliament, "Resolution Embodying the Opinion of the European Parliament on the Proposal from the Commission of the European Communities to the Council for a Regulation on a Community Aid Scheme for Non-documentary Cinema and Television Co-productions," *Official Journal of the European Communities* C288 (1985): 30–31; European Parliament, "Resolution on the Promotion of Film-making in the Community Countries," *Official Journal of the European Communities* 307 (1983): 16–19.

16. Quoted in Michael Tracey, "Popular Culture and the Economics of Global Television," *Intermedia* 16, 2 (1988): 16–17.

17. Quoted in Noam, *Television in Europe,* 302.

18. Cris Shore, "Inventing the 'People's Europe': Critical Approaches to European Community 'Cultural Policy,'" *Man* 28, 4 (1993): 788.

19. Accusations of this type had helped to frustrate many other attempts by the EP and the Commission to involve the EU in cultural and educational policy in preceding years. These included attempts to establish a "European foundation" in charge of promoting "European culture" and to infuse a "European dimension" into national school curricula.

20. At first some of their meetings were held on an informal basis, thereby circumventing the controversial question of constitutional competences.

21. Although a partial denationalization of audiovisual content was clearly what they were after, the Commission and the EP were generally savvy enough not to use this or similarly unconcealed terms. Instead they employed code words and wrapped their audiovisual policy statements in a thick layer of unity-in-diversity rhetoric.

22. See, for instance, European Parliament, "Resolution on the Promotion of Film-making"; European Parliament, "Resolution Embodying the Opinion of the European Parliament on the Proposal from the Commission."

23. Commission of the EC, "Proposal for a Council Regulation on a Community Aid Scheme for Non-documentary Cinema and Television Co-productions," COM(85) 174 final; *Bulletin of the EC,* April 1985, point 1.3.1.

24. On the "metaphors of cultural war," see Chapter 4 by Philip Schlesinger in this volume.

25. Commission of the EC, "Amended Proposal for a Council Regulation (EEC) on a Community Aid Scheme for Non-documentary Cinema and Television Co-productions," COM(85) 800 final; *Bulletin of the EC,* December 1985, point 2.1.125.

26. Wedell, "The Establishment of the Common Market for Broadcasting," 284. See also André Lange and Jean-Luc Renaud, *The Future of the European Audiovisual Industry* (Manchester: European Institute for the Media, 1989); Johan Ryngaert, "Le Conseil 'mixte' culture: un événement vite redimensionné," *Rivista di studi politici internazionali* 216 (1987): 581–590. As is often the case in EU politics, it is difficult to assess the extent to which such opposition enjoyed the tacit support of other member states. Since the countries mentioned (and especially Denmark) seemed so staunchly set against the Commission's audiovisual aspirations, governments that shared similar reserva-

tions could afford to exercise restraint in their display of overt opposition and yet be assured that the Commission's efforts would remain fruitless.

27. Commission of the EC, "Action Programme."

28. Lange and Renaud, *The Future of the European Audiovisual Industry*, 208.

29. Matto Maggiore, *Audiovisual Production and the Single Market* (Luxembourg: Commission of the EC, 1990), 63.

30. Commission of the EC, "A Fresh Boost for Culture in the European Community," *Bulletin of the EC*, Supplement 4, 1987, 14.

31. European Council, "Council Decision of 21 December 1990 Concerning the Implementation of an Action Programme to Promote the Development of the European Audiovisual Industry (Media) (1991–1995)," *Official Journal of the European Communities* L380 (1990): 37–44. See also Commission of the EC, "European Community Audiovisual Policy," *European File,* June 1992, 8.

32. Collins, "Unity in Diversity?" 96 (emphasis added).

33. With the subsequent Amsterdam Treaty, this became Article 151.

34. See Léonce Bekemans and Athanassios Balodimos, "Etude concernant les modifications apportées par le Traité sur l'Union Politique en ce qui concerne l'éducation, la formation professionnelle et la culture," mimeograph, Bruges 1992; Hermann-Josef Blanke, *Europa auf dem Weg zu einer Bildungs- und Kulturgemeinschaft* (Cologne: Carl Heymanns Verlag, 1994); Terry Sandell, "Cultural Issues, Debates and Programmes," in Philippe Barbour, ed., *The European Union Handbook* (Chicago: Fitzroy Dearborn, 1996).

35. A large proportion of the remaining 6 percent, moreover, was made up of viewers watching domestic channels from neighboring countries, often in their own language (e.g., Austrian audiences watching German channels, or Italian immigrants in France watching channels from Italy). See Cathy Stewart and Julian Laird, *The European Media Industry: Fragmentation and Convergence in Broadcasting and Publishing* (London: Financial Times Business Information, 1994), 5.

36. A Commission study found that in 1996 some 16 percent of cinema tickets sold in the EU were for national films in their respective home markets (or, in the case of coproductions, for films shown in the home markets of the participating countries). A mere 6 percent of tickets were sold for films from elsewhere in the EU. The remaining 78 percent of tickets sold to cinema goers in the EU thus were for films originating from overseas, overwhelmingly from the United States. A study by the European Audiovisual Observatory in 1996 came to very similar results. Of the forty commercially most successful films in the EU, only ten were European. In fact, apart from *Trainspotting* (which ranked thirteenth) the first twenty were all from the United States. European Commission, *The European Film Industry Under Analysis: Second Information Report 1997* (Brussels: European Commission, 1997).

37. "MEDIA II—Development and Training. (Draft text as amended by the EP)," *Official Journal of the European Communities* C166 (1995). On top of this came some multinational audiovisual initiatives that were initiated outside the EU framework. The most important of those is the Eurimages program launched in 1989, based on the Council of Europe's Cultural Convention. Eurimages goes further than MEDIA in that it seeks to fund audiovisual coproductions. At the same time, Eurimages funding has remained so modest that its overall impact on the European audiovisual sector can be judged negligible. Until now it has expended a total of Fr 1.125 billion (US$0.156 billion). This

amounts to little more than Fr 100 million (i.e., US$13.8 million, or about 15 million euro) per year on average. See the Eurimages homepage, http://culture.coe.fr/eurimages/.

38. European Commission, "Proposal for a Council Decision Establishing a European Guarantee Fund to Promote Cinema and Television Production," COM(95) 546 final.

39. Marcelino Oreja, "For a Modern Audiovisual Policy in the European Union (Speech at the Closing Plenary of the European Audiovisual Conference, Birmingham, 8 April 1998)," available at: www.europa.eu.int/eac/speeches/oreja2.html. For a more general assessment of the audiovisual situation by the Commission, see European Commission, "Audiovisual Policy: Next Steps (Communication from the Commission to the European Parliament and the Council of Ministers)," COM(98) 446 final.

40. "Commission Green Paper on the Convergence of the Telecommunications, Media and Information-Technology Sectors, and the Implications for Regulation—Towards an Information-Society Approach," COM(97) 623. See also European Commission, "Europe's Way to the Information Society: An Action Plan (Communication from the Commission to the Council and the European Parliament and to the Economic and Social Committee and the Committee of Regions)," COM(94) 347 final.

41. See, for example, Shore, "Inventing the 'People's Europe"; Tobias Theiler, "The 'Identity Policies' of the European Union," Ph.D. dissertation, University of Oxford, forthcoming.

42. An argument along those lines has been put forward with varying nuances and degrees of intensity by different observers of European integration. See Paul Taylor, "The European Community and the State: Assumptions, Theories and Propositions," *Review of International Studies* 17, 2 (1991): 109–125; Alan Milward et al., *The Frontier of National Sovereignty: History and Theory, 1945–1992* (London: Routledge 1993); Andrew Moravcsik, "Why the European Community Strengthens the State: Domestic Politics and International Cooperation," Harvard University, Center for European Studies, Working Paper Series 52, 1994.

43. As I have discussed elsewhere, such identity-centered fears led to a growing popular opposition to a potential EU involvement in areas such as cultural policy, audiovisual policy, and education. Tobias Theiler, "International Integration and National Beliefs: A Psychological Basis for Consociationalism as a Model of Political Unification," *Nationalism and Ethnic Politics* 5, 1 (1999): 46–81.

44. See, for example, Denis McQuail and Sven Windahl, *Communication Models for the Study of Mass Communications,* 2nd ed. (Harlow: Longman, 1993); René Jean Ravault, "Défense de l'identité culturelle par les réseaux traditionnels de 'Coerséduction,'" *International Political Science Review* 7, 3 (1986): 251–280.

PART THREE

EUROPE'S EXTERNAL POLITICAL IDENTITY

6

European Identity,
EU Expansion, and the
Integration/Exclusion Nexus

Iver B. Neumann

Where do we look for a culture-sensitive study of the expansion of the European Union, which can help us understand how this political question came to be framed the way it did, and how the European Commission in the autumn of 1997 came to recommend that membership talks should be opened with Cyprus, Estonia, the Czech Republic, Hungary, Poland, and Slovenia? What do we make of the fact that at its summit in December 1997 the EU decided to open talks with all ten applicant members but refused to establish a closer institutional setup with Turkey? One possibility would be to look to anthropology. As the social sciences were institutionalized from the late nineteenth century onward, it fell to anthropologists to busy themselves with matters we would now refer to by the term *identity*. At the beginning of this century, some of them had taken to leaving their studies in order to visit distant peoples about whose values and social organization the outside world knew little. World War I saw one of their number, a British resident by the name of Bronislaw Malinowski, paying such a visit to the Trobriand Islands off Australia. Instead of returning to Britain, Malinowski, who held an Austrian-Hungarian passport, decided to stick it out in the islands for a considerably longer time than he had originally intended. Thus was born the idea of the lengthy fieldwork, which ever since has been the anthropologists' standard procedure for investigating the identities of a given human collective.[1]

An earlier version of this chapter was previously published in *Alternatives: Social Transformation and Humane Governance* 23, 3 (July–September 1998): 397–416.

Identity Is Relational

I mention this here not because I want to underline one of the favorite themes of my own branch of social science—international relations— namely, the importance of war for the unfolding of history. My point is rather that since anthropologists have trusted their fieldwork method to throw light on that corner of social inquiry which has to do with identity, they have routinely neglected the study of large-scale identities. They have, moreover, shown a particular penchant for studying the powerless. These factors conspire to make anthropological studies of whatever "European identity" may be very rare indeed, and studies of European institutions rarer still.[2] As far as I have been able to establish, in English there exists only one single anthropological monograph on the topic: a study of identity formation not within one of the institutions of the European Union but within the European Space Agency.[3]

The anthropologist who studied the European Space Agency, Stacia Zabusky, happens to be American, and her country of citizenship turned out to be the point around which her fieldwork would turn.[4] It is Zabusky's claim that the employees with whom she ate her lunch negotiated and reproduced their identities as European by contrasting themselves, understood as an "us" or a collective self, with the "them" or "other" of the United States, embodied at these occasions by herself. Thus, as she put it, these people were "making Europe over lunch." Two other anthropologists who have done fieldwork in Brussels report a European Commission employee who said that "Europeanism doesn't exist; there are no cultural roots for it to exist. The only time I feel European is when I'm in the USA."[5]

This way of studying political processes by means of fieldwork may of course be questioned, and it seems certain that we will have to complement this technique by others in order to gain a richer understanding of issues such as EU expansion. We may note, however, the similarity between Zabusky's claim and the views of one of the most eminent political theorists this century has seen, Hannah Arendt. In the 1950s she wrote about the topic in the following manner:

> If it is true that each nationalism (though, of course, not the birth of every nation) begins with a real or fabricated common enemy, then the current image of America in Europe may well become the beginning of a new pan-European nationalism. Our hope that the emergence of a federated Europe and the dissolution of the present nation-state system will make nationalism itself a thing of the past may be unwarrantedly optimistic.[6]

Arendt's musing about whether one indeed has to treat the other as an enemy is of particular relevance here. Zabusky, it seems, was on very friendly terms with most of her informants, among whom she also counted some friends. So let us not assume that the forging of a collective identity and the wider process of social integration of which it is a (crucial) aspect hinges on the production of an enemy. What may, however, safely be assumed is that the integration of a human collective necessarily involves the exclusion of nonmembers. What forms this exclusion takes, how it is performed, and how strong it is insisted upon are questions for empirical inquiry.

In Zabusky's case "Europeanness" was overwhelmingly made a question of diversity. "You Americans are all the same," people would tell her over lunch, "whereas we Europeans are at one in our differences." There are two points to be made about this. First, one recalls that the words *E pluribus unum* are engraved on a number of American state symbols; among Americans, then, there also exists an idea of being at one in diversity. This was treated as irrelevant to the Europeans in question, which goes to show that this particular group of Europeans did not negotiate their identity as such with their American other but among themselves, ostensibly in isolation from the other. One stresses the *ostensibly*, because it is readily seen that collective identity is a relation between two human collectives, that is, it always resides in the nexus between the collective self and its others, not in the self seen in isolation. Second, one notes that the idea of diversity is used not to integrate the United States but, on the contrary, to exclude it. In this case the idea of diversity served the end of limiting diversity. What this begins to suggest is that a collective self marks itself off from its others by a number of what anthropologists following Fredrik Barth call "diacritica."[7] The pair diverse/homogeneous has been viewed as one such diacriticon in the case of European identity. There are others, and what these are is a crucial question to which I return below. Before that, however, the general insights from anthropology seem in need of some analytic embellishment before they can be applied to the issue of EU expansion.

Integration and Exclusion in EU Expansion Practice

According to the Treaty of the European Union, members of the organization have to be states, they have to be democratic, and they have to be European. Since the late 1980s, a very motley crew of states have joined, and even more have applied for membership. As a matter of fact, there hardly seems to be a state in the immediate vicinity of present EU territory that does not harbor a substantial number of citizens who would like their state to join.[8] Two cases stand out as extremes with respect to the way they were handled by the EU. First, there was Morocco's membership application of 1986.[9] The EU dealt with this application in no uncertain terms; Rabat was simply told that the organization was open only to Europeans, and that was that. There was no room for ambiguity, only unequivocal exclusion and marking of Morocco as clearly "non-European." Whereas all other applications have set in train complicated bureaucratic procedures that have led to different kinds of institutional agreements, Morocco's led to nothing. When the EU made agreements with this state at a later date, it was not in a context that stressed the question of future membership.

What is at issue here is not whether I as a chronicler of this event hold Morocco to be European or not. One could easily spin a story of how the cohabitation of Catholics and Moors in Spain up to 1492, the trade ties across the Mediterranean, the years of French colonial administration, and so on make up a common history by dint of which Morocco should be seen as a member of a human collective referred to, for example, as Europe. It is most instructive that such stories of a common history are spun by a number of Europeans, including some authorized by the European Commission, when the context is one of building a Mediterranean region including the EU, the Magreb, the Mashrek, and other riparian states. What is at issue is rather that when the frame happened to be the institutional one of EU expansion, a number of other historical sequences and social constructions of Morocco conspired to make the Commission pass it off in record time as non-European. There is a general point to be made here: Identities are always context bound, and the same speakers may activate very different representations of the same others when the context changes. Identities are fluid not only across time and space but even as they pertain to the same subjects at the same point in space and time.

To return to EU expansion, the other extreme case is that of the former German Democratic Republic, which became a member without an application, a referendum, or even a ratification by the European Community states themselves.[10] The laws and political weight of one of the states that was already a member, namely, the Federal Republic of Germany, was enough to secure membership. It would be a mistake to hold that an unequivocal identity of "Germanness" automatically qualified the human collective of former subjects of the GDR to become members. Indeed, what it means to be "German" is an extremely complicated affair, where *Aussiedler, Vertriebene, Ossie* (evacuees, refugees, former East Germans), and a whole plethora of other subgroups make up the complicated and arguably hierarchized structure that one often refers to homogenizingly as the "German nation."[11] When the EC opted for what was in institutional terms almost unequivocal integration (the only hiccup being the tardiness in expanding the number of seats in the European Parliament to accommodate the representatives of the newcomers), it was because Europeanness was conferred upon them the moment they became citizens of a member state. European identity was seen as secured by their new EC passports. Or to put it another way, because this human collective was treated as part of a member state, the treaty's questions of whether they were European, and incidentally also whether they were democratic, simply were not seen to arise.

Both these recent cases tell us something important about how EU practice "operationalizes" European identity, to use an unlovely term. They also vaguely begin to tell us something about the wider question of which diacritica are activated in order to maintain the boundary between Europe and non-Europe. In order to move closer to this issue, however, one may investigate all the cases of membership applications that have been treated ambiguously. Indeed, there exists an entire belt of applicant states—from Estonia, Latvia, and Lithuania in the north to Turkey, Cyprus, and Malta in the south—that have neither been excluded nor included outright. All of these states have noted that being European is one of the two explicit criteria for membership and, consequently, that representing the state and having it recognized by the EU as European is not only relevant to the application but a prerequisite for its being taken seriously. If one should think otherwise, there is always Morocco to serve as a reminder. I now turn to a two-step discussion of how applicants have positioned themselves. First, I try to demonstrate how Poland, the Czech Republic, and Hungary find themselves at the head of the queue today partly because of the successful identity politics strategy of forging themselves into a "Central Europe."[12] Second, I draw attention to three structural similarities of applicant rhetoric and what they tell us about the discourse on European identity generally.

An Example of Applicant Rhetoric: The Making of "Central Europe"

Whereas the idea that there exists a *Mitteleuropa* hails from the turn of the nineteenth century and has a distinct German flavor to it, the present discourse on Central Europe may be seen to have emerged in the writings of Polish, Czech, and eventually also Hungarian artists and intellectuals from the late 1950s onward. The gist of their argument emerges clearly in Milan Kundera's article from 1980:

> As a concept of cultural history, Eastern Europe is Russia, with its quite specific history anchored in the Byzantine world. Bohemia, Poland, Hungary, just like Austria, have never been part of Eastern Europe. From the very beginning they have taken part in the great adventure of Western civilization, with its Gothic, its Renaissance, its Reformation—a movement which has its cradle precisely in this region. It was here, in Central Europe, that modern culture found its greatest impulse: psychoanalysis, structuralism, dodecaphony, Bartók's music, Kafka's and Musil's new esthetics of the novel. The postwar annexation of Central Europe (or at least its major part) by Russian civilization caused Western culture to lose its vital center of gravity.[13]

This was also the thrust of the original title of Kundera's successful region-building essay, "A Kidnapped West: The Tragedy of Central Europe."[14] Kidnapping is not to be condoned, and especially not when it is conducted against part of an ostensible collective self like "the West." That the West was the addressee of the essay and that it was not intended for perusal in that "Central Europe" of which it was ostensibly a discussion is borne out by Kundera's later insistence that the essay falls into that part of his production which he disowns, because it was tailor-made for Western consumption.

This marking of Western Europe as though it were outside of itself as long as Central Europe remained in the custody of the Soviet Union also revealed a very positive moral assessment of "the European idea." Indeed, most traits ascribed to "Central Europe" can be refound in the rhetorical armory of European federalists (see, e.g., Chapter 1). The controversy was not so much about the Western European other, which was perceived ambiguously as both self and other at the same time (what I will later discuss as liminar), but about the other to the East. It was not a matter of different moral assessments of the Soviet Union as a political entity, which was seen almost universally as morally inferior to "Central Europe." It was, rather, about a question that has taken on renewed urgency after the collapse of the Soviet Union, namely, whether the other was simply confined in time to the Soviet political system or whether the other was "eternal Russia." Moreover, it was about whether Russia was wholly other or whether there was the same kind of ambiguity between self and other in the case of "Central Europe" and Russia as there was between "Central Europe" and the West. In his essay Kundera was very clear about this—the other was not simply the Soviet Union but eternal Russia: "Russia is not just as one more European power but as a singular civilization, an other civilization. . . . Totalitarian

Russian civilization is the radical negation of the modern West."[15] This categorization was also supported by a strand of Hungarian historiography where Europe's history was treated as a tripartite affair, with developments of postulated "Western," "Central," and "Eastern" (that is, mainly Russian) spheres ostensibly being easily separable.[16]

The events of 1989 were greeted enthusiastically by the participants in the discourse on Central Europe. The attempted external differentiation of "Central Europe" from and at the expense of Russia continued as before. Perhaps the most concrete and striking early example of this practice emerged in October 1991, as a self-proclaimed appeal to the EC's Maastricht summit. "Though we should do our utmost to promote democracy in the new Russia," the article starts out in what can only be the prose of Timothy Garton Ash,

> this should not obscure the more immediate and manageable challenge of Central Europe. . . . Historically and culturally, Poland, Hungary, and Czechoslovakia belong to Europe. A Europe which contains Crete but not Bohemia, Lisbon but not Warsaw, is historical nonsense. . . . Yet where would this leave the rest of post-Communist Europe . . . It makes plain, practical sense to start with those that are nearest, and work out to those which are farthest. Poland, Hungary, and Czechoslovakia are nearest not only geographically, historically, and culturally, but also in the progress they have already made on the road to democracy, the rule of law, and a market economy.[17]

So, the three coauthors concluded, "Following the suggestion originally made by the Czechoslovak foreign minister, Jiří Dienstbier, some of the aid to Russia and the other post-Soviet republics should be made in a form which both enables and obliges them to spend it in East Central Europe." Moreover, all other EC concerns should be streamlined to the overriding priority of catering to Poland, Hungary, and Czechoslovakia: "All proposals for a deepening of the present EC of twelve through closer integration must be workable by extension in a community of twenty." Finally, it was asserted that all good things may come together. Privileging "Central Europe" will turn it into "a magnet for South East Europe, for the Baltic states, the Ukraine, and, yes, for the European parts of Russia," and the broadening of the European Community it entails will "help in deepening" the EC's integration process as well.[18] All this was presented by the *New York Review of Books* under the title "Let the East Europeans In!" which yet again stressed that what was good for "Central Europe" is good for "Eastern Europe" as well as for Europe.

Far from being a peripheral part of the discourse, these formulations quickly found their way into the rhetorical armory of people like the Polish minister of foreign affairs. In a general survey of the state of European relations in the spring of 1992, Krzysztof Skubiszewski held that

> as a consequence of the end of the Cold War, contemporary security relations on our continent have lost their simplicity and may be geographically described as concentric circles progressing from the stable nucleus of the countries of the European Communities, the Western European Union and the North Atlantic Alliance, to the most unstable peripheries. . . . The most important danger zone in Europe, with regard to possible military conflicts, is the area extending between Russia, the Ukraine, and Rumania. . . . The association of the three countries [i.e., Czechoslovakia, Hungary, and Poland] with the European Community is relevant to their security but also to that of the West: the hard core of Europe will comprise a bigger territory.[19]

Since 1992 a discursive pattern has already established itself in Europeanwide discourse on EU and also North Atlantic Treaty Organization (NATO) expansion where this kind of perspective has become the starting point of deliberation. "Central Europe" is not only firmly entrenched as a term, but it has also contributed to propelling the states that ostensibly make it to the front of the queue of EU applicant states. Central Europe started as an appeal by Czech, Hungarian, and Polish dissident intellectuals, issued above the heads of the local politicians, to Western civil society. Western intellectuals later took up the bugle call. With the local Communist politicians gone and the former dissidents installed in still warm seats, the arguments of the Central European debate became part of official foreign policy. From there they went on to join the overall European discourse on expansion of the institutions of the EU and NATO.

The debate about "Central Europe" was a moral appeal to Western Europe on behalf of an imagined community, born of frustration with the Soviet hegemony in Eastern Europe. Indeed, the language of the "Central European" project is similar to that of nationalism inasmuch as it tries to turn the political field into a battleground among groups that are not only culturally but more often than not also ethnically defined. Integration of Central Europe is advocated at the price of exclusion of Russia and certain other countries. As will shortly be seen, it is, however, not the case that discourse on Central Europe is all that different from applicant discourse generally. It is above all the efficiency of the Central European campaign that stands out, not its quality. We have here a concrete example not only of the unfolding of identity politics but also of how specific carriers of discourse—in this case first artists and intellectuals, then statesmen—are able to change the framing of one particular discourse in what they consider to be an advantageous direction.

From "Central" to "Western"

We also have here an example of identity politics intentionally applied. The artists, intellectuals, and statesmen who fielded this representation of Central Europe did so by presenting it as what we may call a liminar identity, that is, an identity that hovered on the border (*limes* in Latin) between Eastern Europe on the one hand and Western Europe on the other. Indeed, already the adjectivization itself states as much. As this success played itself out, one could see a wild-goose chase begin all over former Eastern Europe and in certain parts of the former Soviet Union to have one's country subsumed under the term *Central Europe.*

Whereas one reason for this goose chase was a perceived need to partake of the success of the Central European enterprise of the 1980s, there was an additional reason. As Maria Todorova pointed out, after 1990 "Central Europe" was no longer presenting itself simply as different from Russia, but also as different from that other half of the old "Eastern Europe," the Balkans. The Balkans has become a new other to Central Europe, "sometimes alongside with, sometimes indistinguishable from" Russia.[20] Todorova produces as particularly convincing discursive evidence for this a quote from the debate about the pacing of NATO enlargement, where it was argued that NATO "cannot suddenly open its doors to anyone at all. . . . The contiguous and stable Central European belt borders both on the traditionally agitated Balkans and the great Eurasian area, where democracy and market economics are only slowly and painfully breaking away toward their fulfillment. In short, it is a key area for European security."[21]

What we see here, though, is not only the growing relevance of a new other but also the subsumption of this other under the heading of "the East." We see here a homogenization of contexts, or (if one likes) a growing digitalization, whereby relations with the Balkans and Eurasia are treated as being of the same kind. One Balkan response to this othering was to fight the exclusion from Central Europe by trying to be included in it, that is, by fielding itself as an alternative Central Europe.

Another significant development of the 1990s was that the debate about *Mitteleuropa* became a central part of ongoing German negotiations about the place and identity of that country in its European setting.[22] The move of the capital from Bonn back to Berlin is often presented as the epitome of this process, and so a quote from one of

German chancellor Helmut Kohl's Berlin speeches may be used as an example: "In Berlin the paths from north to south, from Western to Eastern Europe cross. We Germans have more neighbors than any other European country. As a result of Germany's central geographical location, we cannot be indifferent to what happens around us."[23]

At present, then, representations of "Central Europe" take on three major forms. First, there is the politically successful one that denotes the Czech Republic, Poland, and Hungary as Central European *and hence* accepted into NATO and first in line for EU membership. We have here a self-representation that has been recognized by Western Europe. Second, there is a politically aspiring representation of Central Europe that is entertained by the belt of countries from Estonia in the north to Bulgaria in the south that insists that Central Europe include not only these three countries but also something more, and most particularly the country where this representation is being forged, be that Slovenia, Romania, or elsewhere. We have here a self-representation usually not recognized by Czechs, Poles, and Hungarians and only variously so by Western Europeans. One may say that negotiations over this representation are intense. Third, there is a politically successful representation of Central Europe known as *Mitteleuropa*, centered on Germany and usually not seen as comprising other spaces. This self-representation is variously, and usually grudgingly, recognized in all other European countries, and so it is largely a politically successful one.

It seems, then, that the vastly successful Czech, Hungarian, and Polish representation of Central Europe, which came to the fore in European politics in the 1980s, is about to be hoisted on its own petard. This is suggested by, first, the very success of the undertaking of becoming an institutionalized part of the European self and, second, the way in which this success lays the discursive space of Central Europe open to the two other representations currently in circulation.

First, the success: The Czech Republic, Poland, and Hungary are already inches away from being fully fledged members of NATO, the geopolitical implications of this being that they become members of the Atlantic community. Although membership in the EU seems unrealistic before 2006 at the earliest, these three countries are widely believed to be on their way in. In terms of political and economic integration, they are drawing closer to current members of the EU by the month. All this seems to suggest that Western European countries have recognized the representation of these three countries as a part of Europe without which Europe cannot be whole. This bond, furthermore, has been institutionalized.

There are two ways of describing this in terms of geographical metaphors like *west* and *central*. One is to say that NATO and the EU will now consist of Western and Central Europe, not only Western Europe as before. But what packed the power into this representation of the Czech Republic, Hungary, and Poland as "Central Europe" was among other things its having been temporarily cut off from Western Europe. With integration into Western European structures, one of the predicaments on which this whole representation was predicated has therefore disappeared. Instead of saying that Central Europe joins Western Europe, then, it would make more sense to say that these three countries are being integrated into Western Europe.

Another reason this may be a more helpful way of describing matters is the existence of the two other representations of Central Europe— German *Mitteleuropa* and the belt of states from Estonia to Bulgaria. With the Czech Republic, Hungary, and Poland ensconced in Western Europe, we can already witness an attempt by the latter to hog the Central European space left by those who have decamped for the West. Indeed, in terms of the only sense in which these three countries could be said to be central to Europe, namely, in the geopolitical one, they cease to be central and begin to be part of the West from the moment NATO membership takes effect. The central geopolitical space between Russia and NATO—to the extent that it can be said to exist at all as a contested area—will be taken up by the three Baltic states, Ukraine, and others. This will inevitably strengthen the claim of these countries to make up Central Europe, and it will strengthen it in the very terms formulated by Czechs, Hungarians, and Poles during the 1980s and 1990s. At the same time, there is every reason to believe that Germany's geographical location will confer on it a role of centrality—or perhaps even greater centrality—than what one sees at the present juncture.

For these reasons, Central Europe seems to be moving away from Prague, Warsaw, and Budapest in the direction of Tallinn, Riga, Vilnius, and Kiev, on the one hand, and in the direction of Berlin, on the other. Of course, the representation of the Czech Republic, Poland, and Hungary as "Central Europe" may continue to coexist with a representation of these countries as Western European ones, in the same way that the five Nordic countries manage to be both Northern European and Western European at the same time. Which identity comes to the fore is, after all, contextual. The absolute digitalization of identity is impossible to bring about, since contexts and hence relations that constitute identity must necessarily be in flux. With two other representations pitching for the same ground, however, there may not be more political mileage to be had out of the representation of Central Europe for the elites of the Czech Republic, Poland, and Hungary, and so this particular representation seems destined to lead a rather shadowy political life compared to the other two. Yet this move from "Central" to

"Western" was ostensibly what the Czech, Polish, and Hungarian artists and intellectuals who resuscitated the term in the late 1950s ultimately wanted. Now that it is happening, it confers on the Czech Republic, Hungary, and Poland the onerous task—known for a long time by other peripheral states in Western Europe (such as the one I know best, Norway)—of proving to be central in some specific issue area or other. It is nice not to be too central, particularly not to be too central in a strategic military sense. It is not nice, however, to be a forgotten country on the periphery of Europe. As members of NATO and the EU, these three countries will still have to take the many small steps that will place them centrally in all those flows that make up European politics. In this they may take Finland's EU record as an example of how it is possible to navigate successfully and Sweden's record as an example of how easily chances are missed. In terms of identity politics, then, the Czech Republic, Hungary, and Poland cannot afford to rest on their Central European laurels but must start forging other Central European roles for themselves.

Applicant Rhetoric: A Structuralist Moment

What we have in the case of the transformation of Central Europe, then, is a turn away from liminarity, a change from what we may call analog identity (where identity consists of a number of graded relationships) to a digitalized identity (where identity hinges on one overriding binary opposition, in this case East/West). If I am allowed a structuralist moment, let me draw attention to three common features of the rhetoric that Central European as well as other applicant states (and also a number of their subjects writing and speaking in unauthorized capacities) avail themselves of when they represent their states as European. The relevant rhetoric is not necessarily tailor-made for the particular purpose of boosting a membership application to the EU, although the element of instrumentality is often there for the asking. Rather, the talk is about the phenomenon of discourse on the self and Europe—how the state's identity in relation to the concept of "Europe" is being constructed. There is, first, always a reference to history. As an example, there is Soviet premier Mikhail Gorbachev's break with previous Russian-language discourse in introducing the idea of a "Common European Home":

> Some in the West are trying to "exclude" the Soviet Union from Europe. Now and then, as if inadvertently, they equate "Europe" with "Western Europe". Such ploys, however, cannot change the geographic

and historical realities. Russia's trade, cultural and political links with other European nations and states have deep roots in history. We are Europeans. Old Russia was united with Europe by Christianity. . . . The history of Russia is an organic part of the great European history.[24]

Gorbachev's invocation of a common history in order explicitly to avoid the fate of exclusion and boost the chances of integration has parallels in all the applicant states. The "realities" of history and geography are invoked in a spirit of self-fulfilling prophecy, and this is hardly surprising, since history and geography alike are socially constructed phenomena.[25] And yet, subjects of applicant states very rarely recognize that this does not mean that they are the last country to the (ostensibly geographical) east that should be counted European. The second common feature of applicant rhetoric is, namely, that not only is the state of the subject European but the next state to the east is not European. As an archetype of this, one notes Metternich's jest that Asia begins at Vienna's Ringstrasse. Czech national identity depends on Slovakia as one of its others, and the dichotomy European/Asian is routinely invoked to demarcate the border between the two.[26] Slovenian discourse not only underlines the "Europeanness" of Slovenia but the "Balkan" character of Croatia.[27] In Croatia one is told that Croatia is in Europe, whereas Serbia is definitely non-Europe.[28] Serbs will underline that they and other traditionally Orthodox Christian states such as Russia and EU member Greece are European, while Bosnia, which insistently is referred to as a "Muslim" state, is not.[29] In Hungarian discourse it is, to put it politely, not uncommon to hear Romania represented as non-European. Romanians, in turn, stress their Europeanness by pointing to the lack thereof where Ukraine is concerned. In Ukraine one is told that Ukraine is Europe and Russia is most certainly non-European. As the chairman of the foreign affairs committee of the Ukrainian parliament, Dmytro Pavlychko, put it, "The integration into the general European structures will move us [i.e., Ukrainians] to Europe, where we were born and grew up as a nation. But we were torn away from there and forced into Asiatic imprisonment. They dressed us in a Muscovite cloak and trained us in the Slavic-Russian language like the grandchildren of Genghis Khan."[30]

Indeed, this structural feature of applicant rhetoric is a very good illustration of how geographical tags such as "east" are not only a question of compass needles but are constituted in political terms. It is firmly grounded in a historical trajectory where "west" is seen as dynamic, whereas "east" is seen as stagnant. There can be little doubt about the strength and persistence of this way of framing the question of European identity. Even in 1916 the leading Russian liberal, Pavel

Milyukov, argued that Russia was better equipped than the Porte to take care of the Straits and Constantinople, quoting a contemporary British writer to the effect that "the presence of the Turk in Europe is incidental. They remain at the end of five hundred years as much strangers as they were at the beginning. European ideals and words, like 'nation,' 'government,' 'law,' 'sovereign,' 'subject,' do not apply to them."[31] The idea of representing one's own state as more "European" than one's more "eastern" neighboring states has a long, if not very illustrious, history. It is hard to think of a better example of how integration (into "the west") is pursued in terms of exclusion (of "the east") than this.

The third common feature of applicant rhetoric has to do with regime homogeneity. It is often said about the so-called Southern expansion of the EU (Greece in 1984, Spain and Portugal in 1987) that their democratic regime type was secured by the admission of these states into the EC. In all three states, it was only a matter of years since the regime type had by common internal and European-wide consensus been nondemocratic. It was argued that it would be harder for nondemocrats in and out of the armed forces to take over the state apparatus once these states were enmeshed in European structures. In the debate about the coming "Eastern expansion" of the EU, this argument is routinely floated, not least by the regimes of the applicant countries themselves. This is true not only for regimes in former Communist states but also for Malta and Turkey. As former prime minister Tancu Çiller told a journalist from *Time* during the run-up to the negotiation of a free trade treaty that was viewed as an important step on the way to membership, failure by the EU to deliver would certainly propel the Islamicist Welfare Party to power and thus tip Turkey further toward the Middle East and away from Europe:

> Now the European Parliament has to make its decision. It can say either yes or no—there is no third alternative. Delay means no to me and to all the people of Turkey; if nothing else, the fundamentalists will make sure that it is understood as a no. And it is not just Turkey that is concerned here: there are also the millions of Turkic-speaking people of Central Asia who are looking at two models: ours or the Iranians'. . . . I see my task as changing the history because Turkey can become a bridge for peace between the two areas. If it does not, the two regions will be divided and in confrontation with each other. We can be the link. We are democratic; we are secular; and our economy is the first open, sophisticated economy in the area. . . . The radicals, the fundamentalists and the extreme rightists will capitalize on any delay in the decision as a no vote and as an objection to Turkey by Europe. They will make sure that is understood by the people. So it is going to strengthen the radicals and may even move them into power—move the anti-Europe, antidemocratization, anti-Westernization, antisecular forces into power. . . . Now it's

me versus them. I represent Westernization, secular government, liberalization, the link with Europe.[32]

Invariably, the incumbent regime is represented as more democratic than (some element of or the entirety of) the opposition. There
is an exception here, namely, Slovakia. On two occasions the prime minister of that state has received notes from the EU expressing worries
about the democratic nature of the regime. By common European consensus, the current Slovakian opposition (including the elected president) is more democratic than the incumbent regime. This state of
affairs deprives the regime of this particular rhetoric. The main point,
however, is that the same conflict between pro- and anti-integration
political forces and the same inscription of this dichotomy in terms of
more and less democratic may be seen in this case as in the others. The
two explicit criteria for membership, Europeanness and democratic
regime type, are treated as two sides of the same coin.

To sum up this structuralist excursion, the first common feature of
applicant rhetoric has to do with the way applicant states insist on their
place in a historical and geographical Europe. The second common feature is the way they attempt to exclude their neighboring states to the
east. This exclusion takes the form of a gambit presented in order to
heighten the chances of being integrated into the European structures
to the west. The third common feature has to do with the way in which
applicant regimes try to integrate their state into European structures in
order to exclude internal elements from taking over and (ostensibly)
changing the regime type. These three common features illustrate the
centrality of the integration/exclusion nexus for the overall discourse
on EU exclusion. In addition, they throw up some of the diacritica by
which the wider issue of European identity is demarcated. Since democracy is an explicit criterion for membership, it is hardly surprising to
find this issue to be prominent among the diacritica. More interesting,
the emphasis that aspiring members of Europe in general and the EU
in particular place on similar historical experiences begs the question
that Arendt could be seen to raise at the outset of this chapter, namely,
to what extent the question of European identity is framed as a question
of national identity writ large.

Applicant Rhetoric and the
EU's Supranational Temptation

It is often maintained that the EU is an alternative to the nation-state,
and in a number of senses this may be a fair point. A lot of the thinking

about the EU and the forging of a European identity is nonetheless invariably colored by the categories of state and nation-state. The idea that the sovereign state is the principle for organizing politics is routinely traced back to its period of gestation between 1492 and 1648. The Western canon called "political theory" may be read as one long meditation on the state and its consequences. For the last 150 years or so, the hegemonic form of the political unit has been the nation-state. Now, when applicant states appeal for membership in Europe by pointing to a common history as somehow conferring upon them a European identity, this is a way of thinking about the integration/exclusion nexus that takes its cue from the structure of national identity. A number of identities are sometimes observably forged without reference to that chronological dimension of identity that is history: gender identities, say, or variants of republican identities. So it is possible to think of European identities' being negotiated without a recourse to a common history. It is easy to understand why much present European discourse is cast in the nationalist mode, but this is not an invariable occurrence.

It is also possible to invoke a common history as a diacriticon of a common identity in the sense that one wants to move away from it—that is, one treats the common history, a postulated former gestation of the collective self, as one of the present self's others. This is, for example, the gist of the emancipatory program for a European identity set out by Habermas.[33] As already touched upon in the case of Morocco, one may also always read history in an inclusionary way, in order to foreground amity or at least commonality and play down enmity.

True, it is possible to leave history out of European identity formation, and it is possible to invoke it in an integrationary way. One notes, however, that this is not the way history is routinely invoked by the applicant countries. Among them the exclusionary mode known from the forging of national identities (but hardly definitional to that mode) as well as from before the advent of nationalism in the late eighteenth century clearly dominates. This may be because each and every applicant state is severally caught up in a logic of identity formation dominated by the historical experience and continued force of nationalism. It may, however, also be because the discourse on European identity at large is in some respects formatted as a nationalist discourse. One must ask whether there exist empirical sequences that may sustain such a claim.

I would argue that such sequences not only exist but that some of them may be seen to be institutionalized by the European Commission itself. I have in mind, first, the work of the Adoninno Committee, active in the early 1980s, which busied itself with the question of European identity. In order to inculcate such a common identity, the committee suggested and had approved an EU hymn, an EU flag, and an EU day.

It also recommended that the EU field European sports teams and so on.[34] It hardly demands much effort to spot the fount of these ideas. We have here distinct attempts to project onto the EU practices that are deemed to have "worked" as vessels of national identities. It would hardly be tendentious to describe such a practice as supranationalist (where *supra* refers first and foremost to scale). Arendt's worrying can hardly be said to have been misplaced; if doubts can be raised about whether the United States is now the main other of European identity formation, the point stands that a nationalist-style, exclusionary mode of talking about European identity formation is very much part of contemporary discourse. It may be, therefore, that one reason applicant members avail themselves of an exclusionary rhetoric is that it sits well with a certain exclusionary strand of overall European discourse.

I want to be very explicit on this point. One phenomenon that has been amply demonstrated since the late 1980s is how the prospect of being recognized first as European and then as a member of the EU has contributed to changing overall political discourse in applicant countries. For two shorthand examples, I refer to the Polish debate on civic-military relations and the Estonian debate on minority policy. In Poland the prestige of the military has traditionally been high. This probably has to do with factors such as the importance of the warfaring *szlachta* (aristocratic class) as a nation-bearing element in the nineteenth century and the role of Józef Piłsudski in the interwar period. From the early 1990s when President Lech Wałesa's political base crumbled, it was therefore not surprising to see him look to the military for support (that this happened despite Solidarity's experiences with the imposition of martial law only adds to the strength of this argument). One of Wałesa's lines was to play down the need for clear-cut civil control with the military. When the opposition was nevertheless rather efficient in fighting this strategy, it was partly because they could refer to the existence of a European "standard" where civil-military relations were concerned and the need for Poland to adhere to that standard in order to be treated as eligible for admission by the EU and also NATO. Thus, Polish internalizations of what represented European "standards" played a role, perhaps a decisive one, in defeating a ploy that had the strength of growing out of national traditions.

In Estonia discourse about Russians in the late 1980s and early 1990s had a heavily racist strand. One theme typical of a number of racist discourses was that of biological contamination. Estonians at home and abroad would remark about how Russian women had been raped by Mongols and Tatars for centuries and so were "contaminated" by an "Asiatic gene pool." At present this thinking has not necessarily disappeared, but it has at least been forced further underground. How did this happen? One major reason was the existence of a European standard of discourse where such views were deemed impermissible. The cultural hegemony of a European standard against racist discourse worked in the direction of changing this particular element of Estonian life. As witnessed by the case of Estonian citizenship laws, this is not to say that Estonia is entirely adhering to the European standard for minority policy as it is held up by the EU, the Organization for Security and Cooperation in Europe (OSCE), and others. The point, however, is that the political discourse of one applicant state was partly changed. A further point may be that by not fully complying with the European standard in question, Estonia has weakened its chances of integration into the EU.[35]

Thus, an EU hegemony does exist, and it has at least to my mind demonstrably changed discourse in applicant states. When it has not changed the proclivity to refer to history as a reservoir of a common European identity, it may be because this notion is part of overall EU and European political discourse. And, I would argue, it is a part that is lodged deeply in the discursive structure of European identity formation. Where Turkey's membership application is concerned, it is apposite to recall that when the epithet of *Europe* cropped up in the second half of the 1400s (related epithets having already made a cameo appearance at the time of Charlemagne), it was specifically within the context of the Turkish threat in the East. For example, Juan Luis Vives (1492–1540), a major humanist, "saw the struggle against the Turks in the context of the classical distinction between Europe and Asia."[36] Elsewhere I have tried to demonstrate how exclusion of "the Turk" has been used as an integrating strategy for Europe.[37] Representations of "the Turks" have changed radically, so the point here is not that Turkey possesses some kind of essence as Europe's other. It is rather that the diacriticon of religion has been invoked so many times and in so many guises that it cannot fail to color the question of how the EU handles the Turkish membership application.

Associations that come with the name *Turkey* directly concern only two applicant states, Turkey and Cyprus. Leaving aside Malta, all the other cases are colored by another historical sequence of exclusion from Europe, that which concerns Russia.[38] It is not merely that Russians "have traditionally been perceived as non-European," a generalization some other scholars have put forth.[39] The case of Russia is not a case of simple leaving out. No matter which social practices a period has foregrounded, whether religious, bodily, intellectual, social, military, political, economic, or otherwise, Russia has consistently been seen as an irregularity. The point may be taken too far. Identity is a fluid, many-stranded, and perpetually negotiated phenomenon, and so all identities are ipso facto ambiguous. Russia has, furthermore, not been alone in being constructed as an ambiguous presence on Europe's border; before the advent of the Napoleonic Wars, this was the lot of all human collectives inhabiting territories stretching from the Baltic to the Black Seas, including some that are now invoked by "Central European" states as their forerunners. And yet Russia stands out for its 500-year history of always just having been tamed, civil, civilized; just having begun to participate in European politics; just having become part of Europe. Since the Enlightenment it has, furthermore, been seen as a pupil and a learner, be that a successful one (the authorized version of the Enlightenment and the present), a misguided one (the alternative version of the Enlightenment), a laggard who should learn but refuses to do so (the authorized version of the nineteenth century), a truant (the twentieth-century view). It is therefore deeply appropriate that since the early 1990s the main metaphor used in European discussions of Russian politics and economics has been that of transition. The dimension of European identity formation in which Russia stands out is not first and foremost the spatial one. The question often asked—Is Russia located inside or outside of Europe?—has usually been answered in the affirmative. To the extent that it has not, it is an easy exercise to establish examples of how countries such as Germany and Spain have also been constructed to be spatially outside Europe; one French saying has it that Africa begins at the Pyrenees. Russia's specificity as Europe's other does thus not reside along the spatial but within the temporal dimension, as the country perpetually seen as being in some stage of transition to Europeanization. When Russia was until recently discussed as not yet ready for membership in the Council of Europe, this construction could be offered in terms of specific contemporary practices in the area of human rights or elsewhere. Its effectiveness in present discourse was, however, reinforced by the rich baggage of the "not yets" and "justs" of half a millennium.

Once asked about the patronage of the EEC, Belgian statesman Paul-Henri Spaak answered that Stalin was its father, inasmuch as fear of the Soviet Union had provided the impetus to hang together rather than hang separately. To wheel out another and perhaps overused quote, the first secretary-general of NATO, Lord Ismay, held that the job of NATO was to keep the Americans in, the Russians out, and the Germans down. Regardless of degree of institutionalization, then, the construction of Europe is tied to the idea of the Russian other. Since exclusion is a necessary ingredient of integration, this is in itself no problem. The temptation remains, however, to play up the alterity of Russia in order to increase the integration of the European self. This is a factor in a number of contemporary debates that have to do with the expansion of the EU and NATO, trade policy, arms control, and the like. Since these issues are tied up with half a millennium's worth of construction of Russia as barbarian, Asiatic, and so on, they seem to call for rather more sensitivity to the question of how the construction of Russia enters into them than what seems to have been shown so far. It lies close to hand to see Russia as a learner, as half Asiatic, as having despotic political institutions, as riding roughshod over its Muslim minorities. Indeed, as shown in the case of the discourse on a "Central Europe," this kind of exclusion of Russia is at the heart of some of the pleas for further integration by the frontrunners among the applicant states. It is tempting, then, for the EU to avail itself of exclusionary rhetoric against Russia in particular because by playing the exclusion/integration nexus this way, it may ease the inclusion of Central European states by stressing the exclusion of Russia. Indeed, this temptation may be represented as part of a wider temptation, whereby the EU would try to boost its legitimacy and its ostensible security of self by copying the experience of European nation-states and try to forge a fully fledged ethnopolitical rhetoric. This is the EU's supranational temptation, whereby it would borrow from nationalism in order to strengthen one particular European identity by emphasizing the exclusion of the human collectives that have historically been its trusted others, Russia and Turkey being prominent among them.

Conclusion

The EU may choose to stress one particular European identity. There is in today's discourse on European identity one strand that emphasizes such a supranational identity as the one to be preferred, or indeed the only one possible. I would argue that identities are necessarily fluid and ever in need of reinscription, that there cannot be such a thing as a European identity in the singular but only a plurality of European identities that will clash and reconstruct one another in the process that is identity politics. This insistence in itself will, however, not keep other voices from trying to tie down and close off the question of European identity in order to make it a uniform concept that refers to a bright march toward a free market haven, a racially homogeneous collective, a discursive structure cleansed of power where bounded individuals realize a perfected democracy, or any other homogenized utopia.

I do not think we will see such a closing down of discourse in the name of some monolithic scheme partly because language itself rails against being totally homogenized, but also partly for the more mundane reason that the institutional structure of the EU seems to develop in what one may call an analog rather than a digital way. Throughout this chapter, I have stressed the ambiguity of the discourse on EU expansion. It should also be noted that the ambiguity of who is in and who is out is mirrored in institutional practices. With all and sundry accelerated schemes by certain member states (Benelux, Schengen), opt-outs by member states from certain policies and prospects (Great Britain, Denmark), overlapping memberships (the WEU, NATO), specific setups on questions political (the European agreements), specific setups on economics (the European Economic Area involving, incredibly, the EU and Iceland, Liechtenstein, and Norway), free trade agreements and promises to open up accession negotiations at certain points in time, the institutional setup is itself reflective of a graded situation. Each of Europe's states stands in some kind of relation to the EU, as core member, member, honorary economic member, almost member, or whatever. The prospect of imposing a supranational identity on this very graded and overlapping set of political entities would, to put it mildly, entail a lot of work. One may think of situations of crisis and war that would help such an undertaking, but it remains unlikely that Europe will succumb to the supranational temptation. That does not mean that the trade-off between exclusion and integration is not central to policymaking. It does mean, however, that a repetition of the attempted demarcation of boundaries between us and them in the digital and exclusionary manner of the nation-state era will probably not be repeated. Instead, discursive and institutional demarcation will tend to be analog, which at least to my mind is something to be celebrated.

Notes

An earlier version of this chapter was presented at the conference "Defining and Projecting Europe's Identity: Issues and Trade-Offs," Institut Universitaire de Hautes Etudes Internationales, Geneva, 21–22 March 1996. I thank Peter Bugge, Tor Bukkvoll, Thomas Hylland Eriksen, David Hogstad, Heikki Patomki, Irena Sumi, Tobias Theiler, Bjorn Thomassen, Maria Todorova, Rob Walker, and particularly Lars-Erik Cederman for their kind help.

1. Anthropologists used to boast that their totemic ancestor was actually interned on the Trobriands. This turns out not to have been so. Although Australian authorities first classified Malinowski as an enemy alien, colleagues intervened on his behalf, and he had his freedom of movement restored. See Jerry D. Moore, "Bronislaw Malinowski," in Jerry D. Moore, ed., *Visions of Culture: An Introduction to Anthropological Theory and Theorists* (Walnut Creek, Calif.: Altamira, 1997), 128–139.

2. Sharon MacDonald, "Identity Complexes in Western Europe: Social Anthropological Perspectives," in Sharon MacDonald, ed., *Inside European Identities* (Oxford: Berg, 1993), 1–26.

3. See Marc Abélès, *La Vie quotidienne au Parlement Européen* (Paris: Hachette, 1992); Marc Abélès and Henri-Pierre Jeudy, eds., *Anthropologie du politique* (Paris: Armand Colin, 1997). See also MacDonald, *Inside European Identities;* Thomas M. Wilson and Estellie M. Smith, eds., *Cultural Change and the New Europe: Perspectives on the European Community* (Boulder, Colo.: Westview, 1993); Victoria A. Goddard, Josep R. Llobera, and Cris Shore, "Introduction: The Anthropology of Europe," in Victoria A. Goddard, Josep R. Llobera, and Cris Shore, eds., *The Anthropology of Europe: Identities and Boundaries in Question* (Oxford: Berg, 1994), 1–40. A study of the European Commission by Maryon McDonald is rumored to be in the pipeline, as are monographs by Annabel Black and Cris Shore. For teasers, see Cris Shore, "Inventing the 'People's Europe': Critical Approaches to European Community 'Cultural Policy,'" *Man* 28, 4 (1993): 779–800; Cris Shore, "Governing Europe: European Union Audiovisual Policy and the Politics of Identity," in Cris Shore and Susan Wright, eds., *Anthropology of Policy: Critical Perspectives on Governance and Power* (London: Routledge, 1997), 165–192.

4. Stacia E. Zabusky, *Launching Europe* (Princeton: Princeton University Press, 1995); Stacia E. Zabusky, "Making Europe Over Lunch," manuscript delivered at the Convention of the European Community Studies Association, Chicago, 1994.

5. Cris Shore and Annabel Black, "Citizens' Europe and the Construction of European Identity," in Victoria A. Goddard, Josep R. Llobera, and Cris Shore, eds., *The Anthropology of Europe: Identities and Boundaries in Question* (Oxford: Berg, 1994), 288.

6. Hannah Arendt, "Dream and Nightmare. Europe and America," *Commonweal* 60, 2-3 (1958): 54.

7. Fredrik Barth, ed., *Ethnic Groups and Boundaries: The Social Organization of Culture Difference* (Boston: Little, Brown, 1969).

8. In all states there are also a substantial number of subjects who do not want the state to join/remain in the EU. One may also investigate this as an integration/exclusion nexus, where these groups fear social exclusion in a growing number of contexts should the state to which they are subject integrate further into the EU. Some of these groups may latch onto the 200-year-old idea that Europe is a project of nations in order to put a European spin on their argument. Giuseppe Mazzini's Young Italy movement had parallels not only in Poland and other nations bit also in the Young Europe movement. A European international of nationalists has existed and may yet appear in a new gestation.

9. That this application was hardly well conceived (among other things, addressed to Jacques Delors, chairman of the Council of Ministers) is of course relevant, inasmuch as it facilitated the ease with which it could be turned down.

10. David Spence, "Enlargement Without Accession: The EU's Response to German Unification." London, Royal Institute of International Affairs Discussion Paper 36, 1991.

11. Diana Forsythe, "German Identity and the Problem of History," in Elizabeth Tonkin, Maryon McDonald, and Malcolm Chapman, eds., *History and Ethnicity* (London: Routledge, 1989), 137–156.

12. This part of the chapter draws on Iver B. Neumann, "Russia as Central Europe's Constituting Other," *East European Politics and Society* 7, 2 (1993): 349–369.

13. Quoted in Ladislav Matejka, "Milan Kundera's Central Europe," *Cross Currents* 9 (1990): 131.

14. Milan Kundera, "The Tragedy of Central Europe," *New York Review of Books*, 26 April 1994, 33–38.

15. Ibid.

16. Jeno Szucz, "Three Historical Regions in Europe," in John Keane, ed., *Civil Society and the State* (London: Verso, 1988), 291–331.

17. Timothy Garton Ash, Michael Mertes, and Dominique Moïsi, "Let the East Europeans In!" *New York Review of Books*, 24 October 1991, 19.

18. Ibid.

19. Krzysztof Skubiszewski, "The Challenge to Western Policy of Change in Eastern Europe," paper presented at the Conference on Britain and the Future of Eastern Europe and the Former Soviet Union, All Souls College, Oxford, 10–12 April 1992.

20. Maria N. Todorova, *Imagining the Balkans* (New York: Oxford University Press, 1997), 160.

21. Václav Havel in *New York Times*, 17 October 1993, E17, quoted in ibid., 156.

22. Jørgen Staun, "Mitteleuropa—Centraleuropa—Mitteleuropa—Tysklands genkomst i midten af Europa," manuscript, Copenhagen, 1998.

23. Kohl, 13 March 1991, quoted in ibid., 37 (my translation).

24. Mikhail Gorbachev, *Perestroika: New Thinking for Our Country and the World* (London: Fontana, 1988), 190.

25. Henri Lefebvre, *The Production of Space* (Oxford: Blackwell, 1991).

26. Ladislav Holy, "Back to Europe: Czech National Tradition and European Values." Manuscript, Charles University, Prague, 1995.

27. Lene Hansen, "Slovenian Identity: State Building on the Balkan Border," *Alternatives* 21, 4 (1996): 473–495.

28. Maria Todorova, "The Balkans: From Discovery to Invention," *Slavic Review* 53 (1994): 453–482.

29. Two obvious points here: first, Bosnia may also be framed as a multi-ethnic state. Second, the use of religion as a diacriticon does not depend on the degree to which religion is practiced—already in 1983 Ernest Gellner remarked that being a Bosnian Muslim did not entail believing that there is no God but Allah, but rather that one had lost that faith. See Ernest Gellner, *Nations and Nationalism* (Ithaca: Cornell University Press, 1983).

30. Dmytro Pavlychko, "Evropa vidchula shcho vona bilsha nish zdavalosh," *Viche* 1 (November 1992).

31. Thomas Riha, *A Russian European: Paul Miliukov in Russian Politics* (Notre Dame, Ind.: University of Notre Dame Press, 1969).

32. "Dancing with the Wolves: Ciller Tells Europe That Now, It's Either Yes or No," *Time* 20 November 1995.

33. Jürgen Habermas, "Citizenship and National Identity: Some Reflections on the Future of Europe," *Praxis International* 12, 1 (1995): 1–15.

34. Kjersti Løken, "EFs strategi for å skape en europeisk identitet," *Internasjonal Politikk* 51, 3 (1993): 349–358.

35. The very mention of standards will call to the fore a number of reactions. What is at issue here is the EU's invocation of standards and the cultural hegemony that makes it able to wield it, not whether there exists a universalist standard per se or whether any one particular standard is good or bad. See Gerrit W. Gong, "The Standard of 'Civilisation,'" in Hedley Bull and Adam Watson, eds., *The Expansion of International Society* (Oxford: Oxford University Press, 1984).

36. Pim den Boer, "Europe to 1914: The Making of an Idea," in Kevin Wilson and Jan van der Dassen, eds., *The History of the Idea of Europe* (London: Routledge, 1993), 37.

37. Iver B. Neumann and Jennifer M. Welsh, "The Other in European Self-Definition: A Critical Addendum to the Literature on International Society," *Review of International Studies* 17, 4 (1991): 327–348.

38. See Iver B. Neumann, "Self and Other in International Relations," *European Journal of International Relations* 2, 2 (1996): 139–174.

39. Gerard Delanty, *Inventing Europe: Idea, Identity, Reality* (Houndsmills, UK: Macmillan, 1995), 11.

7

Liberal Identity and Postnationalist Inclusion: The Eastern Enlargement of the European Union

Frank Schimmelfennig

On 31 March 1998, the European Union opened bilateral intergovernmental conferences on the accession of five Central and Eastern European (CEE) countries: the Czech Republic, Estonia, Hungary, Poland, and Slovenia. At the same time, the EU promised the other five associated countries from this region (Bulgaria, Latvia, Lithuania, Romania, and Slovakia) that it would intensify preparation for their eventual membership and the start of concrete accession talks as soon as they would meet the prerequisites.

I start from the assumption that the analysis of Eastern enlargement is a suitable way to gain knowledge about the collective identity of (the members of) the European Union. After all, the issue of expanding the membership of any organization is strongly influenced by considerations such as "Who are we?" and "What do we stand for?" The answers to these questions will determine the answers to others: "Who belongs to us?" and "Who fits in our organization?" And they will also frame the trade-offs between exclusion and dilution that the organization faces.

I approach the question of enlargement from two different perspectives. In the interest-based "club perspective," identity does not play a role as an explanatory factor. International organizations are instrumental associations designed to maximize the welfare of their members. The trade-off they face is between the costs of congestion, administration, and decisionmaking caused by expansion and the opportunity costs of exclusion. Enlargement will take place only if the members reap net benefits from admitting a new country. I argue that the Eastern enlargement of the European Union is puzzling from this perspective because the expected costs of full membership for the CEE countries exceed the potential benefits of Eastern enlargement for the present EU members.

By contrast, in the "community perspective" identity is the crucial variable. An international organization is thought to represent an international community. The organization is designed to strengthen the community's collective identity and assert the common values on which it is based. Concerning the enlargement issue, the organization is confronted with a trade-off between the risk of diluting its collective identity and the possibility of disseminating its constitutive values and norms and expanding the community. Enlargement will take place when states outside the community reliably share the community values and adhere to its norms.

I argue that the European Union is best understood as the main organization of the European international community. This community is founded upon a "thin" postnationalist collective identity defined by liberal values and norms of domestic and international conduct. The conditions of accession declared by the EU as well as its actual Eastern enlargement policy corroborate the liberal community perspective: The five countries the EU invited to concrete accession talks are similar to EU member states and also distinguishable from other nonmember states when it comes to the internalization of basic liberal norms. The only fact this approach cannot explain is the exclusion of Lithuania from this first-rate group of CEE countries. Moreover, the results of the analysis contradict the assumption that the EU is founded on a "thick" pannationalist identity defined by Western Christian culture.

The Club Perspective on Eastern Enlargement: The Benefits of Exclusion

The interest-based approach to the issues of inclusion, exclusion, and their respective trade-offs is best captured by the theory of clubs. A club is defined as a voluntary group deriving mutual benefit from the sharing of a good characterized by excludable and partially divisible benefits.[1] This definition is held to suit most international organizations. In the case of the EU, the central public good is its internal market and the accompanying legal order. Other EU policies create divisible benefits, above all the Common Agricultural Policy and the regional policies that together account for about 80 percent of the budget and are mainly responsible for the gap between net contributors and net recipients among the member countries.

If an international organization provides divisible goods, membership becomes a problem because additional members are rival consumers. Enlargement can lead to congestion, that is, members cannot use the good as much or as often as they would like to because of other members. International organizations, then, expand only if the costs of increased congestion are matched by equivalent "cost reductions owing to the sharing of provision expense."[2] This applies to all members individually. That is, for a club-type international organization to expand, each member state must expect positive net benefits in order to approve of expansion.

The costs of increased congestion, however, are not the only costs to be balanced. An increase in the number of members also boosts the administrative and decisional costs of the organization. For instance, as the administrative workload of the secretariat and the need for office space grows, a demand for higher budgets is created. Communication and information exchange become more cumbersome because speeches and documents have to be translated into yet another language. More important still, "the addition of a new member will raise the costs of finding agreement in a more than proportional manner" because of greater heterogeneity in the membership.[3]

Thus, in the club perspective, the EU members calculate the trade-off between the costs of congestion, administration, and decisionmaking caused by the inclusion of new members and the opportunity costs caused by their exclusion. The EU decides to expand only if its members expect a net benefit from enlargement.[4]

The costs of decisionmaking and administration are expected to rise sharply in the case of Eastern enlargement. First, heterogeneity within the EU will strongly increase with the accession of CEE countries. The new members will bring with them a peculiar historical, political, economic, and social heritage and the problems of their region. They have a particularly low level of socioeconomic development, struggle with specific problems of transformation from a Communist society, and possess political traditions (long periods of authoritarianism, foreign domination, etc.) that distinguish them clearly from the current EU members.[5] Second, increased heterogeneity will raise the costs of decisionmaking and reduce the probability of consensus. Even (qualified) majorities are more difficult to build because the number of potential blocking coalitions rises disproportionally. The joint-decision trap will be even harder to evade; the opportunity costs of nondecisions will increase.[6] Third, administrative costs will explode because of the rising number of official languages that have to be interpreted (and translated into all other official languages). It is therefore widely agreed that EU organs and policymaking processes would have to be reformed

ahead of Eastern enlargement lest they lead to a breakdown of EU decisional capacities.[7] A reduction of EU commissioners, official languages,
and consensus requirements in European Council decisionmaking are
among the most prominent proposals for reform. Such reforms, however, create costs for the old members (in particular for those that
would see their number of commissioners and the status of their native
languages reduced).

In a club perspective, then, the marginal benefits accruing to the
EU members as a result of Eastern enlargement have to be considerably
higher than the marginal costs of crowding in the use of the shared
good. They would have to balance the disproportionally increasing costs
of decisionmaking and administration as well. Are there enlargement
benefits sizable enough to make the old EU members interested in the
accession of CEE countries?

Economists agree that trade integration with the CEE region will
benefit the EU economies in the aggregate. It opens a new market for
Western European exports in their close proximity. In addition, the supply of cheaper resources and cheaper but qualified labor as well as
economies of scale will reduce costs and strengthen European competitiveness on the world market.[8] But this positive outlook has to be qualified in several ways:

1. "Studies of the long-run output, employment, and welfare
   effects of increased CEE-EU trade in the EU commonly conclude that *the overall impact will remain relatively small.*"[9]
2. *The effects of trade integration will be positive in the aggregate but distributed unevenly* among sectors and countries. EU agriculture,
   textile, and leather as well as metalworking industries will be
   exposed to stiffer competition as a result of progressive market
   integration. EU member countries that specialize in such traditional and resource-intensive industries (like Spain, Portugal,
   Greece, and Italy) will face higher import pressures than others.[10] Moreover, Weise et al. expect political problems because
   the "burdens of adaptation are concentrated mostly on specific
   sectors in which actors are easy to mobilize politically. Profits,
   however, are spread more widely and [are], therefore, less trans-
   parent."[11] Those (mostly northern) countries that will benefit
   most from trade integration will in turn face migration pressures
   for which there is a high potential because of geographical proximity, high unemployment in the East, and high wage differen-
   tials.[12]
3. Most important, however, the *EU members are able to reap the fruit
   of trade integration without granting the CEE countries full member-*

ship.[13] Already under the association regime, the EU has realized a trade surplus with its Eastern neighbors year after year. Western corporations benefit from advantageous terms of trade. Direct investments in the region are growing. What is more, association allows the EU to protect the sectors in which it is particularly vulnerable to competition and to prevent migration more effectively than would be possible after enlargement.

This lack of incentives to include CEE countries as full members is emphasized by the budgetary costs that would follow from Eastern enlargement. In its March 1998 detailed planning for the "Agenda 2000," the European Commission estimated the direct costs of preparing the CEE candidates for EU membership at around ECU 80 billion (US$75 billion) until 2006, more than half of which will be spent for structural policies. Most important, it is obvious that all CEE countries would become structural net recipients. For the foreseeable future, EU transfers to these countries will outweigh by far their contributions to the EU budget. This mainly results from the effects of enlargement on the CAP and the EU's structural and regional policies.

According to Stefan Tangermann, the CAP would be seriously affected because the CEE associates produce only 3 percent of the EU's gross national product (GNP) yet possess 44 percent of the EU's productive land and attain 30 percent of the EU's agricultural production.[14] He expects that agricultural production will expand rather than diminish as a result of economic recovery and that participation in the CAP would give the CEE countries an additional incentive for agricultural production because EU prices in many areas of agriculture are well above world market prices. Furthermore, because of their low levels of wealth and income, the CEE countries would benefit enormously from the structural funds under current conditions. If these policies remained unchanged, the community budget would have to increase by one-third to two-thirds of its current volume depending on the scenario and the calculation.[15] There is a consensus in the academic literature as well as among policymakers that these costs are prohibitive and that a reform of the CAP and the structural policies is an indispensable precondition of enlargement. Any reform, however, will inevitably lead to income reductions for EU farmers as well as either lower transfers to the comparatively disadvantaged EU regions or a reduction of regions eligible for financial support. Three strategies of cost reduction are conceivable (but, as I argue, of limited effect):

1. The EU could *restrict its Eastern enlargement* to the five CEE countries with which it currently conducts accession talks. These

countries are certainly the most prosperous of the CEE region.[16] This group is still much below EU economic standards, however, and comprises some of the most potent agricultural producers of the region.

2. The EU could *accord partial membership* to the CEE countries in order to exclude their participation in the CAP and the structural policies. But this is only a theoretical option. It would be impossible to legitimate politically.[17] Further, it would meet serious practical obstacles. An (even temporary) exclusion of the new members' agriculture from the community, as it was practiced in the case of Southern enlargement, would be much more difficult to implement now because of the internal market. For instance, border controls for all exports from and imports to the Eastern members would have to remain in place.[18]

3. The EU could *postpone enlargement* significantly. The costs of CEE membership will probably diminish over the course of time: The CEE countries will be able to narrow the socioeconomic gap between themselves and the EU; they will approach the GNP levels of the poorer EU members; structural change may make them less agricultural than they are currently. Nevertheless, the CEE countries would still become an EU periphery and would not turn into net contributors to the community budget. Costs may be reduced over time, but they will stay high. Moreover, this strategy affects only the structural policies positively (provided that CEE growth rates continue to exceed EU growth rates). In the case of the CAP, an increase in CEE agricultural productivity would mean an increase in expenses instead.

So the basic question remains: Why should the EU enlarge to the east if enlargement is not necessary in order to reap (most) of the benefits of integration and if it entails potentially enormous decisionmaking and budgetary costs as well as economic problems that could be avoided under the association regime? The two main (stylized) rationalist answers to this question that can be found in some of the academic literature and much of the political rhetoric do not change the cost-benefit calculation of the expansion-dilution tradeoff:

1. *"Without the prospect of EU membership, the CEE countries would not open their markets to the West and thus deprive the EU of the benefits of trade integration."* This answer is unconvincing because of the systemic pressures for world market integration and the highly asymmetrical economic interdependence between the EU and the CEE region. By shield-

ing their economies from integration with the EU, the CEE countries would harm themselves more than the EU.

2. *"Without the prospect of EU membership, the CEE countries would become politically and economically unstable, threatening Western European security and welfare with illegal migration and organized crime."* This answer is not persuasive for three reasons. First, "self-inflicted chaos" is no credible bargaining strategy. It is in the self-interest of the CEE countries to develop stable political and economic systems. Some may not be able to do so. But then, second, countries that do not achieve internal stability on their own and export instability beyond their borders (like Albania or the former Yugoslavia) do not stand a chance to become EU members anyhow. And third, given its resources, why shouldn't the EU be able to defend itself successfully against the spillover of Eastern European instability?

In sum, the trade-offs emphasized by a club-theoretical analysis of Eastern enlargement clearly point toward the exclusion of Central and Eastern Europe from the European Union. It is highly plausible but not even necessary to argue that the expected costs of full membership for the CEE countries exceed the potential benefits of Eastern enlargement. That is because from the point of view of EU members, association constitutes an efficient institutional solution that enables the EU to benefit from the economic integration of EU and CEE markets without having to bear the costs of political integration.

The Community Perspective on Eastern Enlargement: The Commitment to Inclusion

In the community perspective, international organizations represent international communities. International communities are based on, for instance, ethnic ties, a common culture, or shared fundamental norms that shape the collective identity of its member states. The collective identity of the community determines the criteria for membership in the community organizations. A state that adopts the collective identity of the international community is regarded as "one of us" by the community members and is legitimately entitled to join the community organizations. In the community perspective, then, the issues of exclusion and inclusion are not determined by material costs and benefits and by considerations of efficiency, as is the case in the club perspective, but by the degree of mutual identification between the community members and the aspirants and by considerations of legitimacy.[19] Whereas the members of a club fear that expansion "dilutes" efficiency, the members of a community are worried that enlargement undermines their collective identity. I believe that the European Union is founded mainly upon a postnationalist, liberal identity. Consequently, the EU grants membership to those states that share its liberal values and adhere to its liberal norms.

The Liberal Identity of the European International Community

The European Union is the main organization of the European community of states. This European international community is part of a wider Euro-Atlantic or "Western" international community that transcends the geographical borders of Europe and spreads across the Atlantic to include the United States and Canada.[20] The Western international community is most fundamentally based on the liberal values and norms shared by its member states and societies. The belief in and adherence to liberal human rights, that is, individual freedoms, civil liberties, and political rights are at the center of the community's collective identity. Liberal human rights are the "constitutive values that define legitimate statehood and rightful state action" in the domestic as well as in the international realm.[21]

In the domestic realm, the liberal principles of social and political order—pluralism, the rule of law, democratic political participation and representation, as well as private property and a market-based economy—are derived from and justified by these liberal human rights. Only a state that bases its domestic system on these values and principles is regarded as fully legitimate by the Western international community.[22]

In the international realm, liberal values and norms are expressed in the institutions of peaceful conflict management and multilateralist collaboration. The "democratic peace," the fact that consolidated democratic states do not wage war against each other, has its roots in the domestic norms of liberal democratic states. These norms demand that political conflicts be managed and resolved without violence and on the basis of constitutional procedures. As these norms are constitutive for the political culture and collective identity of democratic societies, democratic states tend to externalize them. They want their international relations to be governed by the same norms of nonviolence and rule-based conflict management as their domestic politics. When democratic states deal with each other, they know that all actors are committed to these common values and norms. This knowledge enables them to develop mutual trust, dependable expectations of peaceful behavior.[23]

In time, liberal democracies develop "pluralistic security communities" in which states neither expect nor prepare for organized violence as a means to settle interstate disputes.[24]

The other basic international norm, multilateralism, is defined as a generic institutional form that "coordinates relations among three or more states on the basis of generalized principles of conduct: that is, principles which specify appropriate conduct for a class of actions, without regard to the particularistic interests of the parties or the strategic exigencies that may exist in any specific occurrence."[25]

These "generalized organizing principles logically entail an *indivisibility* among the members of a collectivity with respect to the range of behavior in question" and generate "expectations of 'diffuse reciprocity.'"[26] They correspond to the basic liberal idea of procedural justice, that is, "the legislative codification of formal, reciprocally binding social rules" among the members of society.[27]

The process of *European integration* has produced a particularly highly developed network of multilateralist institutions based on liberal values. The liberal community values have been declared most authoritatively and clearly in Article F of the Treaty on European Union (TEU) as amended by the Treaty of Amsterdam: "The Union is founded on the principles of liberty, democracy, respect for human rights and fundamental freedoms, and the rule of law, principles which are common to the Member States."

The member states regard the TEU as "a new stage in the process of creating an ever closer union among the peoples of Europe" (Article A). Since the foundation of the European Coal and Steel Community in 1951, European integration was meant to create and stabilize a security community that would replace the traditional rivalries and bloody contests among the European powers (cf. the preamble of the ECSC treaty). In its course, community members have not only established a stable democratic peace among them but also a unique "supranational" legal order. The density and strength of the generalized rules governing the relations among the EU members is unparalleled by other multilateral organizations. European law takes direct effect and possesses supremacy with regard to national law. It is enforced by an independent international court, the European Court of Justice, whose decisions are binding upon the member governments.

Thus, in the community perspective, the international relations of Europe have been thoroughly transformed in the process of European integration—not by the intentional erection or the gradual emergence of a European superstate, as the early federalists and neofunctionalists had envisaged, but rather by the "Europeanization of state identities."[28] Katzenstein thus writes:

Respect for human rights, peaceful democracy, an economy based on private property and supported by a generous welfare state, and close connections with neighboring states and NATO as well as other European security organizations define what it means to be a "modern" European state. As institutionalized practices, these norms are so much taken for granted in northern and western Europe that they pass largely unnoticed.[29]

The liberal collective identity of the European international community belongs to the class of postnationalist identities (see Chapter 1 of this volume). Liberal identity is universalistic. Liberal democrats claim that their values and norms are universally applicable and the only legitimate principles of political order and conduct. The liberal community seeks to expand its membership by disseminating its values and norms and by convincing other individuals and societies of their legitimacy. Accordingly, liberal identity is acquirable and changeable. Neither adherence to liberal values and norms nor their rejection is regarded as a "natural" or "immutable" characteristic of a state. The liberal identity is based on values and norms that can be taught and learned, adopted and rejected.

In both respects the liberal community differs from international communities with particularistic identities based on quasi-natural or organic traits such as race (as, for instance, in the national socialist idea of a European order) and culture or religion (as, for instance, in Huntington's "clash of civilizations"). In other words, the liberal identity is not a pannationalist identity. Its cultural content is limited to *political* culture.

At the same time, the liberal collective identity is sufficiently thin to be compatible with various ethnic or cultural identities, a pluralistic authority structure, and different varieties of democratic political systems and market economies. Identification with the European international community does not imply the supersession of nation-states, national identities, or national political traditions. Article F of the TEU as amended by the Treaty of Amsterdam states explicitly: "The Union shall respect the national identities of its Member States."

There is, however, one obvious limit to the universalism and openness of the European international community: the geographical content of European identity. Although the geographical borders of Europe are neither objectively defined (particularly in the East) nor congruent with political borders (most obviously in the cases of Turkey and the Russian Federation), it is clear that a state without European territory (in the widest geographical sense) is not entitled to join the European Union even if it shares the EU's values and norms completely.

What, then, are the exclusion-dilution trade-offs for the European Union as the main organization of the European liberal international community? On the one hand, a restrictive enlargement policy strengthens the collective identity of the EU members by minimizing the risks of diluting the existing community of values and norms. Each round of enlargement has led to the accession of European states that were either skeptical about the creation of an "ever closer union" (like Britain, Denmark, and Sweden) or had not been stable liberal democracies in the past (like Greece, Spain, and Portugal).

On the other hand, a restrictive enlargement policy weakens the collective identity of the EU members by undermining its universalist, liberal mission and its claim to unite the peoples of Europe. Enlargement not only widens the scope of multilateral cooperation and legal integration in Europe, but in former authoritarian countries the prospect of EU membership also helps to speed up and stabilize liberal democratic transformation and to promote the peaceful and norm-based management of domestic and international conflicts.

In the community perspective, the EU is thus faced with the double requirement to put off enlargement until it can be sure that the aspirants reliably share and adhere to the liberal community values and norms *and* to intensively prepare for enlargement in order to support the consolidation of liberal democracy as well as multilateralism and peace in Europe.

Liberal Identity and Eastern Enlargement

Two expectations concerning enlargement follow from the assumption that the members of the European Union possess a postnationalist, liberal collective identity:

1. The conditions of accession set up by the European Union correspond to the liberal values and norms of the European international community.
2. The countries selected for accession talks both match the EU members and distinguish themselves from other nonmembers with regard to their adherence to the liberal community values and norms. European states are excluded from membership only if they do not meet the liberal community standards.

Conversely, neither pannationalist criteria nor considerations of efficiency are expected to determine the enlargement decisions of the European Union. The conditions of accession set up by the EU indeed closely correspond to the liberal values and norms. Whereas the original Article 237 of the EEC treaty accorded all European states the right to apply for membership, subsequent EU declarations and legal acts as well as EU practice have established several more precise prerequisites for a successful application.[30]

First, the EU requires its new members to be democracies that respect the rule of law and human rights (preambles to the Single European Act [SEA] and the TEU, Articles F and O of the TEU). Second, new members must conform to the community principle of an open-market economy with free competition (Article 3a of the EC treaty). But this principle offers members a great deal of leeway with regard to the degree of state involvement and intervention in the economy and does not specify any necessary levels of economic development or capacities. Finally, new members must accept the entire *acquis communautaire*, that is, the entire body of EU law, as well as the *acquis politique* (mainly from the Common Foreign and Security Policy).[31]

These general prerequisites have been reaffirmed with regard to Eastern enlargement. The European Council in Copenhagen explicitly established the accession of CEE states as an EU objective in June 1993, provided that they have achieved "stability of institutions guaranteeing democracy, the rule of law, human rights and respect for and protection of minorities" and "the existence of a functioning market economy" as well as the ability to adopt the *acquis*. They must accept the aims of political, economic, and monetary union as stated in the TEU (but they do not have to meet the criteria of economic convergence required for joining the monetary union).

Yet the conclusions of the European Council in Copenhagen also contain provisions concerning the capacities of both the EU and the CEE associated countries: While the candidates are required to have the capacity to cope with competitive pressure within the EU, the EU must have achieved the capacity to absorb new members without endangering the momentum of European integration.[32] Such conditions appear rather out of place in a community perspective that emphasizes identification and legitimacy. There is some evidence, however, that the capacity-oriented conditions are less important than the institutional conditions.

As to the capacity of the EU, the 1996-1997 intergovernmental conference was supposed to introduce the necessary internal reforms in order to prepare the EU for Eastern enlargement. Obviously, most issues were left undecided. This might have been a good opportunity to postpone the launch of formal accession talks. Instead, the bilateral conferences began as planned. Rather than being made dependent upon progress in institutional and policy reforms, the enlargement timetable itself increases reform pressure.

As to the capacity of the CEE candidates, the European Commission, in its 1997 "Opinions" on the CEE candidates, evaluated their ability "to cope with competitive pressure and market forces within the Union," their "capacity to take on the obligations of membership," and their "administrative and legal capacity" in the medium term, whereas the institutional criteria (democracy, human and minority rights, functioning market economy) were assessed in their present condition.

Although criteria of efficiency figure explicitly in the list of conditions of accession, pannationalist criteria such as a Christian culture or, still more restrictively, an affiliation with Western Christianity are not even mentioned in the relevant documents. It may be, however, that the selection of new members does not follow the explicitly stated conditions of membership. Table 7.1 therefore assembles some relevant data in order to evaluate the expectation that the five countries selected for concrete accession talks (the Czech Republic, Estonia, Hungary, Poland, and Slovenia) both match the EU members and distinguish themselves from the other CEE countries with regard to their adherence to the liberal community values and norms.

The CEE countries' progress in liberal transformation is regularly evaluated and compared by Freedom House, a nongovernmental organization (NGO), and the European Bank for Reconstruction and Development (EBRD). Table 7.1 lists the 1997 ratings by both organizations. These data represent by and large the situation in the CEE countries at the time when the European Commission prepared its opinions on the candidates' suitability for membership. The first group of Freedom House indicators focuses on the political or human rights norms of liberalism; the second group assesses the overall institutionalization of liberal democracy and market economy in the CEE countries. By contrast, the EBRD indicators evaluate only economic transformation and are more technical in character. "Progress in transition" according to the EBRD does not exclude authoritarian political structures. Therefore the EBRD data are used primarily to assess to what extent capacity-oriented economic and technical criteria influence the selection of members.

To a very large degree, the data confirm the community perspective on Eastern enlargement and the expectation that the selection of new members is determined by the liberal collective identity of the EU members. They do not, however, sufficiently explain the exact choice of CEE countries for the first round of enlargement.

With the exception of Slovakia. all associated countries are categorized as "free," whereas all other CEE countries were rated "partly free" or "not free."[33] Since all "free" CEE countries are associated with the EU, a political system in which political human rights and civil liberties

Table 7.1 The Political and Economic Transformation of CEE Countries

Status	Country	Political Rights[a]	Civil Liberties	Freedom[b]	Time[c]	Democracy[d]	Economy	Classification	EBRD Score[e]
EU accession talks	Czech Republic	1	2	Free	7/4	1.38	1.88	Consolidated democracy	3.5
	Estonia	1	2	Free	4/1	2.06	2.13	Consolidated democracy	3.4
	Hungary	1	2	Free	7/4	1.44	1.63	Consolidated democracy	3.6
	Poland	1	2	Free	7/2	1.44	2.00	Consolidated democracy	3.4
	Slovenia	1	2	Free	6/4	1.88	2.38	Consolidated democracy	3.2
EU association	Bulgaria	2	3	Free	6	3.81	5.38	Transitional	2.8
	Latvia	2	2	Free	3	2.06	2.50	Consolidated democracy	3.1
	Lithuania	1	2	Free	6/2	2.06	2.50	Consolidated democracy	3.0
	Romania	2	3	Free	1	3.88	4.63	Transitional	2.7
	Slovakia	2	4	Partly Free	–	3.81	3.38	Transitional	3.3
No association	Albania	4	4	Partly free	·	4.50	4.00	Transitional	2.6
	Belarus	6	6	Not free	–	5.88	6.00	Consolidated autocracy	1.6
	Bosnia- Herzegovina	5	5	Partly free	–	–	–	–	–
	Croatia	4	4	Partly free	–	4.25	3.88	Transitional	3.0
	Macedonia	4	3	Partly free	–	3.88	4.50	Transitional	2.6
	Moldova	3	4	Partly free	–	3.81	4.00	Transitional	2.6
	Russia	3	4	Partly free	–	3.75	3.50	Transitional	3.0
	Ukraine	3	4	Partly free	–	3.88	4.25	Transitional	2.4
	Yugoslavia	6	6	Not free	–	–	–	–	–

Sources: Based on "freedom in the world" ratings by Freedom House, as reported in Adrian Karatnycky, Alexander Motyl, and Boris Shor, eds., *Nations in Transit 1997: Civil Society, Democracy and Markets in East Central Europe and the Newly Independent States* (New Brunswick, N.J.: Transaction, 1997) and European Bank for Reconstruction and Development, *Transition Report 1997: Enterprise Performance and Growth* (London: EBRD, 1997).

Notes: a. Ratings are from 1 (best) to 7.

b. The freedom rating is a combined measure of political rights and civil liberties.

c. The first figure is the number of continuous years the country has been rated "free"; the second figure indicates the number of years the country has had a score of 1 for political rights and a 2 for civil liberties.

d. The democracy rating is composed of ratings for political process, civil society, independent media, rule of law, and government and public administration. Again, ratings are from 1 to 7.

e. This score is the average of eight ratings of progress in transition concerning enterprises (mainly privatization), markets and trade, and financial institutions. The best rating is 4.3, indicating "standards and performance typical of advanced industrial economies."

are basically guaranteed appears to be a sufficient (although not entirely necessary) condition of association with the EU.[34]

It is beyond question, according to these data, that the Czech Republic, Hungary, and Poland had to be among the first countries to be admitted to accession talks. For each group of indicators, they score better than the rest of the CEE countries. First, the Czech Republic, Hungary, and Poland have been rated "free" since the breakdown of Communist rule, and their scores have improved since then. This indicates that liberal norms and values have become rooted in these countries for a longer time than is the case elsewhere. Second, their democracy and economy indices rank highest. Finally, their scores for political rights and civil liberties match those of the current EU members.[35]

Moreover, none of the three Central European countries has been engaged in major territorial and ethnic conflict with its neighbors or major domestic ethnic conflict. All of them have shown the willingness and capability to manage whatever conflicts there were by peaceful means and in accordance with Western norms. Poland granted minority rights to its German-speaking population and made no claims to Lithuanian, Belarusian, and Ukrainian territory that had belonged to its prewar area.[36] The Czech Republic used no force or pressure against Slovak separatism but agreed to a peaceful dissolution of Czechoslovakia. The Hungarian government has stayed away from irredentism despite sizable Hungarian minorities abroad. In the face of considerable domestic opposition and repressive policies against the Hungarian minority in Slovakia and Romania, it has actively and successfully pursued the conclusion of basic treaties with both neighboring countries.

Beyond this group of three, the evidence does not fit the expectations as neatly. To be sure, the invitation of Estonia and Slovenia to the first round of accession talks is perfectly compatible with the assumed postnationalist, liberal selection criteria. Both countries are "free" and "consolidated democracies and market economies" with the same ratings for political rights and civil liberties as the Czech Republic, Hungary, Poland, and the typical EU member. In the liberal community perspective, it cannot be explained, however, why Lithuania was not invited to accession talks together with Estonia and Slovenia (or why Estonia was not excluded from the group of first-rate associates together with Latvia and Lithuania). Lithuania has not only received the same Freedom House ratings as the first-rate candidates but has also received them for a longer time than Estonia. It has been rated "free" as long as Slovenia, and 1 and 2 for political rights and civil liberties as long as Poland. Moreover, its democracy and economy ratings match those of Estonia.

A cross-check based on the economic and technical EBRD indicators of transition supports the general findings. Whereas political transition based on the liberal norms of human rights and democracy usually goes hand in hand with economic transition to a liberal market economy, there are three obvious exceptions: According to the EBRD rating, Slovakia (3.3) should be among the first-rate candidates for accession to the EU, and Croatia and Russia (3.0) should be among the countries associated with the EU. Neither is the case. As suggested by the data, the cause for this discrepancy is their human rights record, which is below the standards of their economic peer group. This finding corroborates the expectation that the adherence to domestic liberal values and norms is a sine qua non for membership and cannot be balanced by purely economic adaptation.

The European Union's own evaluation can be found in the opinions that the European Commission prepared for each of the candidate countries in 1997 (see Table 7.2). Generally, assessments by the expanding organization itself should be treated with caution, as they might be used to rationalize ex post a selection of new members that was based on criteria other than those publicly stated. But this problem should not be overstated. First, one can cross-check the Commission ratings for the political criteria with the independent Freedom House figures. Second, one can test whether the Commission justifies its selection consistently and with regard to the community norms. In particular, it will be interesting to see how the Commission weights the institutional criteria (liberal political and economic order) in comparison with the more functional criteria (the ability to cope with competitive pressure and the implementation of the *acquis*).

The Commission's evaluation of the political criteria is very similar to the Freedom House data. Indeed, in preparing its opinions and reports on the candidate countries, the European Commission draws on NGO information. All countries that Freedom House rates 1 for political rights and 2 for civil liberties are regarded as fulfilling the basic political criteria for membership. This also holds for Lithuania, and even Latvia scores as well as Estonia. By contrast, Bulgaria and Romania are seen as lagging behind in the institutionalization of a liberal political system, and Slovakia is judged to fail on the political score. Although Slovakia fulfills the economic criteria to a very large extent and has transposed and implemented the *acquis* no less than the Czech Republic, Hungary, and Poland, this failure was sufficient for Slovakia to be dismissed as a first-rate candidate.

According to the Commission, all countries of the top group have institutionalized a functioning market economy (the first economic criterion). The Commission considered Estonia not fully able to cope with the competitive pressure of the internal market in the medium term (the second economic criterion) but still put the country in the top

Table 7.2   The European Commission's "Opinions" on the Associated CEE Countries

Status	Country	Political Criteria	Economic Criteria[a]	Acquis[b]
Accession talks	Czech Republic	Yes	Yes	Yes
	Estonia	Yes but accelerate naturalization	Yes but not yet fully able to cope	Considerable progress
	Hungary	Yes	Yes	Yes
	Poland	Yes	Yes	Yes
	Slovenia	Yes	Yes	"Has to make considerable efforts"
Association	Bulgaria	"On its way"	Limited progress/ unable to cope	No
	Latvia	Yes but accelerate naturalization	Considerable progress/ serious difficulties in coping	Some progress
	Lithuania	Yes	Considerable progress/ serious difficulties in coping	Some progress
	Romania	"On its way"	Considerable progress/ serious difficulties in coping	No
	Slovakia	No	Yes but lacking transparency in implementation	Yes

Sources: Based on "Agenda 2000—Summary and Conclusions of the Opinions of Commission Concerning the Applications for Membership to the European Union Presented by the Candidate Countries" (DOC/97/8) as well as "Agenda 2000—Volume I—Communication: For a Stronger and Wider Union" (DOC/97/6). Available at http://europa.eu.int/comm/enlargement/agenda2000/strong/21.htm.

Notes: a. Economic criteria are a functioning market economy and the "ability to cope with competitive pressure in the medium term."

b. *Acquis* refers to the capacity to transpose and implement the *acquis communautaire* in the medium term.

group. This may indicate that in accordance with the logic of appropriateness the institutional criterion trumps the technical criterion. The economies of the countries on the waiting list (other than Slovakia) are found wanting on both accounts. The lack of a functioning market economy and "serious difficulties" of coping with the pressures of the internal market in Latvia and Lithuania seem to have been the main reasons why Estonia was preferred to its Baltic neighbors despite their political aptitude. Moreover, it is obvious that the capacity to transpose and implement the *acquis,* another technical criterion, was of little importance for the selection of formal negotiation partners. Although Slovenia's score on this point fell short of all associated countries except Bulgaria and Romania, it was admitted to the top group because of its good political and economic record.

Finally, there are no indications that the EU treats the CEE countries according to pannationalist criteria of "civilization identity," as Huntington suggests. His proposition that the "European Community rests on the shared foundation of European culture and Western Christianity" does not provide a valid explanation for the EU's enlargement decisions.[37] One might argue, of course, that all first-rate candidates share the Western Christian cultural foundation. Some countries, however, that do not fulfill the necessary liberal accession criteria are not admitted to accession talks even if they do belong to the Western Christian civilization.[38] Furthermore, Bulgaria and Romania are associated with the EU despite their Eastern Christian (or Orthodox) civilization identity. They do not belong to the first-rate candidates because their liberal democratic systems are not yet sufficiently consolidated, not because their culture is Eastern Christian. If one looks beyond the CEE region, the weakness of the pannationalist perspective becomes even more obvious: Orthodox Greece is an EU member, and Cyprus has been invited to accession talks together with the first-rate CEE countries. Finally, it is perfectly justifiable from a liberal community viewpoint that the EU treats Turkey differently from the CEE "pre-ins": Turkey's human rights record ("partly free"; 4 for political rights, 5 for civil liberties) is far worse than that of the associated CEE countries (and also worse than that of most nonassociated CEE countries).

Beyond Eastern Enlargement

Except for the different treatment of Estonia and Lithuania (for largely economic reasons), the process of Eastern enlargement conforms to the expectations derived from a community perspective on the European Union. The analysis strongly suggests that the spread and the firm establishment of liberal values and norms (within Europe) determine the membership and the territorial scale of the European Union. It leads to the conclusion that the European Union is indeed founded upon a postnationalist, liberal collective identity. This identity determines the EU's decisions concerning inclusion and exclusion as well as the trade-off between expansion and dilution it faces. Neither the club-theoretical perspective on the enlargement of international organizations nor the assumption of a pannationalist identity based on Western

Christian culture offers a viable alternative explanation of Eastern enlargement. The empirical scope of this study is limited, though. I therefore offer some initial reflections on whether this chapter's results are also valid for earlier rounds of EU enlargement.

The case that appears to be most similar to Eastern enlargement is the enlargement of the European Community to southern Europe in the first half of the 1980s. Like the CEE countries, Greece, Portugal, and Spain had transformed themselves from authoritarian to liberal democratic systems but could not be expected to increase the net welfare of the EC-9. Furthermore, as mentioned above, the membership of Greece clearly disconfirms the hypothesis of a Western Christian pan-nationalist collective identity.

At first sight, however, the community perspective appears to be less relevant in the two rounds of Northern enlargement in the early 1970s and the early 1990s. After all, the "northern" countries had long been liberal democratic states before they entered into accession talks with the community and became members. Moreover, some of these countries, most notably Norway and Switzerland, have still not joined the EU.

But these peculiarities do not necessarily contradict the account of Eastern enlargement presented here. The EU has always been open in principle to the accession of the "northern" democratic states.[39] On the basis of their liberal identity, the EU has regarded these countries as legitimate members of the European international community and has understood as part of its "mission" to unite the entire community under its organizational umbrella. Yet the trade-off between dilution and exclusion was not absent from northern enlargements. Although there was no risk that the domestic liberal values and norms would be compromised by the northern members, their commitment to the "deepening" of multilateralist cooperation and legal integration could not be taken for granted. Nevertheless, the community was ready to admit countries like Britain, Denmark, Norway, and Sweden, whose skepticism toward far-reaching integration was obvious. (They were required to adopt the *acquis,* of course.) This appears to be another indication of the EU's strong commitment to the inclusion of the entire European liberal community. In general, the cases of belated or failed accession have to be attributed to the lack of interest or the lack of popular consensus in the nonmember states, not to a lack of willingness on the part of the EU.

Notes

1. This definition is an abbreviated version of one in Richard Cornes and Todd Sandler, *The Theory of Externalities, Public Goods, and Club Goods* (Cambridge: Cambridge University Press, 1986), 24f. Clubs are "voluntary in

the sense that members would not join (or remain in the club) unless a net gain resulted from membership"; Todd Sandler and John T. Tschirhart, "The Economic Theory of Clubs: An Evaluative Survey," *Journal of Economic Literature* 18 (1980): 1491. A good is *in*divisible "when a *unit* of the good can be consumed by one individual without detracting . . . from the consumption opportunities still available to others from that *same* unit"; it is excludable if its benefits can be "withheld costlessly by the owner or provider"; Cornes and Sandler, *Theory of Externalities*, 6. The seminal article here is James M. Buchanan, "An Economic Theory of Clubs," *Economica* 32 (1965): 1–14.

2. Cornes and Sandler, *Theory of Externalities*, 159f.

3. Michele Fratianni and John Pattison, "The Economics of International Organizations," *Kyklos* 35 (1982): 252. See also Joseph S. Nye Jr., *Peace in Parts: Integration and Conflict in Regional Integration* (Boston: Little, Brown, 1971), 105f.); and Todd M. Sandler, William Loehr, and Jon T. Cauley, *The Political Economy of Public Goods and International Cooperation* (Denver: University of Denver, 1978), 69.

4. A precise club-theoretical analysis would require an assessment of the costs and benefits of each member state regarding each of the club goods. Here I limit the analysis to a collective and qualitative assessment of those costs and benefits that figure prominently in the enlargement debates. But I consider the results of this assessment sufficiently unambiguous to draw valid conclusions from them.

5. Cf. Michael Kreile, "Eine Erweiterungsstrategie für die Europäischen Union," in Werner Weidenfeld, ed., *Europa öffnen. Anforderungen an die Erweiterung* (Gütersloh, Germany: Verlag Bertelsmann Stiftung, 1997), 212f.

6. Fritz W. Scharpf, "Die Politikverflechtungs-Falle: Europäische Integration und deutscher Föderalismus im Vergleich," *Politische Vierteljahresschrift* 26, 4 (1985): 323–356; Claudia Wilming, *Institutionelle Konsequenzen einer Erweiterung der Europäischen Union. Eine ökonomische Analyse der Entscheidungsverfahren im Ministerrat* (Baden-Baden: Nomos, 1995).

7. Cf., e.g., Werner Weidenfeld and Christian Jung, "Osterweiterung und Handlungsfähigkeit der Europäischen Union: Zwang zur Reform," in Werner Weidenfeld, ed., *Europa öffnen. Anforderungen an die Erweiterung* (Gütersloh, Germany: Verlag Bertelsmann Stiftung, 1997), 11–23; Günther F. Schäfer, "Die institutionellen Herausforderungen einer EU-Osterweiterung," in Werner Weidenfeld, ed., *Europa öffnen. Anforderungen an die Erweiterung* (Gütersloh, Germany: Verlag Bertelsmann Stiftung, 1997), 31ff; Wilming, *Institutionelle Konsequenzen*, 198; Adrian Hyde-Price, *The International Politics of Eastern Europe* (Manchester: Manchester University Press, 1996), 203.

8. Jürgen von Hagen, "The Political Economy of Eastern Enlargement of the EU," in Lorand Ambrus-Lakatos and Mark E. Schaffer, eds., *Coming to Terms with Accession* (London: Center for Economic Policy Research, Institute for EastWest Studies, 1996), 6; Elzbieta Kawecka-Wyrzykowska, "On the Benefits of the Accession for Western and Eastern Europe," in Lorand Ambrus-Lakatos and Mark E. Schaffer, eds., *Coming to Terms with Accession* (London: Center for Economic Policy Research, Institute for EastWest Studies, 1996), 88.

9. Von Hagen, "Political Economy," 6 (my emphasis).

10. Ibid.

11. Christian Weise, Herbert Brücker, Fritz Franzmeyer, Maria Lodahl, Uta Möbius, Siegfried Schultz, Dieter Schumacher, and Harold Trabold,

Ostmitteleuropa auf dem Weg in die EU—Transformation, Verflechtung, Reformbedarf (Berlin: Duncker & Humblot, 1997), 26 (my translation).

12. Ibid., 18.

13. Cf. Michael Dauderstädt and Barbara Lippert, *Differenzieren beim Integrieren. Zur Strategie einer abgestuften Osterweiterung* (Bonn: Friedrich-Ebert-Stiftung, 1995), 12.

14. Stefan Tangermann, "Osterweiterung der EU: Wird die Agrarpolitik zum Hindernis?" *Wirtschaftsdienst* 75 (1995): 485.

15. Cf. Richard E. Baldwin, *Towards an Integrated Europe* (London: Center for Economic Policy Research, 1994), 161–179; Adrian Hyde-Price, *The International Politics of Eastern Europe* (Manchester: Manchester University Press, 1996), 203; Weise et al., *Ostmitteleuropa*, 258.

16. This holds with the exception that Slovakia is more prosperous (in terms of gross domestic product, or GDP, per head in 1997) than Estonia and Poland. See *Frankfurter Allgemeine Zeitung*, 18 September 1998, 29, reporting Eurostat data.

17. Kreile, "Erweiterungsstrategie," 223ff; Tangermann, "Osterweiterung," 486.

18. Tangermann, "Osterweiterung," 486f.

19. For the juxtaposition of rationalist and sociological approaches to the analysis of organizations, see, e.g., Walter W. Powell and Paul J. DiMaggio, eds., *The New Institutionalism in Organizational Analysis* (Chicago: University of Chicago Press, 1991) and James G. March and Johan P. Olsen, *Rediscovering Institutions: The Organizational Basis of Politics* (New York: Free Press, 1989) on the general theory of organizations and Martha Finnemore, *National Interests in International Society* (Ithaca, N.Y.: Cornell University Press, 1996); Connie L. McNeely, *Constructing the Nation-State: International Organization and Prescriptive Action* (Westport, Conn.: Greenwood Press, 1995); and Steven Weber, "Origins of the European Bank for Reconstruction and Development," *International Organization* 48 (1994): 1–38, on the analysis of international organizations.

20. I use the term *European international community* rather than *European community* in order to clearly distinguish the community of values and norms from the formal organization, the European Community. The European international community has more organizations than the EU, e.g., the Council of Europe.

21. Christian Reus-Smit, "The Constitutional Structure of International Society and the Nature of Fundamental Institutions," *International Organization* 51, 4 (1997): 558.

22. As long as these principles are observed, domestic systems are allowed to vary, e.g., with regard to presidential v. parliamentary democracy, the amount of direct democratic elements, or the degree of state interventionism in the economy.

23. John M. Owen, "How Liberalism Produces Democratic Peace," in Michael E. Brown, Sean M. Lynn-Jones, and Steven E. Miller, eds., *Debating the Democratic Peace* (Cambridge, Mass.: MIT Press, 1996), 116–154; Bruce Russett, *Grasping the Democratic Peace: Principles for a Post–Cold War World*, 2nd ed. (Princeton: Princeton University Press, 1995), 31–32; Thomas Risse-Kappen, "Democratic Peace—Warlike Democracies? A Social Constructivist Interpretation of the Liberal Argument," *European Journal of International Relations* 1, 4 (1995): 491–517.

24. Karl W. Deutsch, *Political Community and the North Atlantic Area: International Organization in the Light of Historical Experience* (Princeton: Princeton

University Press, 1957); European Bank for Reconstruction and Development, ed., *Transition Report 1997: Enterprise Performance and Growth* (London: EBRD, 1997); Emanuel Adler and Michael N. Barnett, "Governing Anarchy: A Research Agenda for the Study of Security Communities," *Ethics and International Affairs* 10 (1996): 76; Emanuel Adler, "Imagined (Security) Communities: Cognitive Regions in International Relations," *Millennium* 26, 2 (1997): 263–267.

25. John Gerard Ruggie, "Multilateralism: The Anatomy of an Institution," in John Gerard Ruggie, ed., *Multilateralism Matters: The Theory and Praxis of an Institutional Form* (New York: Columbia University Press, 1993), 11.

26. Ibid.

27. Reus-Smit, "Constitutional Structure," 577.

28. Peter J. Katzenstein, "United Germany in an Integrating Europe," in Peter J. Katzenstein, ed., *Tamed Power: Germany in Europe* (Ithaca: Cornell University Press, 1997), 29–31.

29. Peter J. Katzenstein, "The Smaller European States, Germany and Europe," in Peter J. Katzenstein, ed., *Tamed Power: Germany in Europe* (Ithaca: Cornell University Press, 1997), 262.

30. Pascal Richter, *Die Erweiterung der Europäischen Union. Unter besonderer Berücksichtigung der Beitrittsbedingungen* (Baden-Baden: Nomos, 1997). Cf. also Anna Michalski and Helen Wallace, *The European Community and the Challenge of Enlargement*, 2nd ed. (London: Royal Institute of International Affairs, 1992), 33–36; John Redmond and Glenda G. Rosenthal, introduction to John Redmond and Glenda G. Rosenthal, eds., *The Expanding European Union: Past, Present, Future* (Boulder, Colo.: Lynne Rienner, 1998), 2f.

31. Many authors add that candidates must subscribe to the EU's *finalité politique* as a prerequisite of membership (cf., e.g., Michalski and Wallace, *European Community*, 8, 35; Redmond and Rosenthal, *The Expanding European Union*, 3; Gerd Tebbe, "Wunsch und Wirklichkeit: Das Problem der Osterweiterung," *Europa-Archiv* 49, 13–14 (1994): 389. But since the long-term objectives and the final destination of European integration are undefined and contested among the member states, this does not amount to more than a declaratory commitment to the "ever closer union" proclaimed in the treaties.

32. Cf. Ulrich Sedelmeier and Helen Wallace, "Policies Towards Central and Eastern Europe," in Helen Wallace and William Wallace, eds., *Policy-Making in the European Union*, 3rd ed. (Oxford: Oxford University Press, 1996), 374.

33. Slovakia was rated "free" in 1994–1995 and 1995–1996 but downgraded in 1996–1997.

34. Neither Romania nor Slovakia were "free" countries when they became associated with the EU.

35. The current members are in general rated 1 for political rights and 1 or 2 for civil liberties. The minor exception is Greece, with a rating of 3 for civil liberties.

36. See Wlodek Aniól, Timothy R. Byrnes, and Elena A. Iankova, "Poland: Returning to Europe," in Peter J. Katzenstein, ed., *Mitteleuropa: Between Europe and Germany* (Providence: Berghahn Books, 1997), 39–100.

37. Samuel P. Huntington, *The Clash of Civilizations and the Remaking of World Order* (New York: Simon and Schuster, 1996), 27.

38. This applies to Latvia as well as Slovakia. Croatia, another Western Christian country, has not even associated with the EU.

39. The only exception is the European Community's temporary rejection of British accession in the 1960s. Britain acceded to the EC in 1973.

PART FOUR

EUROPE'S CIVIC
IDENTITY

8

European Identity and Migration Policies

Jef Huysmans

Since the mid-1980s, migration has become increasingly politicized in Western Europe.[1] Population flows and migrants are again a major political question and are the subject of turbulent debates in the public sphere. A wide range of political actors position themselves in terms of different definitions and regulations of migration. In this chapter I look at two interrelated dimensions of the politicization of migration. On the one hand, there is a Europeanization of migration policies. Migration is at the top of the agenda for the European Union, as reflected in the relocation of migration policy in the Treaty of Amsterdam from the intergovernmental framework of the third pillar to a communitarian approach. Migration policy has also been increasingly transnationalized in Europe through, for example, the development of transnational police networks.

On the other hand, the Europeanization of migration policy goes hand in hand with a growing consensus among major political actors to move to a restrictive, control-oriented approach. Often people communicate socioeconomic reasons in justifying this restrictive attitude. Changes in the labor market or the economic recession are formulated as major reasons for limiting the migrant population. More recently, another reason has been offered: security. Particularly since the mid-1980s migration has been regularly packaged as a security problem—as a threat to public order, for example. The 1985 Schengen Agreement, now incorporated in the Treaty of Amsterdam, is an exemplary case of a political discourse that places the problem of migration explicitly in a security context in which questions of border controls, terrorism, crime, drugs, and immigration and asylum are interrelated.

In this chapter I focus on how migration is rendered problematic in the process of securitization, that is, a politicization that fabricates migration into an existential threat. This chapter makes a particular point of portraying the complexity of the security dynamic in which migration emerges in the EU today. More specifically, it develops an argument against cultural reductionist interpretations of the migration phenomenon. The trade-off between exclusion and dilution in the EU cannot be reduced to a question of cultural identity. In other words, the politicization of migration does not rest solely on trading off the survival of national or European cultural identity against a multicultural dilution of the postwar political order in Europe. In the securitizing process, the cultural questions are heavily overdetermined by questions related to the protection of public order and the rule of law on the one hand and challenges to the welfare system on the other.

The first section describes a few key developments in migration policy, which are part of the general context within which the Europeanization of migration developed. The three remaining sections analyze the Western European security dynamic in which migration emerges as an existential threat. More specifically, the sections deal with the way in which the securitization of migration connects questions of internal security, societal security, and challenges to the welfare state.

European Migration Policy

Although it is difficult to generalize about different policies and countries, it could be argued that in the 1950s and 1960s immigrants were primarily an extra pool of workers in the main Western European countries.[2] The economic situation and the labor market required an additional workforce that was preferably cheap and flexible. Countries like France, Germany, and the Netherlands generally used a permissive or even promotional migration policy motivated by the need for extra labor. In contrast to the present situation, in which the question of illegal immigration justifies to a considerable extent the formation of more restrictive migration policies, the legal status of the immediate postwar immigrants was not really a controversial issue. In France, for example, specialized agencies recruited immigrants directly from their country of origin without bothering about the legal status of the "imported" people, which was not of immediate relevance for the domestic economic needs they met. If anything, their illegality contributed to making immigrant workers an even more flexible and inexpensive workforce.[3] This does not mean that states did not try to regulate and normalize the situation of the immigrants, but the debate about their legal status did not have the prominence that would come to characterize it from the 1980s onward.

In the late 1960s and more generally in the 1970s, immigration increasingly became a subject of public concern. This concern developed simultaneously with a move from a more or less permissive or promotional immigration policy to a control-oriented, more restrictive policy. [4] A main indication of this shift was the decision to halt immigration in some European countries.[5] Yet this swing did not immediately radically change the way immigrants were classified. A utilitarian, economic logic determining immigration policy on the basis of changes in the labor market largely defined immigrants, and so they remained categorized first and foremost as guestworkers. The restrictive policies were strongly, although not exclusively, motivated by changes in the labor market—the fall in demand for foreign labor—and by a desire to protect the social and economic rights the domestic workforce had secured in the postwar development of the welfare state.[6]

Although the political rhetoric more regularly than before started linking migration to public order, the most important deviation from a purely utilitarian policy was the granting of permission for family reunions.[7] Whether one interprets this as an attempt to stabilize the immigrant working force that was already present in the domestic society and could not be sent home easily, as an economic approach would suggest, or whether one understands it as motivated by a more humanitarian concern is not that important here. More important is that family reunions drastically changed the nature of the immigrant population. It became clear that a large portion of the guestworkers were there to stay and became part of everyday life in the neighborhood, certainly increasing the public visibility of the immigrant population. Immigration for reasons of family reunion also meant that the immigration stoppage did not result in a radical reduction of the number of immigrants.[8] The temporary guestworkers became, in a sense, permanent guests.[9]

During this period migration policy was hardly an important issue for the European Communities.[10] Although the free movement of workers from third countries, that is, nonmember states, has been a point of discussion since the days when the project of the internal market was formulated, it remained a largely marginal issue in the construction of the internal market.[11] Moreover, free movement of persons in general did not have priority in the development of the internal market.

With regard to the present position, the most significant decision of this period was the European Council's regulation 1612/68, which established the difference between the right of free movement of nationals of member states and the right of free movement of nationals from third countries.[12] Mehmet Ugur argues that it was this decision that laid the foundation for the Fortress Europe in terms of immigration, not the Treaty of Maastricht (1992), which formalized EU citizenship and introduced the question of immigration in the body of treaties.[13] The decision of 1968 articulated the assumption that the free movement of persons in the internal market would be an exclusive right for nationals of member states.[14] The idea that EC citizens should benefit from special rights was confirmed at the 1973 Paris summit, where it was also decided that the EC should formulate a common legislation for foreigners.[15]

The adoption of the action program in favor of migrant workers and their families in 1974 is also mentioned frequently as an important first step toward the development of a common position on migration in the EC.[16] The growing interest in the question of migration was not only a reaction to the oil crises and economic recession but also a result of the first enlargement of the EC to include the UK, Ireland, and Denmark.[17]

On the rare occasions that migration arose as an issue, it concerned the development of a common labor market in which workers could freely and easily move between the member states. This stands in stark contrast to the present situation in which the category "migrant" is more and more difficult to delimit, as the traditional definitions of immigrant workers, their families, asylum seekers, and refugees have become conflated. One reason for this mixing is that asylum and refugee status are increasingly approached as alternative routes for economic immigration in the European Union.[18]

Since the mid-1980s migration policy has experienced a relatively fast Europeanization. In the 1980s migration featured more regularly as an important issue in intergovernmental forums in Europe such as Trevi, the Ad Hoc Group on Immigration, and the Schengen group.[19] Although most of these forums were not part of the European integration process in a strict sense, they certainly contributed to an increasing development of European transnational and intergovernmental policy networks interested in a cooperative regulation of migration.[20] To an extent they did provide the groundwork for a gradual incorporation of migration policy into the constitutional structure of the European Union. As a result of the Single European Act (1986) and the momentum developed in the Schengen group, the Treaty of European Union (1992) introduced a third pillar on Justice and Home Affairs, in which migration became an explicit subject of intergovernmental regulation within the European Union. Soon it became clear that the intergovernmental approach of the third pillar was not the most effective way to develop a common migration policy. The move of migration-related questions from the third to the first pillar became one of the key issues for the intergovernmental conference reviewing the TEU.[21] At the conference the heads of government and heads of state decided to communitarize the sections of the third pillar relating to immigration, asylum, and refugees in the Treaty of Amsterdam.[22]

The growth in attempts to develop common regulations of migration in Western Europe correlates with a strong articulation of an interest in control and restriction.[23] European cooperation in migration institutionalizes a restrictive attitude toward migration. The norms derive their regulative and political significance very much from a discourse articulating a desire both to reduce the permeability of state territory and to reinstate a complex form of state control over population flows by means of, among other things, the welfare system, policing, and border control.[24] The Dublin convention, which came into force on 1 September 1997, deals with determining the state responsible for examining applications for asylum and reads, at first sight, as a humanitarian instrument. It aims at limiting the number of refugees in transit, that is, asylum seekers who are passed from one state to another without any decision on their status. These asylum seekers thus remain in circulation among states, living in special centers that amount to a no-man's-land.[25] The Dublin convention aims at limiting the possibility for states to pass the buck by setting out criteria, including place of application and family links, that determine the state that has to process the application. This can be read (and is indeed sometimes represented) as a more humane way of dealing with asylum seekers; it seeks a quicker and more determinate procedure to deal with the request of asylum and thus reduces the time asylum seekers have to spend in limbo. But the humanitarian significance of the Dublin convention is heavily overdetermined by a policy that tries to limit the number of applications. The convention is replete with negative connotations of the term *asylum,* implying it is an illegitimate way of seeking immigration and emphasizing the member states' interest in "discouraging" refugees who apply for asylum in Europe. In other words, the Dublin convention is also an instrument that restricts the demand for asylum by making the asylum system less appealing and more prohibitive.[26]

Such institutional developments were also shaped and have taken place against the background of a thematic shift in the problematization of migration. As a result of the debates in the 1970s, socioeconomic questions about immigration were gradually displaced by debates focusing on the protection of public order and the preservation of domestic stability, which related migration more explicitly to the crisis of the welfare state and to challenges to the cultural composition of the nation. These themes became increasingly incorporated in the politicization of migration as a security question—a phenomenon I refer to by using Ole Wæver's term *securitization*.[27] The rationality—"that which makes possible for us an intelligibility of practices [here: security practices], an intelligibility which at once traverses and is incorporated in these practices"—within which the link between migration and security emerges is the main subject of the next sections.[28]

Internal Security and Migration

The kernel of the politicization of migration in the European Community is the securitization of the internal market that has been developed by linking the abolition of internal border controls to a challenge of public order by transnational flows of goods, capital, services, and people.[29]

The political realization of the internal market received a crucial boost in the mid-1980s, most explicitly by the Single European Act of 1986. The SEA, together with the European Commission's white paper on the internal market, which identified 289 legislative proposals to establish the internal market, instigated a process of radical change aimed at the completion of a common market by 1992.[30] In the SEA the internal market was defined as "an area without internal frontiers in which the free movement of goods, persons, services and capital is ensured in accordance with the provisions of this Treaty" (Article 13). The key goal of this project was a relatively fast abolition of internal border controls to guarantee free movement.

But in the wake of the SEA, EC policies quickly linked the downgrading of internal frontiers to the necessity of strengthening external border controls. The reasons offered for this connection sounded commonsensical: If we diminish internal border controls, then we must harmonize and strengthen the control at the external borders of the European Community to guarantee a sufficient level of control on who and what can legitimately enter the space of free movement.[31] This is the Europeanization of the old, territorial argument that the political community has a sovereign right to control the penetration of its territory and that this happens in the first place at the external borders of this community. Those who feared that this would lead to a clampdown on international free movement warned that a Fortress Europe was in the making. Capitalizing on this fear, commercial interests in the United States mobilized anti-European-integration feelings.[32] Social movements concerned with the free movement of persons launched the idea of a Fortress Europe in an attempt to oppose the development of a restrictive migration policy.[33]

Although the linkage between diminishing internal border control and strengthening external border control may seem logical in itself, it rests on a contentious assumption: that internal security is guaranteed primarily via border control and that free movement of persons is constituted by doing away with such control. But personal identity controls increased in some countries of the European Community following the abolition of internal border control. Border checks were replaced by more numerous random identity controls across the national territory.[34] It is also not clear that the majority of illegal immigrants are smuggled into a country. Staying in a country after a visa has expired is a more common form of entering illegally.[35] Further, it is doubtful that border control is the main obstacle to the free movement of people in modern societies. The granting of work permits, resident permits, and access to welfare provisions and social assistance are undoubtedly more important instruments for improving or limiting the movement of people.[36]

Nevertheless, this linkage between internal and external borders has played an important role in the spillover of the socioeconomic project from the internal market to the internal security of the European Community. The introduction of the third pillar on Justice and Home Affairs in the TEU and the gradual incorporation of the Schengen Agreement into the *acquis communautaire* and then into the Treaty of Amsterdam explicitly mark this spillover at the formal level.

But the linkage in itself does not fully explain the securitization of the internal market and, by implication, the free movement of persons. The specific border issue has been embedded in a more general problematization of internal security. The major issue has been the assumption that a space of free movement would necessarily provide improved opportunities for terrorists, international criminals, asylum seekers, and immigrants to develop their illegal and criminal activities. Thus, a security knowledge emerged that articulated and institutionalized a continuum in which security policy could move from border issues to terrorism and international crime to migration. As a result, "the issue was no longer, on the one hand, terrorism, drugs, crime, and on the other, rights of asylum and clandestine immigration, but they came to be treated together in the attempt to gain an overall view of the interrelation between these problems and the free movement of persons within Europe."[37]

The security continuum frames the linkage between abolishing internal border controls and strengthening external border controls within a more general problematic of transnational movements challenging the protection of public order and the rule of law in the internal market. This discourse has developed in close relation to the institutionalization of transnational police networks in Europe. Since the mid-1970s, different initiatives such as the informal "clubs" on terrorism and drugs (including the Bern Club and the Police Working Group on Terrorism), the Schengen negotiations, and the 1992 project of the EC have gradually created a network of professionals producing and distributing internal security knowledge that has constituted and legitimated the continuum between borders, terrorism, crime and migration. After all, the police are security professionals who are trained to identify and deal with challenges to public order and the rule of law.[38]

The bureaucratic network constitutes a key dimension of the process of Europeanization of justice and home affairs. According to Didier Bigo, this network operates as a bureaucratic field that has moved beyond the control of individual organizations and actors struggling to fulfill their interests. Although it largely originates from self-interested action of bureaucratic agents related to the police or customs, it now operates as a semiautonomous, intersubjective structure simultaneously constraining and empowering the agents "populating" it. Thus, the network is no longer an aggregation of self-interests but functions as a separate "entity" that exists independent of individual practices and beliefs.[39] The unintended creation of this bureaucratic field has definitely played a critical role in the institutionalization of an internal security field in Europe in which bureaucratic and nonbureaucratic agents struggle over the definition of migration policy, the distribution of resources, and so on.

The successful creation of the spillover from the internal market to an internal security field represents the latter almost as a natural consequence of the completion of the internal market. The internal security field hides the contested and political character of the spillover and the practical struggles that preceded the construction of the field—and that continue. The power of this ideological effect, that is, the dominating grip the field has on the way in which transformative practices can redefine the issue of free movement, is indicated by the difficulties pro-migration movements have had in breaking the security logic.[40]

At present, migration is a nodal point in this internal security field. It allows the security approach to connect a rather technical and professional field that depends heavily on the transnational networking of police, customs, and other bureaucratic, professional organizations to a more general political field. Through migration a multitude of agents—including the media, political parties, governments, social movements, and public opinion institutes—are drawn into the field. Questions of political legitimacy of the postwar order and the determination of values defining the good life partly displace the professional debates about migration control. Thomas Faist thus refers to migration (in the German context) as a meta-issue, that is, a phenomenon that can be referred to as a cause of many problems.[41] Immigration, asylum, and refugees, united under the label *migrant*—allow the agents struggling over power, resources, and knowledge in the field to interrelate a range of disparate political issues.[42]

In the next two sections, I look at how the signifier *migration* has a capacity to connect the internal security logic to questions of cultural and racial identity and to challenges to the welfare state and the general political legitimacy of the postwar political order.[43]

Societal Security and Migration

In the EU the politicization of migration relates the professional, more technical approach of the police to a cultural dynamic in which immigrants, asylum seekers, and refugees challenge the myth of national cultural homogeneity by articulating a multicultural presence in everyday practices. European countries have become countries of immigration in which the cultural identity of both the indigenous people and the immigrants is constantly evolving.[44]

The political rendering of cultural identity, which involves a mixture of questions of multiculturalism, European identity, nationalism, xenophobia, and racism, is a subject of securitization in the EU today. In this societal security dynamic, the nation rather than the state is of primary importance. Instead of being reduced to the sovereignty of the state, some of the security claims in Europe today sustain a reference to the identity of the nation as such, thereby rendering legitimate the protection of cultural identity and the definition of threats to this identity.[45]

In itself the phenomenon of rendering the cultural into the political seems to be primarily articulated in extreme nationalistic and new civilizational discourses in which parties and movements mobilize support for national or civilizational identity on the basis of constructing a cultural enemy.[46] This in itself rather narrow articulation, however, gains much more general political significance by being presented as a serious challenge to domestic stability, the integration of society, and the legitimacy of political regimes.[47] Multiculturalism challenges the integrative and legitimating force of nationalism—nationalism meaning the desire to let cultural and political frontiers coincide—in Western societies.[48] Both opponents and supporters of a more liberal migration policy in the EU accept that migration has a capacity to render problematic the political integration of communities on the basis of national identity.[49]

Risks of social and political disintegration are important sources of mobilizing security institutions and rhetoric. As a result, more general questions of domestic stability may further the mobilization of cultural enmity. New conservatism, including extreme right-wing movements and parties and also civilization discourses like Huntington's, also play an instigating role. They articulate moments of societal instability through their rhetoric of societal decadence and decay and their mobilization and/or expectations of violence, which are to a significant extent framed within a longing for a cultural, spiritual, or racist reintegration of societies.[50] The extensive media coverage of immigrant involvement in riots in urban ghettos and the political rendering of these riots as manifestations of incivility, the revival of the dangerous class, and/or Islamic threats all help create the foundation for reifying a cultural enemy.[51]

In the context of the EU, cultural readings of migration emerge in relation to three themes. The first is the cultural (and possibly racial) significance of border controls and limitations of free movement. The second is the question of integration or assimilation of migrants into the domestic societies of the member states. The third is the relationship between European integration and the development of multicultural societies.

I have already referred to the link between the abolition of internal border controls and the strengthening of external border controls in the context of the construction of an internal security problematic. But borders are polysemic; they differentiate among individuals crossing the border according to more than one criterion.[52] In the EU the issue of border controls has also cultural—and to an extent racial—echoes. This becomes most visible when one has a closer look at the practical policies of controlling the crossing of external borders. Although one often suggests that external borders are fortified for all so-called third-country nationals, this is not what is happening. EU borders are more real for most non-OECD nationals than for members of OECD countries: "Within Europe, there is now a widely held view of cultural closeness and similarity between all the 'nations' of Western Europe, a commonality which is constructed and legitimated by means of signifying and naturalising difference in relation to the population of the peripheries of the world economy who 'for their own good' are requested to remain 'where they naturally belong.'"[53] This differentiation is confirmed in the list determining the third countries whose nationals must possess a visa to enter EU member states.[54]

It could be argued that this differentiation is first of all mediated by class interests and shifts in the labor market. Since Western markets seem to demand especially skilled labor, the restrictive policy aims primarily at unskilled and semiskilled migrants, and these migrants tend to belong to non-OECD countries.[55] But this regulation via the labor market seems to have cultural effects in the sense that members of a skilled labor force tend to be aliens with cultural similarities.

It is sometimes suggested that besides cultural and capitalist criteria, racial criteria also play a role in the regulation of inclusion and exclusion of migrants.[56] A racial policy requires collectivities to be differentiated on the basis of biological, somatic criteria that identify relations of superiority and inferiority. That means that cultural differentiation and thus nationalism do not automatically imply a racial policy.[57] Moreover, that border control and the politicization of migration articulate racial criteria as well does not necessarily mean that the European integration process implies the creation of a new Euroracism, that is, a particular form of racism articulated in an EU-wide context.[58] As Robert Miles and Michel Wieviorka have argued, it is problematic to homogenize the diversity of racist practices in different member states and the racial effects of the European integration process into a Euroracism.[59]

A second theme that brings the question of migration and cultural identity into the EU is the integration of immigrants into domestic societies. A restrictive migration policy is (sometimes) justified as a condition for the successful integration of immigrants.[60] Restriction of migration and successful integration are seen as instruments for stabilizing these societies.[61] Although a policy of integration may be at the heart of progressive forms of multiculturalism that support the integration of immigrants by granting them political rights, for example, it may also confirm—intentionally or unintentionally—a nationalist desire for a culturally homogeneous society.[62] Policies of integrating immigrants do often articulate the assumption, to a greater or lesser extent, that a culturally uniform society existed before migration started, and this may go hand in hand with the expression of a desire for reestablishing the foregone homogeneity.[63] In so doing, integration projects partly place migrants outside the national (or European) social formation of which they are a constitutive part. They have contributed to the creation of the society as it exists today but nevertheless are not fully recognized as citizens of the community; they are latecomers. From here it is not a stretch to assume that nonintegration leads to a destabilization of the social formation.

But even here policies are not determined solely by cultural criteria but are overlaid with racial and labor market criteria.[64] Not all culturally different aliens are similarly rendered problematic in policies of integration. This seems to be confirmed by the common characteristics of the different denotations of *migrant* in different European countries. The label refers to (and renders problematic) different population groups in different European countries (e.g., primarily Turks in Germany and Caribbean and South Asian people in the UK), but the groups always share two characteristics: "They originate from nation states beyond the European definition of the boundary of Europe and from nation states which are included in the diffuse notion of the 'Third World'. . . . This spatial and material origin is overdetermined by a set of signified cultural (e.g. Muslim) and somatic (e.g. 'black' skin) characteristics which constitute further signs of difference, if not inferiority."[65]

The final theme is multiculturalism. The European integration process is increasingly related to the question of constructing multicultural and nonracist societies in Europe. The need for a common migration policy is to an extent justified as an instrument to deal with the revival of racist, xenophobic, and extreme nationalistic practices in Europe, which the European Parliament has been very active in cautioning against.[66] Antiracist and pro-migration movements organize themselves transnationally so as to be in a better position to articulate their interest in a genuine multicultural society in the context of the EU.[67] This interest seems to indicate that the process of Europeanization is based not only on a fear of the return of the fragmented Europe of the nineteenth century and the two world wars, as Wæver argues, but also on a fear of virulent nationalism, racism, and xenophobia such as existed during the Third Reich and the interwar period.[68] The peculiar characteristic of the process is that this haunting past is reactivated via a politicization of migration.

The integration process has also spilled over into a more general discussion about multiculturalism in the form of a debate about postnational citizenship.[69] The politicization of migration is the ethical dilemma that triggers this debate, which concerns the opportunity the European integration process offers for creating a political community where national frontiers do not coincide with political frontiers.[70] But multicultural projects run the risk of slipping into a cultural reductionist rendering of society and migration, thereby making the affirmation and contestation of cultural dimensions of migration the kernel of the politicization of immigration, asylum, and refugees.

Others argue that a European migration policy may offer a chance to depoliticize the question of nationality by locating migration policy in a bureaucratic and, by definition, multinational policymaking structure. But a transfer of migration policy to the EU will not happen without triggering a widespread political debate that could result in a further politicization and, more particularly, confirmation of nationality as a main criterion determining political belonging.[71]

Europe, Security, and the Welfare State

As a result of successive economic recessions and the rise in unemployment since the mid-1970s, the struggle over the distribution of social goods such as housing, health care, unemployment benefits, jobs, and other social services has become more competitive. In this context migrants have emerged not only as rivals in the labor market but also as competitors in the distribution of scarce social goods. At the same time, an increasingly visible articulation of a "welfare chauvinism" conflates questions of social solidarity and redistribution of welfare provisions with privileging nationality. Welfare chauvinism argues for delivering socioeconomic rights first and foremost to nationals of member states of the European Union.[72]

This welfare chauvinism has increased the potential for conflict around social rights for immigrants. It is then not surprising that those who support curtailing social rights of immigrants often also argue that migration is a threat to cultural homogeneity. As Faist remarks:

> Recent political conflicts around social rights of immigrants have often been based on the claim that the willingness to share social goods distributed by the welfare state needs a basis of common feeling. It is thus not surprising that those political actors opposed to (further) immigration, and/or to granting certain social rights to immigrants, have tended to refer to the alleged threat immigrants pose not only as economic competitors in the labour market and for social policies ("they take away our jobs and our benefits") but also as a threat to the cultural homogeneity of the national state.[73]

Welfare chauvinism emerges under radical and more moderate forms. In its radical form, the socioeconomic stigmatization constructs migrants as profiteers who try to illegitimately gain benefits from the welfare system of a community to which they do not belong, thus constituting a strain upon the system itself. The migrant is transformed from a competitor into a perpetrator of welfare fraud.[74] A more moderate version relates the necessity for controlling migration to an economic recession that limits employment opportunities for migrants and proportionally raises the costs for sustaining them. Here migrants are not excluded because they are free riding but primarily because they do not really belong to the home society; a community should first provide benefits and welfare for its "own" people.

In both approaches migrants are no longer simply rivals but *illegitimate* recipients of socioeconomic rights. Irrespective of the legal basis upon which migrants claim access to welfare provisions and social assistance, the label *migrant* functions often as a stigma identifying illegitimate claims to social goods, disqualifying the migrant from full social acceptance.[75] Both views also justify a restrictive migration policy curtailing the access of immigrants, asylum seekers, and refugees to social assistance and welfare rights on the grounds that welfare should not function as a magnet pulling migrants into the country.

The rise of welfare chauvinism makes it clear why asylum seekers—and illegal immigrants—are prime targets in the stigmatization of migration in general. Asylum seekers can be easily depicted as economic refugees abusing the asylum procedure to obtain socioeconomic rights in the host society.[76] Moreover, asylum seekers can obtain social goods, more specifically social assistance benefits, without having contributed to the welfare system, which is to an extent based on an insurance principle: You have to contribute before you receive. This makes them a particularly vulnerable target for welfare chauvinists.[77]

The disqualification of migration is given wider societal significance through the use of metaphors such as the invasion or flood of asylum seekers. In a context of socioeconomic stigmatization in a welfare state struggling to deliver the socioeconomic rights it promised, these metaphors articulate a real threat to the survival of the system. Here socioeconomic constructions of the migration problematic potentially and actually slip into a security logic in which the stigma identifying a not fully socially accepted individual transforms into a signifier identifying a collective inimical political agency.[78]

There is a more subtle linkage that introduces migration as a contested issue in a wider struggle over political legitimacy. Welfare rights are at the heart of the postwar political order in Europe in the sense that the social integration in Western societies, and actually the very constitution of the concept of the social and social solidarity, is tied up with the genealogy of the welfare state and the provision of socioeconomic rights.[79] They have also played an essential role in legitimating political authority in liberal democratic states.[80] In other words, the crisis of the welfare state, which started in the 1970s, cannot be reduced to a question of economic recession or a breakdown of the interaction between rapid economic growth and the creation of social rights. The crisis is in essence a political crisis about the decline of the postwar technology of integrating society and state by creating solidarity among the different classes through redistribution, welfare provisions, and a generalized system of insurance against accidents.[81] Besides the economic recessions, political and social dissatisfaction with interventionism of the welfare state, the "nanny state," have stimulated the crisis. In particular, both the growing articulation of a desire for individual emancipation and the repoliticization of society since the late 1960s and early

1970s have played important roles in stimulating the search for a trans-formation of the postwar political order.[82]

It is in relation to expressions of these political aspects of the crisis of the welfare state that the socioeconomic problematic emphasizing the capacity of the state to deliver social goods can turn into a matter of the survival of the political order and the political elite. The question changes from economic crisis to political crisis in which the survival of the political elite and the political order itself are at stake. The term *migrant* becomes a vehicle for the articulation of different political views about the good political order, ranging from a search for social inte-gration on the basis of cultural tradition (most explicitly in extreme conservative positions) to the radical affirmation of individual emanci-pation on the basis of the right of free movement (for example, some of the more radical liberal positions).[83]

The politicization of migration as a challenge to the welfare state allows the socioeconomic problematization of migration that relies on a utilitarian calculus to slip into a question that touches upon the ker-nel of political identity. Turning migrants into an existential threat is then a particular political strategy seeking social integration and politi-cal legitimacy by reifying an inimical force that endangers the survival of the political community.[84] An urgent need to counter an external inimical challenge (the invasion of migrants, for example) veils the fail-ure of the political order to address the economic recession and stifles the increasing domestic demand for change.

The negative representation of migration in this context is not driven solely by extreme right-wing parties. The established elite located more in the center of the political spectrum also contribute to the stigmatization and securitization of migration.[85] The latter sometimes intentionally or unintentionally transform the migrant into a scapegoat, diverting attention away from the internal political crisis to an external challenge to the political and social order.

Yet securitization of migration can also be manipulated to intensify the general feeling of crisis, thereby supporting political agencies that aim at the radical transformation of the political system. Unlike the political center, which is interested in preserving or gradually changing the existing political order, the extreme right tends to use migration to exacerbate the representation of a political system in crisis—a corrupt, unfair political system that perverts the cultural, social, and political tradition of the people.[86] For the extreme right, the securitization of migration is not a strategy oriented to the status quo but one serving a conservative revolution, that is, a radical transformation of a system in the name of reestablishing a cultural and moral tradition.[87] In other words, securitization becomes a double-edged sword.

Yet I am not arguing that the strong form of securitization of migration, that is, the explicit articulation of inimical relations between an indigenous population and foreigners, dominates the discussion about the future of the welfare state. Rather, I am looking here for an understanding of the potential and actual slippage from a socioeconomic problematization of migration into a securitization of asylum seekers, immigrants, and refugees.

How does the European Union enter this picture? The most obvious indications are statements suggesting or playing on themes that easily relate to the discourse of welfare chauvinism. For example, the Justice and Home Affairs Council stated after its meeting in Luxembourg in June 1994 that it approves of temporary employment of foreigners "only where vacancies in a Member State cannot be filled by national and Community manpower or by non-Community manpower lawfully resident on a permanent basis in that Member State and already forming part of the Member State's regular labour market."[88]

But more important for a discussion of the migration question is that the European integration project is steeped in the problematic of the welfare state. The development of the internal market and the EMU are not just technical economic projects aimed at developing an economic level playing field to improve the competitiveness of the European firms and their attractiveness to foreign investors. They are embroiled in the political game of preserving the legitimacy of postwar political order and regimes. The European Community functions simultaneously as a scapegoat for unpopular decisions and a political attempt to reinstall the loop of economic growth and welfare provisions.[89]

The Europeanization of migration policy—the way in which the European integration process becomes a significant referent in the discussion about and formulation of migration policy—cannot escape this political context. However technically one wants to represent the politicization of migration, it will be enmeshed in a political field in which the nature and transformation of political order and the political legitimacy of governments are the object of struggle.

Conclusion

In the European Union the trade-off between exclusion and dilution in migration policy is not exclusively regulated by either a socioeconomic rendering—the demand and supply of labor—or a cultural rendering of the relation between migrants and nationals of member states. Since the mid-1980s, the socioeconomic approach to migration, which defines migrants primarily as a labor force and regulates migration via labor market determinants, has gradually crossed over to a security approach. Security policy defines migration as a challenge to stability and in the more narrow and radical definition as an existential threat. It regulates migration through a complex network of controls, ranging from border control and policing to welfare entitlements.

But the securitization of migration in the European Union cannot be reduced to a cultural version of the existential threat, that is, migrants jeopardizing the cultural homogeneity of the nation or the quasi-homogeneity of Europe. Societal security questions are heavily overdetermined by an internal security and a welfare problematic. The political rendering of the exclusion/dilution trade-off articulated in the securitization of migration embraces a complex network of themes ranging from the protection of public order, the rule of law, border control, welfare provisions, and rights of social assistance to national and European identity.

Notes

1. I do not consistently distinguish among immigrants, asylum seekers, and refugees in this chapter. Often I use the general terms *migrant* and *migration*. This does not mean that the distinction is not relevant, however (see Chapter 9 in this volume).

2. For a more general overview of the similarities and differences in migration policy in Europe, see among others James F. Hollifield, *Immigrants, Markets and States* (Cambridge: Harvard University Press, 1992); Sarah Collinson, *Europe and International Migration* (London: Pinter, 1993); Russell King, ed., *Mass Migration in Europe: The Legacy and the Future* (London: Belhaven, 1993); Martin Baldwin-Edwards and Martin A. Schain, eds., *The Politics of Immigration in Western Europe* (Ilford, UK: Frank Cass, 1994).

3. For an interesting argument along these lines with regard to France, see Claude-Valentin Marie, "Entre économie et politique: le 'clandestin,' une figure sociale à géométrie variable," *Pouvoirs* 47 (1988): 75–81.

4. For example, Anthony Fielding, "Migration, Institutions and Politics: The Evolution of European Migration Policies," in Russell King, ed., *Mass Migration in Europe: The Legacy and the Future* (London: Belhaven, 1993), 43; Hollifield, *Immigrants*, 66–73.

5. One main reason often given to explain the shift is the oil crisis and the changes in socioeconomic conditions that it produced. As Robert Miles has indicated, however, it is difficult to generalize for all the countries of Europe. He has shown, for example, that the problematization of the migrant presence in Britain and Switzerland happened already in the mid-1960s. He has also argued for restraint in reproducing a straightforward link between economic and political processes. Robert Miles, *Racism* (London: Routledge, 1989), 118.

6. For example, in Germany, H. H. Blotevogel, U. Müller-ter Jung, and Gerald Wood, "From Itinerant Worker to Immigrant? The Geography of Guestworkers in Germany," in Russell King, ed., *Mass Migration in Europe: The Legacy and the Future* (London: Belhaven, 1993), 88.

7. For example, in France, Marie, "Entre économie et politique," 83ff.; in European Commission initiatives, Mehmet Ugur, "Freedom of Movement vs. Exclusion: A Reinterpretation of the 'Insider'–'Outsider' Divide in the European Union," *International Migration Review* 29, 4 (1995): 980ff.; in the UK, see Roxanne Lynn Doty, "Immigration and National Identity: Constructing the Nation," *Review of International Studies* 22, 3 (1996): 246ff.

8. On numbers, see, for example, Russell King, "European International Migration 1945–90: A Statistical and Geographical View," in Russell King, *Mass Migration in Europe: The Legacy and the Future* (London: Belhaven, 1993), 19–39.

9. For an interesting reflection on this paradoxical position of the migrant, see Abdelmalek Sayad, *L'Immigration ou les paradoxes de l'altérité* (Brussels: De Boeck, 1991).

10. For a more extensive overview of migration policy and European integration, see, among others, G. Korella and P. Twomey, eds., *Towards a European Immigration Policy* (Brussels: European Interuniversity Press, 1995); Rey Koslowski, "European Union Migration Regimes, Established and Emergent," in Christian Joppke, ed., *Challenge to the Nation-State: Immigration in Western Europe and the United States* (Oxford: Oxford University Press, 1998), 153–188.

11. Ugur, "Freedom of Movement," 964–999.

12. Ibid., 967.

13. "What happened in the period corresponding to the establishment of the Single Market was the transformation of what used to be an elite expectation into a commonly held grassroot perception." Ibid., 977.

14. For a discussion of the legal aspects, see Herwig Verschueren, "Migranten Tussen Hoop en Vrees in het Eengemaakte Europa," *Panopticon* 12, 2 (1991): 137–143.

15. Henri Etienne, "The Commission of the European Community and Immigration," in G. Korella and P. Twomey, eds., *Towards a European Immigration Policy* (Brussels: European Interuniversity Press, 1995), 148.

16. For example, Giuseppe Callovi, "Regulation of Immigration in 1993: Pieces of the European Community Jig-saw Puzzle," *International Migration Review* 26, 2 (1992): 355–356.

17. Ibid.

18. Monica den Boer, "Moving Between Bogus and Bona Fide: The Policing of Inclusion and Exclusion in Europe," in Robert Miles and Dietrich Thränhardt, eds., *Migration and European Integration: The Dynamics of Inclusion and Exclusion* (London: Pinter, 1995), 92–111.

19. Didier Bigo, "The European Internal Security Field: Stakes and Rivalries in a Newly Developing Area of Police Intervention," in Malcolm Anderson and Monica den Boer, ed., *Policing Across National Boundaries* (London: Pinter, 1994), 167–169; Didier Bigo, *Police en réseaux. L'expérience européenne* (Paris: Presses de Sciences Po, 1996); Collinson, *Europe and International Migration*, 110–115.

20. Bigo, *Police en réseaux,* 112–145, 196–208.

21. See, for example, European Commission, *Commission Opinion: Reinforcing Political Union and Preparing for Enlargement* (Brussels: European Commission, 1996), 11–12.

22. A. Duff, *The Treaty of Amsterdam* (London: Federal Trust, 1997), 3–58; Monica den Boer, "Step by Step Progress: An Update on the Free Movement of Persons and Internal Security," *EIPASCOPE* 2 (1997): 8–11.

23. Ugur, "Freedom of Movement vs. Exclusion"; Gallya Lahav, "The Devolution and Privatization of Immigration Control: The State and Third-Party Regulatory Agents," paper presented at the International Studies Association annual convention, Minneapolis, 17–21 March 1998; Robert Miles and Dietrich Thränhardt, eds., *Migration and European Integration: The Dynamics of Inclusion and Exclusion* (London: Pinter, 1995); Jean-Pierre Alaux, "Comment les démocraties occidentales préparent la société plurielle. En Europe: 'sécurité d'abord,'" *Le Monde diplomatique*, February 1991, 20–21; Gérard Soulier, "Droit d'aisle et Grand Marché. L'Europe aux Européens," *Le Monde diplomatique*, July 1989, 11.

24. Ayse Ceyhan, "Towards a Bifocal Control: Border and Welfare Controls in the United States and in France," paper presented at the International Studies Association annual convention, Minneapolis, 17–21 March 1998; John Crowley, "Where Does the State Actually Start? Border, Boundary and Frontier Control in Contemporary Governance," paper presented at the International Studies Association annual convention, Minneapolis, 17–21 March 1998.

25. Didier Bigo, ed., "Circuler, enfermer, éloigner. Zones d'attente et centres de rétention des démocraties occidentales," special issue of *Cultures et Conflits* 23 (1996).

26. José Bolten, "From Schengen to Dublin: The New Frontiers of Refugee Law," in H. Meijer, J. Bolten et al., *Schengen: Internationalisation of Central Chapters of the Law of Aliens, Refugees, Privacy, Security, and the Police* (Antwerp: Kluwer, 1991), 8–36.

27. Ole Wæver, "European Security Identities," *Journal of Common Market Studies* 34 (1996): 103–132. Among others, see Bigo, *Police en réseaux;* Bigo, "The European Internal Security Field"; den Boer, "Moving Between Bogus and Bona Fide," 92–111; Monica den Boer, "The Quest for European Policing: Rhetoric and Justification in a Disorderly Debate," in Malcolm Anderson and Monica den Boer, eds., *Policing Across National Boundaries* (London: Pinter, 1994), 174–196. The term *securitization* is coined by Ole Wæver, "Securitization and Desecuritization," in Ronny Lipschutz, ed., *On Security* (New York: Columbia University Press, 1995), 46–86.

28. Pasquale Pasquino, "Criminology: The Birth of a Special Knowledge," in Graham Burchell, Colin Gordon, and Peter Miller, eds., *The Foucault Effect: Studies in Governmentality* (London: Harvester Wheatsheaf, 1991), 247.

29. For example, Didier Bogo, "Bond of Union: Military Involvement in Internal Security," paper prepared for the International Studies Association annual convention, Minneapolis, 17–21 March 1998.

30. European Commission, *Completing the Internal Market. White Paper from the Commission to the European Council,* Milan, 28–29 June 1985, COM 85310, final, Brussels, 14 June 1985.

31. W. De Lobkowicz, "Intergovernmental Cooperation in the Field of Migration—from the Single European Act to Maastricht," in J. Monar and R. Morgan, eds., *The Third Pillar of the European Union: Cooperation in the Fields of Justice and Home Affairs* (Brussels: European University Press, 1994), 99–122; Malcolm Anderson, *Frontiers: Territory and State Formation* (Cambridge: Polity, 1996), 186–187.

32. Jacques Delors, "European Integration and Security," *Survival* 33, 2 (1991): 103; Brian T. Hanson, "What Happened to Fortress Europe? External Trade Policy Liberalization in the European Union," *International Organization* 52, 1 (1998): 55–85; Jacques Decornoy, "Un Commerce extérieur au service de

quelle politique? Ni 'fortresse' ni 'passoire': un champ de bataille," *Le Monde diplomatique*, January 1989, 16–17; Martin Wolf, *The Resistible Appeal of Fortress Europe* (Washington, D.C.: American Contemporary Institute for Public Policy, 1994); Lester Thurow, *Head to Head: The Coming Battle Among Japan, Europe and America* (New York: William Morrow, 1992).

33. P. Ireland, "Facing the True 'Fortress Europe': Immigrant and Politics in the EC," *Journal of Common Market Studies* 29, 5 (1991): 457–480; Didier Bigo, "Europe passoire, Europe fortresse. La sécurisation et humanitarisation de l'immigration," in Rea Andrea, *Immigration et racisme en Europe* (Brussels: Complexe, 1998).

34. Didier Bigo, "L'illusoire maîtrise des frontières," *Le Monde diplomatique*, October 1996, 10.

35. J. Salt, "A Comparative Overview of International Trends and Types, 1950–80," *International Migration Review* 23, 3 (1989): 431–456.

36. Ceyhan, "Towards a Bifocal Control"; Crowley, "Where does the state actually start?"; Mike King, "Le Contrôle des différences en Europe: l'inclusion et l'exclusion comme logiques sécuritaires et économiques," *Cultures et Conflits* 26/27 (1997): 35–49.

37. Bigo, "The European Internal Security Field," 164.

38. Bigo, *Police en réseaux;* John Benyon, "Policing the European Union: The Changing Basis of Cooperation on Law Enforcement," *International Affairs* 70, 3 (1994): 497–517; Malcolm Anderson, Monica den Boer, and Gary Miller, "European Citizenship and Cooperation in Justice and Home Affairs," in Andrew Duff, John Pinder, and Roy Pryce, eds., *Maastricht and Beyond* (London: Routledge, 1994), 112–118. For more in general about transnational police cooperation, see James Sheptycki, "Policing, Postmodernism, and Trans-nationalism," *British Journal of Criminology* 38, 3 (1998): 483–503.

39. Bigo, *Police en réseaux.*

40. This does not imply that these movements are not successful in raising other issues, such as granting political rights to immigrants. But once a debate is pulled into the security field, there is a real difficulty in taking it out again or showing the arbitrary and ideological dimensions of the securitization. On critical social movements in the migration area, see Ireland, "Facing the True 'Fortress Europe'"; Catherine Wihtol de Wenden, "Immigrants as Political Actors in France," in Martin Baldwin-Edwards and Martin A. Schain, eds., *The Politics of Immigration in Western Europe* (Ilford, UK: Frank Cass, 1994), 91–109.

41. Thomas Faist, "How to Define a Foreigner? The Symbolic Politics of Immigration in German Partisan Discourse, 1978–1992," in Martin Baldwin-Edwards and Martin A. Schain, eds., *The Politics of Immigration in Western Europe* (Ilford, UK: Frank Cass, 1994), 52.

42. See also Didier Bigo, "Sécurité et immigration: vers une gouverne-mentalité par l'inquiétude?" *Cultures et Conflits* 31 (1998): 13–38; Jef Huysmans, "Security—Technique or Techniques? A Discussion of the Complexity of the Meaning of Security," paper prepared for the conference "Risque, menaces et peurs de l'immigration—sentiments d'insécurité et processus de sécurité," Centre d'etudes et de recherches internationales, Paris, 1997.

43. The signifier is one of the two dimensions of a sign: signifier and signified. The *signifier* refers to the expressive dimension of language (e.g., the word *Europe* spoken, written, symbolized, etc.). The *signified* refers to the content of language (e.g., the meaning of *Europe,* such as "European integration").

See Algirdas J. Greimas and Joseph Courtés, *Sémiotique. Dictionnaire raisonné de la théorie du langage* (Paris: Hachette, 1993).

44. Marco Martiniello, *Sortir des ghettos culturels* (Paris: Presses de Sciences Po, 1997), 20–25; Jocelyne Cesari, *Faut-il avoir peur de l'islam?* (Paris: Presses de Sciences Po, 1997).

45. That is what is expressed by the term *societal security.* Ole Wæver, Barry Buzan, Morten Kelstrup, and Pierre Lemaitre, eds., *Identity, Migration and the New Security Agenda in Europe* (London: Pinter, 1993); Barry Buzan, Ole Wæver, and Jaap de Wilde, *Security: A New Framework for Analysis* (Boulder, Colo.: Lynne Rienner, 1998), 119–140.

46. Cesari, *Faut-il avoir peur de l'islam?*

47. Martin O. Heisler and Zig Layton-Henry, "Migration and the Links Between Social and Societal Security," in Ole Wæver, Barry Buzan, Morten Kelstrup, and Pierre Lemaitre, eds., *Identity, Migration and the New Security Agenda in Europe* (London: Pinter, 1993), 148–166.

48. Martiniello, *Sortir des ghettos culturels,* 14.

49. See, for example, Jürgen Habermas, "Citizenship and National Identity: Some Reflections on the Future of Europe," *Praxis International* 12, 1 (1992): 1–19; Yasemin N. Soysal, *Limits of Citizenship: Migrants and Postnational Membership in Europe* (Chicago: University of Chicago Press, 1994); Sayad, *L'Immigration ou les paradoxes de l'altérité;* Dominique Schnapper, *L'Europe des immigrés* (Paris: Edition François Bouvin, 1992); Daniel Weinstock, "Nationalisme et philosophie libérale: peut-on limiter l'immigration afin de protéger une culture," in Klaus-Gerd Giesen, *L'Ethique de l'espace politique mondial: Métissages disciplinaires* (Brussels: Bruylant, 1997), 49–72.

50. Göran Dahl, *Radical Conservatism and the Future of Politics* (London: Sage, 1999); Jürgen Habermas, *The New Conservatism* (Cambridge: MIT Press, 1989); Samuel P. Huntington, *The Clash of Civilizations and the Remaking of World Order* (New York: Simon and Schuster, 1996); John McCormick, *Carl Schmitt's Critique of Liberalism* (Cambridge: Cambridge University Press, 1997).

51. On the fear of suburbs in Western societies and the issue of migration, see Henri Rey, *La Peur des banlieues* (Paris: Presses de Sciences Po, 1996).

52. Etienne Balibar, "Qu'est-ce qu'une 'frontière'?" in Marie-Claire Caloz-Tschopp, Axel Clevenot, and Maria-Pia Tschopp, eds., *Asile—Violence—Exclusion en Europe. Histoire, Analyse, Prospective* (Geneva: Section des Sciences de l'Education de l'Université de Genève, 1994), 339.

53. Miles and Thränhardt, *Migration and European Integration,* 9, 10.

54. The list was requested under Article 100c of the TEU.

55. Robert Miles, *Racism After "Race" Relations* (London: Routledge, 1993), 179–181.

56. For a polemic example, see A. Sivanandan, "Racism: The Road from Germany," *Race and Class* 34, 3 (1993): 67. On the rationalization of xenophobia in Europe, see Gilbert Rochu, "Du contrôle des frontières au racisme ordinaire," *Le Monde diplomatique,* June 1995, 19.

57. Miles, *Racism;* Michel Wieviorka, *L'Espace du racisme* (Paris: Seuil, 1991).

58. J. N. Pieterse, "Fictions of Europe," *Race and Class* 32, 3 (1991): 4–10; A. Sivanandan, *Communities of Resistance: Writings on Black Struggles for Socialism* (London: Verso, 1990), 153–160.

59. Robert Miles, "Explaining Racism in Contemporary Europe," in Ali Rattansi and Sallie Westwood, eds., *Racism, Modernity and Identity: On the Western Front* (Cambridge: Polity, 1994), 189–198; Michel Wieviorka, "Racism in Europe:

Unity and Diversity," in Ali Rattansi and Sallie Westwood, eds., *Racism, Modernity and Identity: On the Western Front* (Cambridge: Polity, 1994), 185–188.

60. Ugur, "Freedom of Movement vs. Exclusion"; Bigo, 'L'Illusoire maîtrise des frontières."

61. Miles, *Racism After "Race" Relations*, 175–185.

62. For a radical argumentation along these lines in the context of the Belgian migration debate, see J. Blommaert and J. Verschueren, *Het Belgische Migrantendebat* (Antwerp: International Pragmatics Association, 1992); J. Blommaert and J. Verschueren, *Debating Diversity: Analysing the Rhetoric of Tolerance* (New York: Routledge, 1998).

63. Often one distinguishes between integration and assimilation of aliens. Although that distinction is not further developed in this chapter, with "integrationist discourses and practices" I refer primarily to those with assimilationist tendencies.

64. Miles, *Racism After "Race" Relations*, 185–190.

65. Ibid., 207.

66. Virginie Guiraudon, "Multiculturalisme et droit des étrangers dans l'Union Européenne," in Riva Kastoryano, ed., *Quelle identité pour l'Europe? Le multiculturalisme à l'épreuve* (Paris: Presses de Sciences Po, 1998), 143–166; Patrick Ireland, "Migration, Free Movement, and Immigrant Integration in the EU: A Bifurcated Policy Response," in S. Leibfried and P. Pierson, eds., *European Social Policy* (Washington, D.C.: Brookings Institution, 1995), 257; European Parliament, *Report Drawn Up on Behalf of the Committee of Inquiry into Racism and Xenophopia* (Luxembourg: Office for Official Publications of the European Communities, 1991).

67. Ireland, "Facing the True 'Fortress Europe'"; Riva Kastoryano, "Participation transnationale et citoyenneté: les immigrés dans l'Union Européenne," *Cultures et Conflits* 28 (1997): 59–73.

68. Wæver, "European Security Identities."

69. Paul Close, *Citizenship, Europe and Change* (London: Macmillan, 1995); Marco Martiniello, "European Citizenship, European Identity and Migrants: Towards a Post-national State?" in Marco Martiniello, ed., *Migration, Citizenship, and Ethno-national Identities in the European Union* (Aldershot, UK: Avebury, 1995); E. Meehan, *Citizenship in the European Community* (London: Sage, 1993).

70. Rémy Leveau, "Espace, culture, frontière. Projection de l'Europe à l'extérieur," in Riva Kastoryano, ed., *Quelle identité pour l'Europe* (Paris: Presses de Sciences Po, 1998), 247–259; Jean-Marc Ferry, "Que'est-ce qu'une identité postnationale?" *Esprit* 59, 7(1990): 80–90; Jean-Marc Ferry, "Pertinence du post-national," *Esprit* 60, 11 (1991): 80–93; Jean-Marc Ferry, "Une 'philosophie' de la Communauté," in Jean-Marc Ferry and Paul Thibaud, *Discussion sur l'Europe* (Paris: Calmann-Lévy, 1992), 127–218; Habermas, "Citizenship and National Identity."

71. Guiraudon, "Multiculturalisme et droit des étrangers," 158–166; Virginie Guiraudon, "Citizenship Rights for Non-citizens: France, Germany, and the Netherlands," in Christian Joppke, ed., *Challenge to the Nation-State: Immigration in Western Europe and the United States* (Oxford: Oxford University Press, 1998).

72. Faist, "How to Define a Foreigner?"; Ayse Ceyhan, "Migrants as a Threat. A Comparative Analysis of Securitarian Rhetoric: France and the United States," in Victor Gray, ed., *A European Dilemma: Immigration, Citizenship, Identity* (New York: Berghahn Books, forthcoming); Ceyhan, "Towards a bifocal con-

trol"; Grete Brochmann, "Control in Immigration Policies: A Closed Europe in the Making," in Russell King, ed., *The New Geography of European Migrations* (London: Belhaven, 1993), 103.

73. Thomas Faist, "Boundaries of Welfare States: Immigrants and Social Rights on the National and Supranational Level," in Robert Miles and Dietrich Thränhardt, eds., *Migration and European Integration: The Dynamics of Inclusion and Exclusion* (London: Pinter, 1995), 189.

74. Faist, "How to Define a Foreigner?" 61.

75. On the general recognition of social rights for immigrants in Western Europe, see Soysal, *Limits of Citizenship*. On stigma, see Ervin Goffman, *Stigma: Notes on the Management of Spoiled Identity* (London: Penguin Books, 1990).

76. Den Boer, "Moving Between Bogus and Bona Fide."

77. Faist, "How to Define a Foreigner?" 61–62.

78. On the invasion metaphor, see among others, ibid., 61.

79. Jacques Donzelot, *L'Invention du social. Essai sur le déclin des passions politiques* (Paris: Seuil, 1994).

80. Ibid.; François Ewald, *Histoire de l'Etat Providence* (Paris: Grasset, 1996); Claus Offe, *Contradictions of the Welfare State* (London: Hutchinson, 1984).

81. Donzelot, *L'Invention du social,* 185–263; Jürgen Habermas, *Legitimation Crisis,* translated by Thomas McCarthy (London: Polity, 1976).

82. Donzelot, *L'Invention du social,* 185–263.

83. Weinstock, "Nationalisme et philosophie libérale."

84. For more extensive discussion, see Jef Huysmans, "The Question of the Limit: Desecuritisation and the Aesthetics of Horror in Political Realism," *Millennium* 27, 3 (1998): 569–589.

85. For a radical analysis of this phenomenon in the context of the Belgian migration debate, see Blommaert and Verschueren, *Het Belgische Migrantendebat;* Blommaert and Verschueren, *Debating Diversity.*

86. Dahl, *Radical Conservatism;* Göran Dahl, "Will 'The Other God' Fail Again? On the Possible Return of the Conservative Revolution," *Theory, Culture and Society* 13, 1 (1996): 25–50.

87. Christian Semmler, "Pourquoi l'extrême droite perce," *Le Monde diplomatique,* September 1998, 5; Christian de Brie, "Le Terreau de l'extrême droite," *Le Monde diplomatique,* May 1988, 1, 13. On the diversity of the extreme right in contemporary Europe, see Geoffrey Harris, *The Dark Side of Europe: The Extreme Right in the 1980s,* 2nd ed. (Edinburgh: Edinburgh University Press, 1994); Aurel Braun and Stephen Scheinberg, eds., *The Extreme Right: Freedom and Security at Risk* (Boulder, Colo.: Westview, 1997). On the worldview of the extreme right, see Helmut Reinalter, Franko Petri, and Rudiger Kaufmann, eds., *Das Weltbild des Rechtsextremismus: die Strukturen det Entsolidarisierung* (Vienna: Studienverlag, 1998).

88. Quoted in Ireland, "Migration, Free Movement, and Immigrant Integration," 262.

89. Anna Leander and Stefano Guzzini, "European Economic and Monetary Union and the Crisis of European Social Contracts," in Petri Minkkinen and Heikki Patomaki, eds., *The Politics of Economic and Monetary Union* (Helsinki: Finnish Institute of International Affairs, 1997), 131–161.

9

European Asylum Policies and the Search for a European Identity

Vera Gowlland-Debbas

In this chapter I focus on the recent prioritization of immigration and asylum on the European agenda and the relationship between the securitization of these issues—inter alia by being linked to the European response to global security questions such as drug trafficking, terrorism, and other international crimes—and the overall process of European integration and search for a European political identity.[1] The leading question is whether policies aimed at exclusion in the name of preservation of a mythical European identity are not paradoxically resulting in a dilution of this identity.

There are two key elements to the approach I adopt here. The first is the international law perspective. The purpose is not to engage in fine legal argumentation but to show how international law can be used as a supplemental tool to shed light on European responses to asylum and immigration issues and their security dimension. For on the one hand, the assumption of international legal obligations inevitably sets constraints on states who have constructed their identity on such foundations as democracy and the rule of law; such obligations—realpolitik arguments to the contrary—do have an impact on and the tendency to color policy decisions. On the other hand, international law has also been used by these same states to legitimate policy designs: In the field of immigration and asylum the creation of new legislative barriers has served to reinforce policies aimed at exclusion.

The second element is the importance of maintaining the conceptual difference between migrants and asylum seekers. The particular nature of the European response to population flows has been marked more by the pressures of asylum seeking than immigration; consequently, asylum rather than immigration has constituted the important challenge to the pillars on which Europe has built its identity.

The Conceptual Distinction Between Migrants and Asylum Seekers

The conceptual difference between migrants and asylum seekers is of course well known, but it is nevertheless important in this context to emphasize this distinction once again, for the two categories have been consciously or unconsciously blurred in recent European rhetoric and public perceptions.

It has been said that migrants are movers par excellence. In contrast the basic absence of a real freedom of choice and movement is the essence of the refugee's condition. Although it is not easy in practice to determine which movements are coerced and which are not—and it is perhaps more accurate to speak of a continuum, for there is a whole range of complex situations between voluntary and involuntary migration—nevertheless the status of refugees in its broad sense is based on the notion of "disfranchisement or breakdown of basic membership rights" since it pertains to groups of persons outside their state of origin who have been effectively deprived of the formal protection of their government.[2]

International law thrives on abstractions, and the concept of statehood is one such abstraction. But so is the essential legal link, the umbilical cord, binding an individual to his or her state. The problem is that the severance of this link (whether de facto through loss of protection or de jure through loss of nationality) results in an anomaly, a malfunction of the interstate system.

The first consequence of this malfunction is that where the loss of protection from one's country of origin results in a refugee condition, other states will be faced with claims for interim substitute protection. To address such claims, a universal system of protection was elaborated in the immediate aftermath of World War II that took the form of multilateral agreements providing for the grant of refugee status in juridical terms and for the eventual integration of these individuals into another state. This edifice was capped by international supervisory machinery to ensure observance of these undertakings and to promote improvement of the position of refugees. It is important to emphasize here that the main pillar of this system—the 1951 convention on the status of refugees and its update, the 1967 protocol—was forged mainly by Western European states as part of their political and ideological designs in the framework of the Cold War. This convention, once considered to be Eurocentric, has now become universalized with some 137 states as parties.

The second consequence of the specificity of the refugee condition is that it presents states with a conundrum, for unlike migrants, these individuals, even if unwanted, cannot be returned to their country of origin, at least not until the conditions that have led to their coerced movement have been removed.

The existence of this anomaly in the interstate system—because of the claim of these individuals to protection and their inability to reintegrate their countries of origin—places tremendous pressures on the traditional basic premises of international law and relations, namely, the sovereign rights of states to control admission into their territories. These individuals have of course no guarantee that they will be admitted, for the irony of the system lies in that while the right to leave any country, including one's own, was central to demands made of Eastern Europe in Western European Cold War rhetoric, one corollary of this right, namely, the right to asylum, did not succeed in establishing itself as an unconditional subjective right of the individual. Nevertheless, the discretion of a state to decide on who should be admitted and who denied entry is tempered by certain important limitations, such as the principle of *nonrefoulement* embedded in Article 33 of the 1951 refugee convention (the obligation of a state not to return a refugee to a territory where her or his life or freedom would be threatened on certain defined grounds), as well as the meting out of certain human rights standards and social benefits to those who are admitted into the territory.

Herein lies the dilemma confronting European states in their choice between inclusion and exclusion. For while migrants and asylum seekers alike constitute cross-border movements and pose problems of entry and presence, when nations are faced with asylum-seeking populations this choice cannot be totally discretionary, since the response can no longer be based on intrinsic policy factors alone—that is, domestic economic, political, and social factors or, in the case of Europe, linked to the development of an internal market—but must be determined by extrinsic factors, that is, response to external conditions and to the need to assume international obligations freely undertaken.

As a result, European states are pressured into at least considering asylum applications for the purpose of distinguishing between bona fide and fake refugees, the fake being presented as the free riders. That the 80–95 percent or so of asylum seekers who fall into the latter category may well not fit the convention definition of a well-founded fear of persecution but nevertheless still be worthy of protection, as, for example, those fleeing armed conflicts, internal violence, or generalized violations of human rights, is not made at all clear to the general public, who tend to assimilate these individuals to illegal aliens or drug traffickers.

Migrants Versus Asylum Seekers and the Link Between Population Flows and Security Issues

The distinction between asylum and immigration is also important to the question of securitization of population flows. It has been shown how recent European migration policies have become dominantly constructed in terms of security with the protection of public order as a core theme.[3]

Yet I would like to point out that asylum—as opposed to migration policies originally grounded on economic motives—was from the start placed not only, and even not primarily, within a human rights framework but within a security logic. Security considerations were in fact built into the international refugee protection system.

While protection of refugees would seem to fall squarely into the realm of human rights, nevertheless refugee law developed separately from human rights law. Insofar as "refugeehood" was premised on the crossing of borders and impacted on other states, it was interlinked with the question of territorial asylum, which of course developed as a counterpart to the law on extradition—par excellence related to security matters and the need to distinguish between the political offender and common criminals.

One can trace historically the attempt to distinguish between those deserving of protection and those who were considered unworthy.[4] In pleading that "a permanent residence ought not to be denied to foreigners who, expelled from their home, are seeking refuge," Hugo Grotius, the so-called father of international law, writing in 1625, underlined that asylum is "for the benefit of those who suffer from undeserved enmity not those who have done something that is injurious to human society."[5]

The security concerns of the predominantly Western European states who gathered together in 1951 permeated the refugee convention and weighed in the balance with humanitarian concerns for refugee protection. From the start it was accepted that not only should one arrive at a universal definition of a refugee for purposes of application of the convention, but that one should also filter out the deserving from the undeserving. This is understandable in the immediate aftermath of World War II in a Europe rampant with quislings and war criminals, not to speak of the common criminal offender.

These security concerns are reflected in the various provisions of the 1951 convention. First, the so-called exclusion clauses ensured that certain categories of asylum seekers would remain outside the ambit of refugee protection. Article 1D, for example, refers to those who were receiving aid from UN agencies other than the United Nations High Commissioner for Refugees (UNHCR) at the time the convention was concluded. This is obviously directed to the exclusion of Palestinian refugees, considered too explosive an issue in the volatile Middle East context. But also excluded from the benefits of the convention are those who have committed crimes against peace, war crimes, or crimes against humanity; those who have committed a serious nonpolitical crime prior to admission; and those who are guilty of acts contrary to the purposes and principles of the United Nations (Article 1[F]).

Second, even in its formulation of the principle of *nonrefoulement*—the core of refugee protection—the convention excludes from its application a "refugee whom there are reasonable grounds for regarding as a danger to the security of the country in which he is, or who having been convicted by a final judgement of a particularly serious crime, constitutes a danger to the community of that country" (Article 33[2]).

Other provisions reflecting concerns for national security or public order were those on expulsion (Article 32), provisional measures essential to national security in the case of particular persons in time of war or other grave and exceptional circumstances (Article 9), and illegal entry (Article 31) (which, however, does not affect the eligibility of illegal entrants). Other instruments have made exceptions also in respect to the mass influx of persons.[6]

Despite the ambiguity and scope of these provisions, they are intended to provide safeguards for the asylum state. The convention thus contains its own balancing mechanisms, weighing the interest of the individual refugee in obtaining protection from persecution against the interest of the receiving state in maintaining security and public order; in short, weighing humanitarian against security concerns.

When the political interests of Western European states coincided with humanitarian concerns, the security aspects certainly remained in the background. The refugee definition laid down in the convention—that is, a person who has a well-founded fear of persecution on certain defined grounds—corresponded well at the time to the image of the political opponents of Eastern European regimes. The liberal who jumped over the Berlin wall in search of freedom and democracy in the West, the Hungarian in 1956, or Czech in 1968 posed no threat to Western Europe, either physically or culturally. He or she was easily integrated. On the contrary, the greater the number of refugees, the more indication of persecution in the East, the more victory points scored by Western European rhetoric.

In this sense, it may be said that the linking of migration and the new types of asylum seekers in a security logic is of recent vintage. Nevertheless, and herein lies the difference between asylum and migration, the incorporation of security concerns into international legal instruments, that is, the translation of political perceptions of threats into legal mandatory language, however vague may be phrases such as "reasonable grounds for regarding as a danger to the security of the country" concerned, or notions of public order, transforms discretionary choices of states into ones to which outer limits have been set, in the same way as discretionary choices in admissions policies have been constrained, as discussed above.

Emerich de Vattel once said that a nation "has the right, and is even obliged, to follow in this matter [admission of refugees] the rules of prudence. But this prudence should not take the form of suspicion nor be pushed to the point of refusing an asylum to the outcast on slight grounds and from unreasonable and foolish fears. It should be regulated by never losing sight of the charity and sympathy which are due to the unfortunate."[7]

That the so-called margin of appreciation of states in deciding on questions of security and public order is not unlimited has been emphasized by both international and regional courts on a number of occasions. In a case brought before the Permanent Court of International Justice in 1935 concerning certain decrees adopted by the senate of the free city of Danzig that would have left the courts to fill in the gaps in both criminal law and procedure by reference to "sound popular feeling," the court stated: "It is true that a criminal law . . . sometimes leaves the judge not only to interpret it, but also to determine how to apply it. . . . But [discretionary power] should not be extended to the point beyond which it would render valueless the rule that fundamental rights may not be restricted except by a law."[8]

The European Court of Human Rights, while recognizing that the European Convention of Human Rights leaves the contracting parties an area of discretion, stated with reference to the emergency powers of states:

> It falls in the first place to each Contracting State, with its responsibility for "the life of [its] nation", to determine whether that life is threatened by a "public emergency" and, if so, how far it is necessary to go in attempting to overcome the emergency. . . . Nevertheless, the States do not enjoy an unlimited power in this respect. The Court . . . is empowered to rule on whether the states have gone beyond the "extent strictly required by the exigencies" of the crisis. . . . The domes-

tic margin of appreciation is thus accompanied by a European super-vision.[9]

The manner in which a number of national courts have balanced humanitarian and security considerations in dealing with asylum cases is reflected in the case of *State of Netherlands v. Vastiampillai,* which illustrates the limits of discretion in asylum law.[10] In this case the Dutch supreme court had to consider an appeal on the question of whether the possession of 3.7 grams of heroin by a Sri Lankan Tamil arrested in the Netherlands was a particularly serious crime within the wording of article 33(2) of the 1951 convention and hence outweighed the principle of *nonrefoulement.* The court balanced the interests of the state in safety and welfare with that of the asylum seeker in *nonrefoulement* and rejected the secretary of state's intention to introduce an objective criterion, namely, that any violation of the law on drugs would constitute such a particularly serious crime. It considered that this must be answered on the basis of the concrete circumstances of the case and that in this case the crime committed was not so serious as to exclude the refugee from the benefits of Article 33(1). There have been similar cases since.

Asylum Seekers Versus Migrants and the European Response to Population Flows

That this edifice of international legal protection has reduced the margin of appreciation of European states in determining such onetime discretionary factors as who to admit on national territory or intrinsic factors of national security or public order has considerably colored the European response to migration and created a paradoxical situation. In today's climate the 1951 convention system, which Europe itself was preeminent in shaping, is no longer a convenient mechanism. Rather, since European states have agreed to play by the rules of the 1951 convention, this has led them to grant asylum to refugees who conform to the convention definition.

Yet the adoption of policies of exclusion, as a result of numerous political and sociological factors, has meant presenting the debate as one between real refugees and fake ones. To separate one from the other, however, means processing asylum claims through costly determination procedures. In consequence, there has been a noted tendency to apply the 1951 convention definition, already a narrow one, in a very restrictive fashion, the net result being that the percentage of asylum seekers deemed to be bona fide refugees has dropped dramatically in all European countries, in some cases as low as 3–5 percent of asylum seekers. The huge edifice of refugee determination procedures is therefore relevant to increasingly smaller segments of the asylum-seeking population. States are then faced with the question of what to do with the large majority of those who are determined not to be convention refugees and who nevertheless cannot be returned to their countries of origin because of the insecure conditions prevailing there. In some cases these individuals are granted temporary protection, which even if institutionalized in national law remains a protection that can be and has been ended at the host state's discretion (as the case of Bosnian refugees has well illustrated); in other cases they disappear underground.

This dilemma therefore has determined European policy responses that consist in significantly reducing the chances of the asylum seekers accessing national territory or, once they are in national territory, of accessing refugee determination procedures by means of the erection of physical and legal barriers. This implies in many cases abandonment of the traditional protection system based on a separation of the deserving from the undeserving and has taken the form of particularized asylum practices or concepts that lie outside the international protection regime: artificially created "international" airport zones, "manifestly unfounded" applications that justify immediate return at the border, or so-called safe third country or safe country of origin principles that are considered not to transgress the *nonrefoulement* obligation. Such policies also go hand in hand with deterrence measures, for example, detention of "irregular" asylum seekers or the cutting off of social benefits.

A series of conventional arrangements reached within the inner and outer circles of Europe—the Schengen Agreements, the 1990 Dublin convention, the projection of parallel agreements with non-EU members; and the assimilation of the Schengen *acquis,* now part of the institutional law of the European Union by virtue of the Amsterdam Treaty—have institutionalized these ad hoc attempts to restrict access to national territory and refugee determination procedures.[11] Under the Dublin convention, for example, the responsibility for processing asylum claims has been narrowed, on the basis of enumerated criteria, to one state alone out of all EU member states, though the latter are all parties to the 1951 convention and 1967 protocol and hence bear individual responsibility under those instruments. The logic of the Dublin convention invites asylum seekers to play Russian roulette: They have one chance out of fifteen to hit on the right asylum state, and rejection in the assigned state responsible for determining asylum claims means exclusion from the rest of the EU area. In the absence of effective harmonization of laws, however, the likelihood of a downward spiral of asylum laws is real. The Schengen *acquis* is designed to limit the right of refugees to choose their place of asylum within the region and even to seek asylum. This is ensured by such measures as the safe third country concept, visa requirements for countries on the verge of producing not immigration but refugee flows (e.g., former Yugoslavia), and sanctions on those carrying undocumented aliens. But the restrictions on the right to seek asylum now affect even more radically nationals of member states of the European Union, who have seen their right to apply for asylum in another member state restricted to certain exceptional situations.[12]

All these measures are extraneous to the system set in place by the international system of refugee protection that depends on determining whether a person is eligible for the bestowal of refugee status (from which all kinds of benefits flow) and serve to considerably weaken the present system. European states are not thereby solving the refugee problem but merely deflecting the flow to increasingly outer areas, as even non-EU members, such as Switzerland or countries from Eastern Europe, are compelled to resort to similar measures. In parallel with the adoption of measures that effectively prevent the operation of the international protection system based on asylum, European states have attempted to cope with the refugee dilemma by other means: promotion of concepts such as "protection in the region," or "in-country protection" (so-called safe havens or protected areas), with all the consequent drama this has entailed in some regions such as Srebenica in Bosnia.

The European Response to Asylum Seeking and the Search for a European Identity

I come to the link between the asylum issues discussed above and the issue basic to this volume of the search for a European identity. If there is one certifiable aspect of European cultural identity—of European belongingness—it is the discourse based on the rule of law and enjoyment of human rights and fundamental freedoms that has been upheld as the basis of genuine democracy. There is in addition a much-vaunted common understanding of what is meant by these terms. This European commitment to rule of law, human rights, and democracy, to which has been added "prosperity through economic liberty and justice," underlies all institutional development in the region, from the preamble to the 1949 statute of the Council of Europe to the 1990 OSCE charter of Paris for a new Europe. These continue to provide the pillars on which European identity has been built, notwithstanding future risks of dilution through expansion of membership outside the inner circle.[13] These guiding principles also underlie the European Union. Article 6 (ex Article F) of the Treaty on European Union as amended by the Treaty of Amsterdam declares:

1. The Union is founded on the principles of liberty, democracy, respect for human rights and fundamental freedoms, and the rule of law, principles which are common to the Member States.
2. The Union shall respect fundamental rights, as guaranteed by the European Convention for the Protection of Human Rights and Fundamental Freedoms signed in Rome on 4 November 1950 and as they result from the constitutional traditions common to the Member States, as general principles of Community law.

These terms have not just remained at the level of rhetoric but have been given substance through the jurisprudence of regional courts.[14] It is because of the strengthened protection and judicial procedures afforded by human rights law that the European Court of Human Rights has been faced with a growing number of asylum cases in recent years that it has examined from the perspective of obligations under the European Convention of Human Rights.

In this framework the issue of how to cope with asylum seekers is placing Europe in a quandary. In the name of preservation of this heritage based on consensus on certain values and purported dependence on cultural homogeneity, the states of Europe have been forced into policies of cultural exclusion. But by the development of what has been termed a two-tier human rights system—that is, one that grants citizens the most sophisticated protection from human rights abuses yet excludes from full human rights protection unwanted aliens, branded as "illegal" or those in an "irregular" situation—Europe faces the risk of undermining this very identity.

The result is a striking dissonance between, on the one hand, the values that lie at the core of European identity and that are continually evolving in the direction of strengthening the rule of law, democracy, and human rights and, on the other, developments in European policy and legislation concerning asylum seekers (although it should be said that European states are by no means alone in this respect, if one takes into account developments in the United States, Canada, Australia, and New Zealand, to name a few). As a result of exclusion policies, asylum law is being developed as an exception to or tangentially to the evolution of regional and universal human rights law, the net result being that asylum seekers may find themselves outside the orbit of the expanding protection given by international human rights law to individuals in general.

This is not the place to evaluate these developments in detail in the light of international law, but I wish to illustrate briefly this contrast between the positive developments in human rights law and developments in the treatment of asylum seekers by giving the examples of the spatial extension of human rights protection, the extension of the beneficiaries of human rights protection, the acknowledgment by human rights law of nonstate actors, and the erosion of the sphere of domestic jurisdiction and so-called withering away of national sovereignty.

The Spatial Extension of Human Rights Protection

Recent developments in international human rights law have acknowledged extension of the state's obligations in human rights protection beyond its own borders. In Article 1 of the European Convention of Human Rights, the parties undertake to secure the rights and freedoms defined in section 1 to everyone "within their jurisdiction." This term has been defined as not being limited to "national territory." The European Commission, for example, in dealing with the obligations of Turkey under the convention stated that "the High Contracting Parties are bound to secure the said rights and freedoms to all persons under their actual authority and responsibility, not only when that authority is exercised within their own territory but also when it is exercised abroad."[15] That the obligations of states to ensure respect for the provisions contained in these instruments apply to the treatment of persons under their authority—that is, under their "jurisdiction"—even if acting outside national territory, is confirmed on the universal level by the Committee on Human Rights in its "General Comments on Articles 2 and 41 of the Covenant on Civil and Political Rights."[16] Moreover, in its famous Soering decision, the European Court of Human Rights even extended the extraterritorial obligation on the European state parties not to return a person to a state that was not party to the convention in which violations of the European convention might occur.[17] This principle has been applied by the court in asylum cases in upholding the convention's obligations under Article 3, which prohibits torture and inhuman and degrading treatment.[18]

Yet in seeking to restrict their obligations toward asylum seekers, European states have narrowed the spatial application of the very principle that lies at the heart of human rights protection of asylum seekers, namely, the principle of *nonrefoulement*. This policy of narrowing the scope of jurisdiction is not limited to European states, as illustrated by the U.S. Supreme Court decision in *Sale v. Haitian Centers Council Inc.*, in which the Court took a wholly different approach to the territorial scope of the 1951 convention in considering the case of the interception on the high seas by U.S. customs authorities of Haitian stowaways, or boat people: "A treaty cannot impose uncontemplated extraterritorial obligations on those who ratify it though no more than its general humanitarian intent. Because the text of Article 33 cannot reasonably be read to say anything at all about a nation's actions toward aliens outside its own territory, it does not prohibit such actions."[19] This has not been the interpretation either of UNHCR or of a foremost human rights authority, Theodor Meron, who, while recognizing that "most of the provisions of the Refugee convention, in contrast to those of the political Covenant, may be primarily territorial in character, in the sense that they apply to claimants who have reached the soil of the state of asylum," nevertheless concludes that "keeping in mind Article 33 of the Refugee Convention—when a state undertakes to exercise its jurisdiction to enforce its laws on the high seas by returning potential asylum seekers to the country they are fleeing, the Convention, and not only its spirit (as the Court suggested) is breached."[20]

Although no similar case confronts EU states on such a large scale, such fictions as international airport zones, the imposition of visa requirements, and sanctions on carriers serve to restrict in spirit if not in law the spatial dimension of refugee protection from *refoulement*.

The Extension of the Beneficiaries

The whole idea of human rights is that they pertain to everyone by virtue of his or her nature as a human being. It follows that the international measures to secure their protection must be anchored in the principle of universality and cannot be limited in their effect to the citizens of one country or of a group of countries but extend to everyone within the jurisdiction. This is reinforced by the prohibition of discrimination that is the core of many human rights treaties, including the 1951 refugee convention. Legitimate distinctions are of course allowable in certain cases, provided they aim at the creation of true equality by taking into consideration the factual inequalities of certain vulnerable groups or for making necessary distinctions between aliens and nationals, for example, as regards the right to vote. Even in respect to the latter, however, the general trend has been to seek to reinforce the protection of human rights instruments with regard to nonnationals, as reflected in the United Nations "Declaration on the Human Rights of Individuals Who Are Not Nationals of the Country in Which They Live."[21]

Whereas, however, the general tendency has been to reinforce the concept of nondiscrimination, and in particular to expand the individual's access to protection by means of new instruments that reinforce human rights law concerning such groups as children, women (in vulnerable situations), the indigenous, and the disabled, policy and legislation regarding asylum seekers has sought to create a special category of aliens in an "irregular" situation who are singled out for certain treatment and are removed from the pale not only of human rights law but even of refugee law. The term *irregular* has been given an extensive scope, encompassing not only those who enter the territory illegally but covering also a wide variety of situations, in some cases even including those asylum seekers who are in the process of awaiting the outcome to their appeal from a negative asylum decision. This so-called irregular situation entitles asylum states to ignore the general reach of human rights law by resorting to such practices as detention and penalization of illegal entry, leading in some cases to outright inhuman and degrading treatment of asylum seekers and disregard of the rights of refugee children and the concept of family unity.

The Extension of Responsibility for
Human Rights Violations by Nonstate Actors

The obligation not only to respect but also to guarantee the human rights laid down in the international instruments imply positive obligations on the part of the state even where this concerns violations of human rights by individuals acting in a nonofficial capacity. That human rights law has come to recognize the responsibility of the state for the acts of nonstate entities acting within its jurisdiction where the state fails in its obligations of "due diligence" has been reflected in jurisprudence, such as the famous *Rodriguez Velasquez* decision.[22] The European Commission of Human Rights has also considered that the obligations under Article 3 of the convention applied in a case where those who hold substantial power within the state, even though they are not the government, threaten the life and security of the individual.[23]

This evolution of human rights law is again not reflected in developments in European asylum law. For evident reasons in order to restrict the field of application of the 1951 convention, European states have tended to refuse to consider as falling within the purview of the definition of persecution central to the determination of refugee status persecution carried out by nonstate actors. As a result, refugee status in a number of European countries, with certain exceptions, has been denied, for example, to individuals fleeing persecution at the hands of militias or to women fleeing societal persecution.

Moreover, confronted with new manifestations of racism fueled by private parties and the rise of xenophobic and neo-Nazi tendencies, aimed particularly at certain groups of foreigners and asylum seekers in the very countries in Europe that have long considered themselves to be the hallmarks of democracy, governments have shown reluctance to assume responsibility for the prevention of such acts on grounds of freedom of expression. This is reflected in the reservations of some states about Article 4 of the convention on the elimination of racial discrimination, in which they are required, inter alia, to condemn all propaganda and all organizations that are based on ideas or theories of racial superiority, to take positive measures to eradicate incitement to or acts of such discrimination, and to penalize such acts by private individuals or bodies as opposed to state officials.[24]

The Erosion of "Statist" Conceptions of International Relations

In order not to create a situation in which European values may appear to be threatened, states have sought to prevent asylum seekers from reaching borders when the pressure of meeting international obligations becomes too demanding.

What is remarkable is that in this framework states are effectively extending their jurisdiction in order precisely to deny it, and with it the obligations that flow from it. This produces a very interesting phenomenon, in that while current discourse centers on the demise of the nation-state—the shrinking of the sphere of domestic jurisdiction, erosion of state sovereignty, the strengthening of supranational and universal institutions, globalization of international economic relations— asylum seeking in Europe has been marked by a reinforcement of that last bastion of state sovereignty: the right of the state to decide whom to admit and whom to expel.

Europe is defending access to national territory not only through reinforcement of the outer borders of fortress Europe but even in areas outside of or increasingly remote from these borders, such as the country of origin itself, for instance through control at foreign airport departure points.

European policies in the field of asylum *are* being justified in terms of national and regional legislation—in other words, the discourse continues to be that of the rule of law. Whatever the merits of these legal arguments, it is the spirit underlying these legal developments and the grave risk of undermining the *ideological* underpinnings of European identity that are of concern.

The European Court has stated in regard to the European Convention of Human Rights:

> The purpose of the High Contracting Parties in concluding the Convention was not to concede to each other reciprocal rights and obli-

gations in pursuance of their individual national interests, but to realise the aims and ideals of the Council of Europe, as expressed in its Statute, and to establish a common public order of the free democracies of Europe with the object of safeguarding their common heritage of political traditions, ideals, freedom and the rule of law.[25]

In fact, however, Europe may be in the process of creating a form of cultural relativism in reverse—not in the sense of the rejection of universal values that do not conform to cultural particularities, which is the discourse of some Third World states, but in the implicit denial of the application of *universal* values to certain third-state nationals who seek entry. Concerning the question of European identity, we would do well to keep in mind an observation by Stephen Legomsky:

> Immigration laws are about as central to a nation's mission as anything can be. They are central because they literally shape who we are as a people. They are central also because they function as a mirror, reflecting and displaying the qualities we value in others. For both reasons, decisions on immigration policy put us to the test as no other decisions do. They reveal, for ourselves and for the world, what we really believe in and whether we are prepared to act on those beliefs.[26]

Notes

1. This linkage has been a constant leitmotiv: In response to contemporary global challenges, the joint action plan signed in Madrid on 3 December 1995 included among its objectives more effective countering of illegal immigration and weaknesses in the asylum system. The presidency's conclusions following on the Madrid European Council meeting on 15 and 16 December 1995 concerned the creation of an area of freedom and security for EU citizens, identifying—and thereby linking—as priority areas for extended cooperation terrorism, drugs and organized crime, judicial cooperation in criminal matters, and the combating of illegal immigration. The Treaty on European Union as amended by the Amsterdam Treaty, cites in Article 2 (ex Article B) as one of the objectives of the EU: "to maintain and develop the Union as an area of freedom, security and justice, in which the free movement of persons is assured in conjunction with appropriate measures with respect to external border controls, asylum, immigration and the prevention and combating of crime."

2. See, generally, James Hathaway, "A Reconsideration of the Underlying Premises of Refugee Law," *Harvard International Law Journal* 31 (1990): 129–183; and James Hathaway, "Reconceiving Refugee Law as Human Rights Protection," in Vera Gowlland and Klaus Samson, eds., *Problems and Prospects of Refugee Law* (Geneva: Graduate Institute of International Studies, 1992), 9–30.

3. See Chapter 8 in this volume.

4. The term *unworthy* of protection is used in the Swiss asylum legislation, for example.

5. *De Jure belli ac pacis*, translated by F. W. Kelsey, book 2, ch. 21, sec. 5.

6. See, for example, United Nations Declaration on Territorial Asylum adopted by the General Assembly on 14 December 1967, which gives as an exception to the principle of *nonrefoulement* "overriding reasons of national security or in order to safeguard the population, as in the case of a mass influx of persons." As an example of national legislation in the same vein, see Article 9(1) of the Swiss asylum law of 5 October 1979 (as amended on 20 June 1986), 1987 *Recueil officiel des lois fédérales* 1677.

7. Emerich de Vattel, *Le Droit des gens ou principes de la loi naturelle appliquée à la conduite aux affaires des nations et des souverains* (1758).

8. *Consistency of Certain Danzig Legislative Decrees with the Constitution of the Free City,* Permanent Court of International Justice, Series A/B, No. 65, December 4, 1935, 52–53.

9. *Ireland v. the United Kingdom,* European Court of Human Rights (ECHR), Series A, Vol. 25, para. 207, 1978.

10. *Staat der Nederlanden v. V.* (13 May 1988, Supreme Court First Chamber No.13.220), Nederlanden Jurisprudentie, no. 910, 3133.

11. See "Convention Applying the Schengen Agreement of 14 June 1985, Schengen, 19 June 1990"; "Convention Determining the State Responsible for Examining Applications for Asylum Lodged in One of the Member States the Community, Dublin, 15 June 1990," *Official Journal of the European Communities* C254/1 (1997); Protocol Integrating the Schengen Acquis into the Framework of the European Union Annexed to the Treaty on European Union and to the Treaty Establishing the European Community, 10 November 1997," *Official Journal of the European Communities* C340 (1997).

12. See "Protocol on Asylum for Nationals of Member States of the European Union Annexed to the Treaty on European Union and to the Treaty Establishing the European Communities," *Official Journal of the European Communities* C340 (1997).

13. The preamble of the statute of the Council of Europe mentions "reaffirming their devotion to the spiritual and moral values which are the common heritage of their peoples and the true source of individual freedom, political liberty and the rule of law, principles which form the basis of all genuine democracy." Article 3 declares that "every Member of the Council of Europe must accept the principles of the rule of law and of the enjoyment by all persons within its jurisdiction of human rights and fundamental freedoms." The connection between human rights and democracy is further emphasized in the preamble of the European Convention on Human Rights.

14. See, e.g., J. G. Merrils, *The Development of International Law by the European Court of Human Rights,* 2nd ed. (Manchester: Manchester University Press, 1993), 125.

15. *Cyprus v. Turkey,* ECHR, Decisions and Reports 2 (1975), 125, 136; 13 (1977), 85ff. See also *Loizidou v. Turkey,* ECHR, Series A, Vol. 310 (1995), 24.

16. UN Doc. CCPR/C/21/Rev.1/Add.6, at 4 para.12 (1994). With respect to Article 2(1), the committee stated that the term *within jurisdiction* does not imply that the state party concerned cannot be held accountable for violations of rights under the covenant that its agents commit upon the territory of another state, whether with the acquiescence of that state or in opposition to it.

17. *Soering Case,* ECHR, Series A, No. 161 (1989).

18. See, e.g., *Chahal v. UK,* ECHR, Series A, No. 22 (1996-V).

19. U.S. Supreme Court, 113 S.Ct. 2549 (1993), P.2565; see *International Legal Materials* 34 (1995): 575.

20. Theodor Meron, "Extraterritoriality of Human Rights Treaties," *American Journal of International Law* 89 (1995): 80–81. See also the statement by Louis Henkin: "It is incredible that states that had agreed not to force any human being back into the hands of his/her oppressors, intended to leave themselves—and each other—free to reach out beyond their territory to seize a refugee and to return him/her to the country from which he sought to escape." "Notes from the President," *ASIL Newsletter,* September-October 1993, 1.

21. Adopted by General Assembly Resolution 40/144 of 13 December 1985.

22. The case of *Rodriguez Velasquez, Inter-American Yearbook on Human Rights, 1988,* 986.

23. See *Ahmed v. Austria,* ECHR, Series A, No. 23 (1996-VI).

24. See in this respect the case of *Jersild v. Denmark,* the landmark judgment of the European Court of Human Rights of September 1994, ECHR, Series A, No. 298 (1995). The court had to deal with a case concerning a television documentary in the form of an interview made by the applicant and intended to describe the attitudes of a group of young people calling themselves the Greenjackets. Three of the youths who were encouraged to express racist views containing highly abusive and derogatory terms about immigrants and ethnic groups in Denmark were convicted under the Danish penal code. This was a clear statement by the Danes that the right to protection against racial discrimination took precedence over the right to freedom of expression. The ECHR found this interference into freedom of expression to be "prescribed by law" and pursuant of a legitimate aim, namely, the "protection of the reputation or rights of others." The court did, however, find against Denmark on the grounds that the documentary in question did not have as its *purpose* the propagation of racist views and ideas.

25. *Austria v. Italy* (1961), Yearbook of the European Convention on Human Rights, IV, 1961, 138.

26. Stephen H. Legomsky, "Immigration, Equality, and Diversity," *Columbia Journal of Transnational Law* 31 (1993): 335.

PART FIVE

———

CONCLUSIONS FOR
THEORY AND POLICY

10

Exclusion Versus Dilution: Real or Imagined Trade-Off?

Lars-Erik Cederman

In search of the European Union's identity, this volume has assessed boundary formation in three broad policy areas, each one loosely associated with a Maastricht pillar. Whether the flows comprise goods, diplomatic messages, or migratory movements, the EU's self-images emerge in its interaction with the "non-European" environment. We have already seen that there is evidence of both inclusion and exclusion at the EU's external interfaces. Does it all add up to a coherent picture? Albeit far from the final word on European identity formation, the current volume allows us to observe general patterns of boundary crystallization that more narrowly construed studies cannot.

Using the four boundary principles that I introduced in Chapter 1, this concluding chapter provides an overview of the theoretical and empirical landscapes explored by the contributions to this volume. Focusing especially but not exclusively on the international relations literature, it reassesses some common assumptions from integration theory. The first section compares inclusion and exclusion processes across issue areas; the second focuses on these processes at the national and European levels of aggregation. A concluding section summarizes the main findings and discusses their consequences for future theorizing about European integration.

Comparing External Identity Formation Across Issue Areas

Are certain issues inherently more inclusive than others? Do issue-specific exclusion-dilution trade-offs spread from one area to another?

What are the consequences of such conceptual entanglements? Do they lead to overall consistency or new, "higher-order" trade-offs? It may come as a surprise that our findings contradict, or at least qualify, the standard answers to these questions. First, it cannot always be assumed that each issue area is driven by its own immutable logic. Second, while integrationists usually see connectedness among issues as an inherently good thing, it appears that such spillover can have unexpectedly adverse effects. Third, the authors' empirical and theoretical observations draw attention to the underlying conceptual tensions among issue areas.

The Exclusiveness of Issue Areas

Despite their disagreements about the relative importance of the security and economic policy realms, both realists and liberals in international relations theory believe that issue areas possess general characteristics that make them more or less cooperative and, by extension, more or less prone to institutionalized inclusion. According to well-known realist principles, all international issues fall into either one of two broad categories: high and low politics.[1] These two realms are often used as a shorthand for security and military matters on the one hand and economic and technical cooperation on the other. From a traditional realist perspective, the former is not only more conflictual and exclusionary but also much more central to world politics than the latter. Thus, realist commentators tend to deny, or at least play down, the prospects for "security regimes," since in their view the security area is generally characterized by more competition, offensive strategies, high stakes, and a general lack of transparency.[2]

Although they take issue with the realist claim that high politics dominates low politics, liberals agree with their opponents' assessment of the comparatively more conflictual nature of security affairs.[3] Instead of questioning the inherent qualities of issue areas, the disagreement pertains to whether threats or wealth-related factors drive international outcomes. In their critique of the realist orthodoxy, Robert Keohane and Joseph Nye insist that overall military power is not always easily transferable. In opposition to the realist postulate of an "issue hierarchy," they propose disaggregated structural models highlighting issue-specific power. Although Keohane and Nye realize that issue areas include a subjective element depending on the way they are conceived of by political actors, the authors tacitly assume that they rest on an underlying "reality."[4] Likewise, while acknowledging that misperception and conflicting political goals may thwart international problem solving, students of "epistemic communities" retain the underlying assumption that there is a unique, "rational" way of approaching issue areas.[5]

Transferring the conventional logic to the EU's pillars, we would expect trade within the first pillar to be inherently more inclusive than the security contents of the second pillar. Yet the picture that emerges is much less clear-cut. Despite all the protectionist rhetoric in the debates about trade and media, both Schlesinger and Theiler do find that the long-term trend favors more liberal policies (see Chapters 4 and 5). But the conclusion that the security area differs significantly from other ones is far from self-evident.

Although Neumann and Schimmelfennig (Chapters 6 and 7) register important examples of exclusionary reasoning in the area of external security and enlargement, the overall trend along those policy dimensions points in a postnational direction. In fact, their analyses do not imply that the EU's external relations are marked by an inherent tendency toward closure.

Moreover, it is far from obvious that all identity formation has to happen in reaction to an external, non-European "other." Whereas Neumann regards pannationalism as endemic but ultimately impractical because of Europe's incoherent and variable institutional architecture, Schimmelfennig finds such warnings overdrawn. Observing that pannationalism has proven to be mostly ineffective on the European level, he asserts that the participants of the Eastern enlargement debates have overwhelmingly subscribed to a postnationalist logic. Although this does not eliminate the existence trade-offs in the second pillar, it suggests that the room for reactive identity formation is quite limited. To illustrate, the Helsinki summit's decision in December 1999 to allow Turkey as a candidate for admission to the European Union allays the fears that the EU is becoming a Christian club.[6]

Likewise, Ole Wæver has also criticized the alarmist tone in writings cautioning against pannationalist invocations of Europe's "other."[7] If the trade-off has so far been avoided, it is thanks to a peculiar rhetorical move. Instead of practicing territorial exclusion, Wæver asserts, contemporary integration discourse transcends the need to single out an enemy by shifting identity formation from the spatial to the temporal realm. European integration, seen from this perspective, is fundamentally a historical project aiming at the sublimation of balance of power and its harmful side effects.

According to this fundamentally constructivist view, then, no issue area is exclusive in a "hardwired" sense. Rather, certain ways of reasoning formulate issues in a way that leads to the detection of dilution threats. For example, without prejudging the case, Schlesinger explores the divergent conceptions of cultural trade. Partly reflecting economic stakes and partly ideological predilections, Americans are prone to view media products as mere goods, whereas most Europeans insist on viewing them as sensitive "programming materials" bound to have a direct impact on collective identities. Adhering to the latter way of framing this sector, European Commission president Jacques Delors turned his critique against free trade in media products into an anti-Hollywood crusade.[8]

Because of their ambiguous standing as comparatively "new" areas of integration policy, it is even less clear what to make of issues such as immigration and citizenship. Huysmans's analysis illustrates that they are subject to continuous reinterpretation (see Chapter 8). More precisely, the exclusion-dilution trade-off tends to get more severe the closer the politicization process comes to the securitization or criminalization pole, though the socioeconomic one also lends itself to an exclusive logic based on alleged threats to employment and social benefits.[9]

Given the present selection of cases, ostensibly commercial matters tied to the first pillar do not appear to be more resistant to trade-off-based reasoning than second-pillar matters. The European Commission and other integrationists launched a concerted effort to construct threatening scenarios in the media sector, for example. Policies relating to the movement of people, in contrast, have a more ambiguous status and have gradually drifted in a more exclusionary direction, although the Amsterdam's Treaty's incorporating them in the first pillar may help turn the securitization process into a more open economistic logic. If we accept that policy debates are at least partly open to construction and reinterpretation, then it becomes crucial to study the spread of issue definitions. Do issue areas rub off against each other, or does the (re-)construction process proceed independently for each issue?

Issue Linkage and Spillover

In the international political economy literature, issue linkage is usually seen as a cooperation-enhancing mechanism. The classic formulation offered by Keohane and Nye presents linkage strategies, together with agenda setting and transnational institutions, as the main mechanisms producing cooperation under "complex interdependence."[10] These points can be seen as a generalization of Ernst Haas's neofunctionalist notion of "spillover," predicated on the locomotive role of supranational organizations and the transfer of loyalty to a transnational elite.[11]

While anti-integrationist backlashes have dampened their earlier optimism, postnationalist scholars and policymakers of neofunctionalist persuasion still view spillover as an inherently positive phenomenon contributing to an "ever closer union." Whether employed as an integration-promoting tactic or dressed up as a social-scientific process, spillover serves as the main engine generating further integration through an "expansive logic" spreading from one issue area to the other. According to Haas's original formulation,

> Lack of agreement among governments can give rise to increased delegated powers on the part of [supranational] institutions. Dissatisfaction with the results of partial economic steps may lead labor and industry to demand new central action. Supranational institutions and national groups may create situations which can be dealt with only through central action, unless the nations are willing to suffer deprivations in welfare.[12]

Though Haas focuses primarily on wealth-driven spillover in this instance, the concept is more generally taken to designate the spread of integration policies from one issue to another. As a combination of economics and politics, the Schuman Plan serves as the prototypical instance of this process. Rather than attacking the problem of pacifying Germany head-on through federation, Monnet proposed an indirect approach starting with coal and steel, which after various detours led to the Rome Treaty. More recently, the debate has been extended to the Single European Act, which, according to the new wave of neofunctionalist analyses, could be seen as another instance of spillover.[13] Taking issue with this interpretation, however, intergovernmentalists rely on changes in states' strategies and preferences as an explanation of the SEA and the Maastricht Treaty.[14]

How does the issue-constructivist logic differ from these two traditional approaches to integration? In opposition to the claims of intergovernmentalism, it accepts the autonomous operation of spillover. Yet unlike neofunctionalism, the securitization perspective emphasizes the possibility of "illiberal" issue linkage. To be sure, Haas postulates the existence of "incomplete" types of issue interconnectedness, such as "tactical" and "fragmented" linkage strategies, but in his case the assumption is that there is a unique, "rational" way of putting issues together.[15] Wæver's observations about the recent tendency to broaden the security concept to encompass various nontraditional issues serves to illustrate how an ostensibly "progressive" reinterpretation of traditional issue borders may actually lead to unintended results: "By treating, for example, the environment or immigrants as security problems, these issues are conceptualized in a specific way with connotations drawn from 'security.'"[16] Rather than being "immune" to redefinition, then, issue areas may "infect" each other through metaphorical and rhetorical repackaging.[17]

Cautioning against "naturalization" of spillover, Huysmans traces one such less than benign case of spillover from the SEA initiative and the free movement of people to the "need" to protect the public order of the EU through criminalization, or even securitization, of migration. Thus, in this instance, "the successful creation of the spillover from the internal market to an internal security field represents the latter almost as a natural consequence of the completion of the internal market" (Chapter 8). Whether representing a conscious strategy or not, issue linkages of this type tend to hide ideological constructions, thereby concealing the contested and political character of the process.[18]

But the link between the common market and immigration operates in the other direction as well. In a study of trade and French identity politics, Suzanne Berger shows how concerns with immigration fed back into the controversy over the "new protectionism" either through a putative employment-related connection or through Le Pen's right-wing activism based on explicit security arguments: "Whether the intrusion feared is a flood of immigrants from North Africa or the goods of East Europe and the developing world or Japanese cars or the wheat of North America, the terms used to castigate the state's irresponsibility in lowering the guard against the dangers of the outside world are strikingly similar."[19]

Though not explicitly studied in this book, monetary integration constitutes perhaps the most important case of spillover flowing from the Single European Act. Viewed as a necessary complement to the deepening of the market initiative, the currency reform has for the most part been debated from a strictly economic viewpoint. By focusing the debate on technical issues, such as the convergence criteria and optimal currency areas, this significant instance of spillover risks obscuring other intensely political aspects, such as "polity-building" and the future of the European welfare state.[20]

These examples suggest that far from always being inclusive, spillover strategies may have illiberal consequences, or at least repercussions unintended by their postnationalist promoters. Because of their liberal proclivities, the proponents of issue linkage often fail to see how trade-offs may travel from one issue to another and how this may lead to illiberal outcomes.

Tension Across Issues

Neofunctionalist spillover may result in tricky policy dilemmas and considerable conceptual tension across issue areas. For example, laissez-faire liberals often combine an uncompromising belief in economic openness with exclusion in other areas. Though variation across issues is not necessarily a sign of an incoherent overall ideology, the enthusiastic support for free trade and foreign direct investment of the past British conservative governments under Margaret Thatcher and John Major stood in stark contrast to their highly restrictive immigration policies. It is precisely this tension between liberal postnationalism and illiberal ethnonationalism that made Thatcher's hold on power increasingly slippery, for her strategy of accepting the Single European Act without endorsing its implied spillover into other issue areas backfired.

Ultimately, the failure to manage the ideological conflict highlighted by European integration caused her downfall. The same dilemma came back to haunt the man who exploited it in his own bid to succeed her. But until the European divide started to threaten party unity, this ideological eclecticism had proven to be surprisingly robust, certainly more successful than David Held expected it to be. Writing in the late 1980s, he pinpointed Thatcher's underlying success recipe as "the uncoupling or separation of the instrumental or performative dimension of the state, that is, the state as an instrument for the delivery of goods and services, from consideration of the state as a powerful, prestigious and enduring representative of the people or nation. Thatcher has sought to draw upon and reinvigorate the symbols and agencies of the latter while systematically attacking the former."[21]

Helped by the Falklands/Malvinas war and the popular press, Thatcher masterfully manipulated national symbols to her own political advantage and launched a "massive reorganization of the apparatus for maintaining law and order," trends that were ardently pursued by the Major government.[22] The successor Labour government under Tony Blair did little to resolve this Thatcherite contradiction.

The Swiss case also shows this "embedded liberalism" in operation.[23] In Chapter 3 Sciarini, Hug, and Dupont reveal that despite the commitment to free trade liberalism, important sectors of the Swiss domestic economy, such as agriculture, are indeed protected from foreign competition, though more recently steps have been taken toward liberalization of agriculture and other sectors. There is even less consistency once international cooperation and immigration policies are factored in. The authors trace this apparent divergence back to the foundational institutions on which the Swiss political system rests: federalism, direct democracy, and neutrality. Far from promoting an unambiguously liberal policy, the tendency toward decentralization and consensus leaves plenty of room for trade-off-sensitive minorities to control specific items on the state's agenda. Recent events have shown that such tensions may be more than academic. The highly sensitive affair following the revelation that Swiss authorities received Jewish gold confiscated by Nazi Germany has shaken the foundations of the Swiss political system and shed light on the fragile basis on which the Swiss political identity rests.[24]

It comes as no surprise that the European Union is not immune from cross-issue inconsistencies involving coupled trade-offs. Protecting the EU from external threats in one area may actually undermine attempts at constructing a European identity along other issue dimensions. Gowlland-Debbas provides a striking example of how the alleged trade-off between exclusion of asylum seekers and the "protection" of Europe's public order within the confines of the Schengen Agreement may create a less obvious, but no less serious, threat to Europe's identity (Chapter 9). According to Gowlland-Debbas, this goal conflict expresses itself as "a striking dissonance between, on the one hand, the values that lie at the core of European identity and that are continually evolving in the direction of strengthening the rule of law, democracy, and human rights and, on the other, developments in European policy and legislation concerning asylum seekers."

As a consequence, Gowlland-Debbas maintains, "Europe may be in the process of creating a form of cultural relativism in reverse—not in the sense of the rejection of universal values that do not conform to cultural particularities, which is the discourse of some third world states, but in the implicit denial of the application of *universal* values to certain third-state nationals who seek entry." By extension, then, the commonly postulated trade-off in immigration erodes the assertions about Europe's fundamentally democratic nature, for by failing to live up to the human rights principles that it purports to defend, the EU will find it harder to deny applicant countries membership on the grounds that their allegedly lacking democracy would "dilute" Europe's democratic status.

To conclude, this section has shown that the exclusiveness of issue areas is at least to some extent manipulable. Far from being unambiguously progressive, spillover may lead to highly unexpected issue linkage that reverses the initially liberal logic of the process. This is so because trade-offs are interlinked both within and between the pillars of the EU.

Comparing Identity Formation
Across Levels of Integration

If Europe's boundary-formation process differs across issue areas, the inclusiveness of policies may also vary with the specific level of integration. It is thus appropriate to focus on a parallel set of questions pertaining to the "vertical" rather than "horizontal" logic of identity formation: Are the national levels of integration inherently more inclusive than the European one, or vice versa? Do trade-offs at the national level have a tendency to spread up to the supranational level, or does the spread follow the opposite, top-down logic? What are the repercussions of such interlevel connections? In particular, if the diffusion processes fail to penetrate the system, do tensions remain between trade-offs at the national and European levels?[25]

The answers to these questions depend on the theoretical perspective adopted (cf. Chapter 1). As a rule, postnationalists are affirmative in their expectations of inclusive identities regardless of scale. Pan-Europeanists, by contrast, anticipate inclusive policies among the EU's member states in order to sustain internal cohesion but the opposite tendency in its external boundary. An ethnonationalist approach suggests exclusive national identities while leaving open the particular choice as regards Europe's identity. The assumptions of bounded integration, finally, are more open-ended at both levels: Here much hinges on the social construction of the issue at hand, although this perspective emphasizes the difficulty of transcending the nation-state.

The Exclusiveness of Integration Levels

In the most ardently "Euro-optimistic" integration literature, there is a tendency to equate any agreements promoting integration with liberal inclusiveness. Such a postnationalist perspective partly reflects a desire to depict the EU in as positive a light as possible, and it is partly predicated upon a fundamental belief in liberalism. But just because cooperation and identity formation move to a higher level of aggregation, it does not follow logically that these processes become more inclusive. In fact, the opposite may sometimes be the case. Although they explore behavioral patterns rather than identity shifts, studies in regime theory confirm this observation. For example, Vinod Aggarwal's analysis of the global textile regime makes a useful distinction between cooperation and liberalism. Observing that international cooperation and protectionism sometimes go hand in hand, Aggarwal draws the conclusion that international regimes often serve anything but liberal purposes. The developed world's protectionist trade practices intended to block cheap Third World textile products are a case in point.[26]

The distinction between postnationalism and pannationalism allows us to make a similar point. While both these positions open the door to supranational identity formation, they differ as to how they conceive of a European identity. Whereas Pan-Europeanists insist on a sharp and fixed cultural boundary at the European level, liberal postnationalists reject reasoning of this kind. Though accepting such an identity provided it is "thin," the latter view the construct as a pragmatic step toward global cooperation and community-building.

The empirical chapters above have shown that Pan-Europeanist thinking is by no means absent from the specific integration debates traced in this volume. In trade and audiovisual markets, Schlesinger and Theiler account for how the French government tried to push other member states into accepting a protectionist line in media and agricultural trade. Likewise, according to Neumann, there was, and may still be, a temptation to resort to Pan-Europeanist reasoning in the enlargement question.

But it is perhaps the issues originally associated with the third pillar that best illustrate the most important potential of pannationalist reasoning. Though, legally speaking, European citizenship derives directly from its national counterpart, the controversies surrounding immigration tacitly rest on the assumption that the EU as a whole needs to be protected against the influx of "non-Europeans." Indeed, since the mid-1970s there has been a trend toward tightening of national border controls, both with respect to general immigration and asylum policies, although there are significant national variations.[27] Although the Amsterdam Treaty calls for a harmonization of the member states' policies on visas, asylum, immigration, and external border controls, these changes will not enter into force until the end of a five-year transition period. At the moment of writing, it is therefore possible to speak only of an "emerging" European immigration regime.[28] Yet it would be imprudent to write off the fears that a veritable Pan-Europeanist "Fortress Europe" will crystallize in immigration policy. There can be little doubt that interstate cooperation in this area is driven by distinctly illiberal motivations, thus illustrating yet another case where cooperation has to be separated from liberal outcomes.[29]

The Swiss case provides a particularly telling comparative example of how officials have attempted to erect strict external barriers while maintaining internal mobility. According to Sciarini and his collaborators, recent proposals divide migrant workers into concentric circles, with the EEA as its core, surrounded by the Western world and the Third World, respectively. This classification would mean that Swiss immigration policy would be driven by explicitly ethnic-cultural considerations (see Chapter 3). Reflecting this state-level observation, Huysmans's analysis traces a similar tendency in the EU's treatment of "third-country nationals." In this case the integration process appears to take on a Pan-Europeanist quality in solidifying Europe's outer boundary into an at least implicitly culture-coded barrier.[30]

Connections Between Levels of Integration

Denouncing exclusion as superfluous and dangerous, postnationalists often emphasize the role of international organizations in promoting liberal norms and eradicating dilution fears. At the international level, this top-down account depends on a postulated learning effect orchestrated by international organizations.[31] To use a European illustration of this general point, there can be little doubt that the convergence criteria associated with EMU have had a liberalizing impact on member states' economic policies. Furthermore, the European Union has already helped to and will continue to solidify human rights and democracy in newly admitted states with brief experiences of these norms. The Southern expansion of the EU undoubtedly promoted and consolidated democracy in Greece, Spain, and Portugal. Though mechanistic extrapolation should be avoided, it appears likely that the mere prospect of an Eastern extension of the European integration process has already helped democracy to take root in Eastern and Central Europe, a process that might even extend to Turkey in the long run. European institutions, in particular the Council of Europe, have also had an impact on the citizenship laws in this part of the world.[32]

But once trade-offs are taken into consideration, this diffusionist view needs qualification, for if inclusive practices may spread, the same also applies to exclusionist ideas and policies. Such an illiberal development can be postulated to operate both upward to or downward from the European level.[33] To begin with the possibility of constructed trade-offs percolating from the member states up to the European Union, it is not hard to find examples drawn from the EU's three pillars. From the very outset, agricultural protection has been an important feature of European integration. By and large, the Common Agricultural Policy reflects a long-standing French tradition of sectoral mercantilism. It is in this context that one should see Schlesinger's account of the European Commission's attempt to launch a Euro-mercantilist agenda in media trade. To a large extent, this diffusion process derives from the influence of French politicians over policymaking in the European Commission, in particular Delors and his cabinet.[34] But as Theiler explains, the diffusion process never took off because the French efforts to export their particular approach to "cultural defense" ultimately fell upon deaf ears within the EU.

Attempts at bottom-up transfer of identity-driven trade-offs are also visible in security affairs. For example, such a process applies to the admission debates. Neumann traces how, once inside the EU, newly admitted states tried to "highjack" the EU's enlargement agenda to serve their own ethnonationalist agendas.[35] Yet of the policy areas considered in this volume, immigration represents perhaps the most important case of diffusion of exclusionary practices. Despite considerable convergence toward stricter national regulations, there is still significant variation in the European immigration regime and thus plenty of room for convergence mechanisms to work.[36]

Despite the inchoate character of the European immigration regime, there is already plenty of evidence of such pressures, especially on current or future member states in Eastern and southern Europe. Many states that belong to the former group allow for visa-free travel for nationals from Russia and the post-Soviet republics.[37] Yet it is unlikely that such liberal arrangements can be maintained, since these states have no option but to accept the Schengen *acquis* as a whole after the Amsterdam Treaty incorporated it in the EU's legal framework. Moreover, states in southern Europe have come under increasing pressure not only to strengthen their border controls but also to tighten their immigration regulations.[38]

The most crucial underlying difference pertains to the member states' reliance on ethnonational or territorial conceptions of nationhood.[39] Because of the deep ideational anchoring of such principles, it seems far-fetched that the EU's civic identity would come to reflect that of one of its least liberal member states, say, Germany. If there is a trend in European discourse, it points away from Pan-Europeanism, as illustrated by the European outcry against the Austrian coalition government including Jörg Haider's xenophobic Popular Party in February 2000. Furthermore, the government of Gerhard Schröder has committed itself to sweeping reforms that would at least partly liberalize the German immigration regime.[40]

Even in the absence of an explicitly cultural framing of these policy issues, there is still a considerable risk that the emergent European regime will consolidate the trend toward national restrictiveness and make it impossible for single member states to experiment with more inclusive practices. Indeed, the mere introduction of citizenship on the European agenda opens up new possibilities for reframing not only political membership but also the nexus between politics and culture. This phenomenon is captured by Huysmans's discursive concept of Europeanization. In that informal but significant sense, there is already a bidirectional process at work connecting national with European conceptions of citizenship and immigration.

Tension Between Levels of Integration

We have seen that perceived policy trade-offs at the national and European levels are linked in a nontrivial way. Incompatibility between the levels of integration create these links. Whether such differences create pressures for homogenization ultimately depends on the social actors' approach to identity formation. To see this, it is necessary to revisit the four paradigmatic perspectives introduced in Chapter 1.

It might intuitively seem as if all ethnonationalists would be strictly opposed to a cultural identity beyond the nation-state. But this impression is mistaken, for while assuming the members states' identities to be culturally defined, ethnonationalist reasoning can be combined with a tactical support of European identity formation. In fact, it is possible to rationalize a case for either a thick or a thin European identity based on such principles.

First, the EU is often regarded as the ultimate guarantor of national sovereignty. By creating a protective wall excluding American media products, external military threats, or "non-European" immigrants, the EU secures the identity of the national communities rather than that of the EU as a whole. It is important to distinguish tactical invocation of Europe's cultural identity from genuine Pan-Europeanism, although the former may actually inadvertently play into the hands of the latter. For example, Theiler concludes that the fragility of the French government's initial support for a Pan-European culture might have derived from a deeper ethnonationalist commitment to France's own cultural identity.

Second, a thin, inclusive European identity may also be useful to ethnonationalist intergovernmentalists. Again, the reason for such a fallback position is primarily tactical. By lobbying for enlargement of the EU, ethnonationalists hope to "dilute" its structure, thus rendering integration impossible in the future. It is widely believed that the Thatcher government's inclination toward enlargement derived from a desire to thwart efforts at deepening the European integration process.[41] In other words, national-level trade-offs may prompt a tactical denial of such dilemmas within the Union.

Of course, far from every ethnonationalist is happy with such strategies of "vicarious" nationalism. Both Le Pen's followers in France and many British Euro-skeptics view even the thinnest conception of Europe as a direct threat to their cherished national identities.

These possibilities illustrate that identity-related puzzles crucially depend on how culture is conceived and operationalized in practice. In contrast, postnationalists have a more straightforward approach to identity-related contradictions: In their eyes, there is not necessarily a single clear locus of boundary formation, and to the extent there are identities, they are of the thin, postnational kind both within the national and all-European contexts. Moreover, national and European identities do not exclude each other but are fluid and partly overlapping constructs. Rather than replicating the logic of traditional sovereignty on a larger scale, this vision of postnational identity formation endorses loose forms of federalism and other forms of subsidiarity as an opportunity to circumvent the boundedness of state-level citizenship (see Calhoun's discussion in Chapter 2).

Yet from the perspective of bounded integration, this postnationalist vision represents too simple a view. Without endorsing the ethnonationalist identities as a logical necessity, these scholars emphasize that boundaries do have functional advantages that cannot be dispensed with without creating contradictions. Perhaps the most serious contradiction relates to the EU's "democratic deficit." Students of bounded integration criticize postnationalists for expecting thin, inclusive identities to develop unproblematically through political practice. Furthermore, they question the viability of democracy in the absence of cultural boundaries once the cultural closure of the nation-state has started to wither away.

Without resorting to essentialism, Schlesinger emphasizes the difficulties of establishing a European-wide political culture. While conceptually elegant, Habermasian constitutional patriotism is fraught with practical difficulties. Given the lack of a European community feeling and the deeply entrenched patterns of nationalist media consumption, it is highly unlikely that "deliberative democracy" would emerge spontaneously through political practice.[42] The problem is that most political theories, including liberal postnationalist visions, presume implicitly that a bounded polity already exists.[43] It is not clear how these liberal theories apply in cases where this assumption does not hold. Postnationalists argue that a multiperspectival, multilevel European polity, for example, could rely on nonelectoral means of democratic governance.[44] Yet from a boundary perspective, the European Union's legitimacy and effectiveness remain in question in terms of both democratic and effective governance.[45]

Effectiveness relates to problems of control and free riding. Since most postnationalist theorists of citizenship emphasize "rights" rather than "duties," it is often forgotten that clear boundaries constitute a functional solution to tricky coordination dilemmas. Thus, creating even an incompletely formed European polity calls for the formation of boundaries.[46] The analogy with the formation of the European nation-states is instructive. Even though the circumstances differed considerably from today's Europe, it is hard to conceive how tax collection, binding majority decisions, and foreign policy functions could be carried out without at least a diffuse boundary.[47]

Rogers Brubaker's account of the parallel development of state structures and citizenship in nineteenth-century Germany illustrates this point. Although the states' internal barriers to movement, such as guilds and municipal citizenship regulations, were swept aside by the giant broom of history, states' external boundaries crystallized in the same period. Not unlike the contemporary worries of Europeans about the potentially conflictual consequences of wealth-driven immigration from the rest of the world, the German states needed to stave off "immigration dumping" among townships. Nevertheless, the states' difficulties in controlling migratory flows in and out of their territories prompted the development of state citizenship: "The citizenry was externally exclusive as well as internally inclusive."[48]

Even the postnationalists' favorite example of multicultural democracy, Switzerland, casts doubts on the compatibility of federalism and inclusiveness. Although most postnationalists seem to be well aware of the selective nature of Swiss liberalism, Sciarini, Hug, and Dupont go beyond that realization by arguing that the exclusionary features of Switzerland's external boundary may have been part and parcel of the state formation process itself. Thus, one would have to admit that "even a national identity based on 'constitutional patriotism' needs some barriers to protect itself" (Chapter 3).

Indeed, these authors suggest that both the success and the exclusive tendencies of the Swiss approach to multiculturalism rest on the institutional pillars that liberal integrationists hail as the way around identity trade-offs. Apart from their frequent reliance on federalism, postnationalists embrace direct democracy through referenda as an identity-reinforcing antidote to the democratic deficit.[49] Yet far from having unambiguously liberal repercussions, the decentralized structure of Switzerland's federalist system appears to have strengthened protectionism in various policy areas such as public procurement and may have made incorporation of immigrants harder than it would have been in a more centralized system.

By the same token, Sciarini and his colleagues indicate that while direct democracy served a central role in promoting loyalty to the confederation, the institution of referenda also opened up possibilities for nationalistic, and sometimes even xenophobic, attempts to block Switzerland's involvement in international political cooperation, the liberalization of agricultural trade, and especially the loosening of a strict immigration regime. Finally, Switzerland's staunch commitment to neutrality offers little hope for those who want to strengthen the EU's common foreign and security policy. It is no coincidence that Delors was haunted by a vision of the EC as a "big Switzerland with gigantic economic power, few diplomatic and no defense capabilities."[50]

All this does not mean that the EU has nothing positive to learn from Switzerland. On the contrary, this country remains one of the few successful instances of multinational governance, and as such its achievements are considerable. The Swiss experience shows how language groups can be made to "cohabit" under the same roof without any serious tensions.[51] Still, the findings of Chapter 3 serve as a helpful reminder that while democracy can in principle be secured under culturally diverse conditions, implementing a viable system of multilevel governance sometimes comes at the price of exclusion. Rather than denying the existence of such trade-offs, taking them seriously may offer a better understanding of the hurdles threatening to derail progress toward a truly open and liberal Europe.

Conclusion

This book has adopted a self-consciously constructivist perspective in its pursuit of Europe's elusive identity. In so doing, it has striven to describe and demystify debates about political loyalty and culture. Rather than reifying either national or European cultural "essences," we have made a focused attempt to scrutinize the external logic of identity formation at both the national and supranational levels.

Yet constructivist approaches to integration do not necessarily expect that supranational identity formation will follow a smooth process. In fact, it appears to be much harder to construct Europe's identity in reaction to a non-European other than hopeful policymakers and critical theorists alike have led us to believe. As we have seen, the European Commission's attempt to depict the United States as a cultural enemy received little support from the member states. In many cases scholars' warnings that the EU is about to be transformed into a Fortress Europe across the board seem exaggerated. This volume has shown that such a process of externalizing identity formation requires much more than "identity talk."

Far from presenting a unified picture, the process, or rather processes, of identity formation vary according to the particular policy area under scrutiny. In fact, not much by way of a coherent European identity exists, at least not in the "thick," cultural sense. If there is any chance that a more unified identity will one day emerge, it is likely to be a much thinner, postnationalist one. The chapters in this book indicate that there are already tendencies in this direction. For one, the enlargement debates have converged on an inclusive attitude that emphasizes political culture rather than Christianity and Europe's "cultural heritage." There are, however, potential exceptions to this trend: The EU's emerging immigration regime exhibits markedly exclusive tendencies.

Despite the strong issue dependence, it would be wrong to infer that each policy area is inherently associated with a particular logic of identity construction. Indeed, not only identities but also the boundaries of the issues and the mechanisms operating within them are socially constructed. True, issue definitions governing the reasoning of policymakers and scholars often acquire a high degree of stability, and much useful analysis can be conducted within such bounds. But when no such epistemic consensus exists, it becomes necessary to endogenize the cognitive principles defining the boundaries of issues, their internal operating principles, including possible identity trade-offs, and the way they are linked to other issues. Failure to do so is likely to lead to premature cognitive closure, thus obscuring underlying ideological assumptions. A prominent example of "issue constructivism," the securitization perspective could "make politicians, activists and academics aware that they make a *choice*, when they treat something as a security issue. Threats and security are not objective matters, security is a way to frame and handle an issue."[52]

Having rejected essentialism as an analytical position, whether national or Pan-European, the main question remains whether postnationalist or bounded integration offers the best general guide to supranational identity formation. The emphasis on boundaries constitutes a better analytical starting point than postnationalism because it refrains from ruling out European cultural identity formation as a matter of assumption, while at the same time expressing healthy skepticism about its practical viability. Moreover, unlike postnationalist universalism, the bounded approach anticipates important issue-specific variations.

What conceptual consequences do these insights have for integration theory? Because intergovernmentalism, especially in its culturally explicit classical version, subscribes to ethnonationalist principles, it is of little help as a guide to supranational identity formation. Flatly denying the possibility of loyalty shifts beyond the nation-state, these scholars' reference to a "logic of diversity" fails to uncover the mechanisms that supposedly maintain its boundedness.[53] A similar insensitivity to the boundary problematic is present in both liberal intergovernmentalism and rationalist perspectives drawn from comparative politics. Because of their heavy reliance on the assumption of presocially defined rational actors, at both the national and European levels, identities remain hardwired into the analytical framework.[54]

Among the paradigms of integration theory, Haas's neofunctionalism and Deutschian transactionalism remain exceptional as frameworks that endogenize identities, though they can be faulted for overstating the extent to which identities can change.[55] Moreover, the neofunctionalists' strongly materialist assumptions overlook the possibility of noninstrumental processes of identity change and stasis.[56] Although this volume has shown that the Pan-Europeanist attempts to create a non-European "other" have so far turned out to be quite ineffective in most policy areas, the mere fact that such policies were attempted illustrates the need to analyze reactive identity formation. Perhaps the theory of multilevel governance comes the closest to capturing the issue-specific geometry of European identity formation.[57] But while such perspectives have had much to say about patterns of policymaking and governance, they have often underestimated the difficulties of transcending the identity locus of the nation-state.

To find theories targeting identity issues at the large, macrohistorical scale of "polity building," one has to turn the attention to historical sociology. While constructivism has usually been associated with fluid collective identities, sociologically inspired theories of European integration approximating the principles of bounded integration have started to appear.[58] Such a focus has many advantages, since it promises to uncover the social mechanisms responsible for the formation and maintenance of collective self-images.[59]

This volume has merely started to explore one set of such mechanisms, namely, those linking Europe's identity to its external environment. A comprehensive analysis of identity formation, however, requires a broader account of processes operating *inside* the European Union. These include language policies, educational institutions, media establishments, party systems, and other political organizations making up a nascent European civil society.[60]

Still, we know little about how internal and external processes of identity formation interact at the European and national levels.[61] Systematic comparisons and evolutionary tracing of both European and non-European historical analogies could help identify complex patterns made up of interlocked and partially contradictory social mechanisms. This volume used Switzerland as a reference case, but the list of potentially fruitful comparisons is long. In particular, such perspectives could circumvent the obvious methodological difficulty caused by the EU's sui generis character.

Pending more comprehensive studies, however, I hope that this book has convinced the reader that policymakers and analysts of European polity formation ignore the boundary problem only at their own peril. Because of the profundity of the epochal changes under way and the inadequacy of our current conceptual resources, we are confronted with a theoretical challenge of no lesser proportions than the one that inspired the classical social theorists of the nineteenth century.

Notes

1. See, e.g., Stanley Hoffmann, "Obstinate or Obsolete? The Fate of the Nation-State and the Case of Western Europe," *Dædalus* 85 (1966): 862–915.

2. Robert Jervis, "Security Regimes," in Stephen D. Krasner, ed., *International Regimes* (Ithaca: Cornell University Press, 1983).

3. Charles Lipson, "International Cooperation in Security and Economic Affairs," *World Politics* 37 (October 1984): 1–23; Robert Axelrod and Robert O. Keohane, "Achieving Cooperation Under Anarchy: Strategies and Institutions," *World Politics* 35 (October 1985): 226–254. These and other essays are reprinted in David Baldwin, ed., *Neorealism and Neoliberalism* (New York: Columbia University Press, 1993).

4. Robert O. Keohane and Joseph S. Nye, *Power and Interdependence* (Cambridge: Harvard University Press, 1977), 65.

5. Ernst B. Haas, *When Knowledge Is Power* (Berkeley: University of California Press, 1990). For an overview, see Emanuel Adler and Peter M. Haas, "Epistemic Communities, World Order, and the Creation of a Reflective Research Program," *International Organization* 46 (1992): 367–390.

6. "Delighted Turks Face Some Big Adjustments," *Financial Times,* 13 December 1999.

7. Ole Wæver, "European Security Identities," *Journal of Common Market Studies* 34 (1996): 103–132.

8. Indeed, from an anthropological perspective, the securitization of trade is more than just an instrumentalist ploy to protect material interests. Douglas and Isherwood analyze how this approach to goods emphasizes "their double role in providing subsistence and in drawing the lines of social relationships." Mary Douglas and Baron Isherwood, *The World of Goods: Towards an Anthropology of Consumption* (London: Allen Lane, 1979), 60.

9. Gowlland-Debbas points out that because of the tight legal link to national security, the securitization logic operated much earlier in the area of asylum law (see Chapter 9).

10. Keohane and Nye, *Power and Interdependence.*

11. Jeppe Tranholm-Mikkelsen, "Neo-functionalism: Obstinate or Obsolete? A Reappraisal in the Light of the New Dynamism of the EC," *Millennium* 20 (1991): 1–22.

12. Ernst Haas, *The Uniting of Europe: Political, Economic and Social Forces* (Stanford: Stanford University Press, 1958), 283–317. For a recent evalution of spillover as a concept, see Robert O. Keohane and Stanley Hoffmann, "Institutional Change in Europe in the 1980s," in Robert O. Keohane and Stanley Hoffmann, eds., *The New European Community: Decisionmaking and Institutional Change* (Boulder, Colo.: Westview, 1991).

13. See, e.g., Wayne Sandholtz and John Zysman, "Recasting the European Bargain," *World Politics* 42 (1989): 95–128.

14. Andrew Moravcsik, "Negotiating the Single European Act: National Interests and Conventional Statecraft in the European Community," *International Organization* 45 (1991): 651–688; see also his more recent work: Andrew Moravcsik, *The Choice for Europe: Social Purpose and State Power from Messina to Maastricht* (Ithaca: Cornell University Press, 1998); Joseph M. Grieco, "The Maastricht Treaty, Economic and Monetary Union and the Neo-Realist Research Programme," *Review of International Studies* 21 (January 1995): 21–40.

15. Haas, *When Knowledge Is Power;* see also Ernst B. Haas, "Why Collaborate?" *World Politics* 33 (1980): 347–405.

16. Wæver, "European Security Identities," 106.

17. See Paul A. Chilton, *Security Metaphors: Cold War Discourse from Containment to Common House* (New York: Peter Lang, 1996).

18. See also Michael Newman, *Democracy, Sovereignty and the European Union* (London: Hurst & Company, 1996), 163; and Andrew Geddes, "Immigrant and Ethnic Minorities and the EU's 'Democratic Deficit,'" *Journal of Common Market Studies* 33 (June 1995): 197–217

19. Suzanne Berger, "Trade and Identity: The Coming Protectionism?" in Gregory Flynn, ed., *Remaking the Hexagon: The New France in the New Europe* (Boulder, Colo.: Westview, 1995), 195–210.

20. See, e.g., Joseph H. H. Weiler, *The Constitution of Europe: "Do the New Clothes Have an Emperor?"* (Cambridge: Cambridge University Press, 1999), 326–327.

21. David Held, *Political Theory and the Modern State* (Cambridge: Polity Press, 1988), 140.

22. Ibid., 141. A similar, though somewhat less pronounced disparity could be observed between Labour's commitment to social inclusion and their willingness to go along with restrictive measures in immigration. See Geddes, "Immigrant and Ethnic Minorities," 207. For a theoretical account of the "historical coalition between nationalism and neoliberalism," see Wolfgang Streeck, "Neo-Voluntarism: A New European Social Policy Regime?" in Gary Marks, Fritz W. Scharpf, Philippe C. Schmitter, and Wolfgang Streeck, eds., *Governance in the European Union* (London: Sage, 1996), 68.

23. John G. Ruggie, "International Regimes, Transactions, and Change: Embedded Liberalism in the Postwar Economic Order," *International Organization* 36 (1982): 379–415. For a penetrating discussion of the contraction between "renationalization" of immigration policy and globalization-driven "denationalization" of liberal economic regimes, see Saskia Sassen, "The *De Facto* Transnationalization of Immigration Policy," in Christian Joppke, ed., *Challenge to the Nation-State: Immigration to Western Europe and the United States* (Oxford: Oxford University Press, 1998).

24. See William Hall, "Nazi Gold Affair Reveals How Swiss Hate to Be Led," *Financial Times*, 26 February 1997, 2.

25. While this volume has primarily focused on the shift from national to European boundary formation, it deserves to be reiterated that there are additional levels to consider, notably subnational or regional developments. Also, the exposition presumes that national and European processes of identity formation can be at least analytically separated despite being interdependent. Nevertheless, it is possible to conceive of a situation in which they become so entangled that it is no longer possible to theorize them as separate entities.

26. Vinod K. Aggarwal, *Liberal Protectionism: The International Politics of Organized Textile Trade* (Berkeley: University of California Press, 1985). See also Robert S. Keohane, *After Hegemony: Cooperation and Discord in the World Political Economy* (Princeton: Princeton University Press, 1984), 189–190.

27. See Chapters 8 and 9. Cf. also, e.g., Christian Joppke, "Immigration Challenges the Nation-State," in Christian Joppke, ed., *Challenges to the Nation-State: Immigration to Western Europe and the United States* (Oxford: Oxford University Press, 1998).

28. Rey Koslowski, "European Migration Regimes: Emerging, Enlarging, and Deteriorating," *Journal of Ethnic and Migration Studies* 24 (1998): 735–749.

29. Gary P. Freeman, "The Decline of Sovereignty? Politics and Immigration Restrictions in Liberal States," in Christian Joppke, ed., *Challenges to the Nation-State: Immigration to Western Europe and the United States* (Oxford:

Oxford University Press, 1998), 91. See also Koslowski, "European Migration Regimes," 738.

30. It is also important to distinguish between "immigration" and "immigrant" policy, i.e., between admission policies targeting newcomers and policies of integration of those immigrants already residing in the territory in question. Cf. Tomas Hammar, "Introduction," in Tomas Hammar, ed., *European Immigration Policy: A Comparative Study* (Cambridge: Cambridge University Press, 1985). Because of the focus on the EU's outer boundaries, this volume analyzes the former rather than the latter. The member states' "immigrant" policies appear to be more inclusive than their immigration regulations. For an influential argument that it is possible to discern a new postnational approach to integration of third-country citizens, see Yasemin N. Soysal, *Limits of Citizenship: Migrants and Postnational Membership in Europe* (Chicago: University of Chicago Press, 1994).

31. The actors propelling these processes may reside in either intergovernmental or nongovernmental organizations. Especially in the latter case, transnational movements, such as Greenpeace, have been found to influence governmental policies through lobbying through the same states' civil societies. See Margaret E. Keck and Kathryn Sikkink, *Activists Beyond Borders: Advocacy Networks in International Politics* (Ithaca: Cornell University Press, 1998).

32. Jeffrey T. Checkel, "Norms, Institutions, and National Identity in Contemporary Europe," *International Studies Quarterly* 43 (1999): 83–114. See also Weiler, *The Constitution of Europe*, 335, for the argument that because of the institutional crowding of the European human rights regime, the European Union's role "has reached a point of diminishing returns."

33. For an analytical overview of processes operating in both directions, see Checkel, "Norms, Institutions, and National Identity," 88.

34. George Ross, *Jacques Delors and European Integration* (Cambridge: Polity Press, 1995).

35. It is not only small states that allow their cultural and nationalist sensitivities to influence the EU's overall policy. It is widely believed that it was Germany's reunification, together with an ethnic approach to sovereignty, that led the country to recognize unilaterally Croatia's secession from the Yugoslav federation. The German initiative created a fait accompli that forced the EU to recognize Slovenia and Croatia. See Beverly Crawford, "Explaining Defection from International Cooperation: Germany's Unilateral Recognition of Croatia," *World Politics* 48 (July 1996): 482–521.

36. Joppke, "Immigration Challenges the Nation-State." The differences pertain not just to the principle of exclusion but also to the infrastructural capacity to control borders. In this respect the countries along the EU's southern and eastern borders are particularly vulnerable.

37. Koslowski, "European Migration Regimes," 740.

38. Ibid., 741. See also Rey Koslowski, "European Union Migration Regimes, Established and Emergent," in Christian Joppke, ed., *Challenge to the Nation-State: Immigration in Western Europe and the United States* (Oxford: Oxford University Press, 1998), 179; and Martin Baldwin-Edwards, "The Emerging European Immigration Regime: Some Reflections on Implications for Southern Europe," *Journal of Common Market Studies* 35 (1997): 497–519.

39. Rogers Brubaker, *Citizenship and Nationhood in France and Germany* (Cambridge: Harvard University Press, 1992).

40. Yet it should not be overlooked that because of its direct dependence on national membership criteria, the European category of citizenship is indirectly influenced by national laws. Thanks to the German principle of *jus sanguinis* together with the internal openness of the EU, ethnic Germans from Eastern Europe and the former Soviet Union acquire automatic citizenship rights that allow them to reside and work in any part of the EU. See Koslowski, "European Union Migration Regimes, Established and Emergent," 178.

41. Cf., e.g., Neill Nugent, "The Deepening and Widening of the European Community: Recent Evolution, Maastricht, and Beyond," *Journal of Common Market Studies* 30 (September 1992): 311; Anna Michalski and Helen Wallace, *The European Community: The Challenge of Enlargement* (London: Royal Institute of International Affairs, 1992), 56–57; Heather Grabbe and Kirsty Hughes, *The 1996 IGC: The British Debate* (London: Royal Institute of International Affairs, 1996), 8.

42. For an application of the concept to the European Union, see Rainer Schmalz-Bruns, "Deliberativer Supranationalismus: Demokratisches Regieren jenseits des Nationalstaats," *Zeitschrift für Internationale Beziehungen* 6 (1999): 185–244. On deliberate democracy in general, see Jon Elster, ed., *Deliberative Democracy* (Cambridge: Cambridge University Press, 1998) and Joshua Cohen and Joel Rogers, *Associations and Democracy: The Real Utopias Project* (London: Verso, 1995).

43. Wolfgang Streeck, "Inclusion and Secession: Questions on the Boundaries of Associative Democracy," in Joshua Cohen and Joel Rogers, *Associations and Democracy: The Real Utopias Project* (London: Verso, 1995). See also Robert A. Dahl, *Democracy and Its Critics* (New Haven, Conn.: Yale University Press, 1989).

44. For an argument along these lines emphasizing social movements, see Doug Imig and Sidney Tarrow, eds., *Contentious Europeans: Politics and Protest in a Composite Polity* (Lanham, Md.: Rowman and Littlefield, 2000). Cf. Thomas Banschoff and Mitchell P. Smith, "Introduction: 'Conceptualizing Legitimacy in a Contested Polity,'" in Thomas Banschoff and Mitchell P. Smith, eds., *Legitimacy and the European Union: The Contested Polity* (London: Routledge, 1999). For a more philosophical argument, see also Jürgen Habermas, "Citizenship and National Identity: Some Reflections on the Future of Europe," *Praxis International* 12, 1 (1992): 1–19; Jürgen Habermas, *Die Einbeziehung des Anderen: Studien zur politischen Theorie* (Frankfurt: Suhrkamp, 1996).

45. Fritz W. Scharpf, *Governing in Europe: Effective and Democratic?* (Oxford: Oxford University Press, 1999).

46. Wolfgang Streeck, "Einleitung: Internationale Wirtschaft, nationale Demokratie?" in Wolfgang Streeck, ed., *Internationale Wirtschaft, nationale Demokratie: Herausforderungen für die Demokratietheorie* (Frankfurt: Campus Verlag, 1998).

47. See, e.g., Samuel F. Finer, "State-Building, State Boundaries and Border Control," *Social Science Information* 13 (1974): 89–126. Obviously, the main difference setting today's external exchange processes apart from those of earlier eras is the nonuse of force. Whereas warfare served an important function in instilling a national identity in early modern Europe, today's European Union cannot resort to such means given its foundational quality as a "security community." See Ole Wæver's analysis in "European Security Identities," and Ole Wæver, "Insecurity, and Asecurity in the West European Non-war

Community," in Emanuel Adler and Michael Barnett, eds., *Security Communities* (Cambridge: Cambridge University Press, 1998).

48. Brubaker, *Citizenship and Nationhood*, 71. Cf. Joppke, "Immigration Challenges the Nation-State."

49. See, e.g., Vernon Bogandor, "Direct Elections, Representative Democracy and European Integration," *Electoral Studies* 8 (1989): 205–216; Michael Zürn, "Über den Staat und die Demokratie im europäischen Mehrebenensystem," *Politische Vierteljahresschrift* 37 (1996): 27–55. For a review of the literature on integration and referendums, see Simon Hug, "Integration Through Referendums," *Aussenwirtschaft* 52 (1997): 287–310.

50. Ross, *Jacques Delors and European Integration*, 92.

51. The conflict over and creation of the twenty-fifth canton, Jura, in the 1970s is the only recent exception to the otherwise comparatively smooth resolution of linguistic and cultural conflicts in Switzerland.

52. Wæver, "European Security Identities," 108.

53. Stanley Hoffmann, "Obstinate or Obsolete?" See also Raymond Aron, "Old Nations, New Europe," in Stephen Richards Graubard, ed., *A New Europe?* (London: Oldbourne Press, 1964); and Dominique Schnapper, "The European Debate on Citizenship," *Dædalus* 126 (1997): 199–222.

54. On liberal intergovernmentalism, see Moravcsik, *The Choice for Europe*, and on perspectives drawing on rationalistic approaches to "domestic" comparative politics, see Simon Hix, "The Study of the European Union II: The 'New Governance' Agenda and Its Rival," *Journal of European Public Policy* 5 (1998): 38–65.

55. Yet this critique fails to perceive important nuances in these authors' work. For example, Ernst Haas's more recent writings express a more ambivalent attitude to supranational integration. Cf. Ernst B. Haas, "Nationalism: An Instrumental Social Construction," *Millennium* 22 (1993): 505–545. Similarly, despite his modernist tendencies and stress of pluralist security communities, it would be a mistake to classify Deutsch as a "Euro-optimist." After all, his view of "amalgamated" integration was much less sanguine. See, inter alia, Karl W. Deutsch et al., *Political Community and the North Atlantic Area* (Princeton: Princeton University Press, 1957), 160–161.

56. See the discussion of instrumental and noninstrumental constructivism in Chapter 1.

57. See, e.g., Gary Marks, Fritz W. Scharpf, Philippe C. Schmitter, and Wolfgang Streeck, eds., *Governance in the European Union* (London: Sage, 1996).

58. See, e.g., Stefano Bartolini, "Exit Options, Boundary Building, Political Structuring," European University Institute, Working Paper SPS No. 98/1, 1998; Adrian Favell, "A Politics That Is Shared, Bounded, and Rooted? Rediscovering Civic Political Culture in Western Europe," *Theory and Society* 27 (1998): 209–236.

59. The recent literature on causal mechanisms includes Arthur L. Stinchcombe, "The Conditions of Fruitfulness of Theorizing About Mechanisms in Social Science," *Philosophy of the Social Sciences* 21 (1993): 367–388; Peter Hedström and Richard Swedberg, eds., *Social Mechanisms: An Analytical Approach to Social Theory* (Cambridge: Cambridge University Press, 1998).

60. The paradigmatic historical study is Eugen Weber, *Peasants into Frenchmen: The Modernization of Rural France 1870–1914* (Stanford: Stanford University Press, 1976). There is also a growing literature on the internal

sources of Europe's identity. See, e.g., M. Rainer Lepsius, "Nationalstaat oder Nationalitätenstaat als Modell für die Weiterentwicklung der Europäischen Gemeinschaft," in Rudolf Wildenmann, ed., *Staatswerdung Europas* (Baden-Baden: Nomos, 1991); Jürgen Gerhards, "Westeuropäische Integration und die Schwierigkeiten der Entstehung einer europäischen Öffentlichkeit," *Zeitschrift für Soziologie* 22 (1993): 96–110; Peter Graf Kielmansegg, "Integration und Demokratie," in Markus Jachtenfuchs and Beate Kohler-Koch, eds., *Europäische Integration* (Opladen: Leske und Budrich, 1996); Tobias Theiler, "The European Union and the 'European Dimension' in Schools: Theory and Evidence," *Journal of European Integration* 21 (1998): 307–341.

61. Though see Linda Colley, *Britons: Forging the Nation, 1707–1837* (London: Pimlico, 1992) and Richard Münch, *Das Projekt Europa: Zwischen Nationalstaat, regionaler Autonomie und Weltgesellschaft* (Frankfurt: Suhrkamp, 1993).

Acronyms

BABEL	Broadcasting Across the Barriers of European Languages
CAP	Common Agricultural Policy
CEE	Central and Eastern European
EBRD	European Bank for Reconstruction and Development
EC	European Community
ECHR	European Court of Human Rights
ECSC	European Coal and Steel Community
EEA	European Economic Area
EFDO	European Film Distribution Office
EFTA	European Free Trade Association
EMU	Economic and Monetary Union
EP	European Parliament
EPU	European Payments Union
EU	European Union
GATS	General Agreement on Trade in Services
GATT	General Agreement on Tariffs and Trade
GDP	gross domestic product
GNP	gross national product
NAFTA	North American Free Trade Agreement
NATO	North Atlantic Treaty Organization
NGO	nongovernmental organization
OECD	Organization for Economic Cooperation and Development
OEEC	Organization for European Economic Cooperation
OSCE	Organization for Security and Cooperation in Europe
PSE	production subsidy equivalent
SEA	Single European Act
TEU	Treaty on European Union
UNHCR	United Nations High Commissioner for Refugees
WTO	World Trade Organization

Selected Bibliography

European Identity Formation

Delanty, Gerard. *Inventing Europe: Idea, Identity, Reality.* London: Macmillan, 1995.

De Witte, Bruno. "Building Europe's Image and Identity." In A. Rijksbaron, W. H. Roobol, and M. Weisglad, eds., *Europe from a Cultural Perspective.* The Hague: UPR, 1987.

Duroselle, Jean-Baptiste. *L'Idée d'Europe dans l'histoire.* Paris: Denoël, 1965.

García, Soledad. *European Identity and the Search for Legitimacy.* London: Pinter, 1993.

Habermas, Jürgen. *Between Facts and Norms.* Cambridge: MIT Press, 1996.

———. *Die postnationale Konstellation: Politische Essays.* Frankfurt: Suhrkamp, 1998.

Hoffmann, Stanley. *The European Sisyphus: Essays on Europe, 1964–1994.* Boulder, Colo.: Westview, 1995.

Journal of Common Market Studies 34, 1 (Spring 1996). Special issue on European identity.

Journal of European Public Policy 6, 4 (1999). Special issue on constructivism.

Kastoryano, Riva, ed. *Quelle identité pour l'Europe? Le multiculturalisme à l'épreuve.* Paris: Presses de Sciences Po, 1998.

Laffan, Brigid. "The Politics of Identity and Political Order in Europe." *Journal of Common Market Studies* 34 (1996): 81–102.

Lenoble, Jacques, and Nicole Dewandre, eds. *L'Europe au soir du siècle: Identité et démocratie.* Paris: Éditions Esprit, 1992.

Lepsius, M. Rainer. "Nationalstaat oder Nationalitätenstaat als Modell für die Weiterentwicklung der Europäischen Gemeinschaft." In Rudolf Wildenmann, ed., *Staatswerdung Europas.* Baden-Baden: Nomos, 1991.

Münch, Richard. *Das Projekt Europa: Zwischen Nationalstaat, regionaler Autonomie und Weltgesellschaft.* Frankfurt: Suhrkamp, 1993.

Olsen, Johan P. "Europeanization and Nation-State Dynamics." ARENA Working Paper 9. Oslo, 1995.

Rougemont, Denis de. *The Making of Europe.* New York: Stein and Day, 1965.
Scharpf, Fritz W. *Governing in Europe: Effective and Democratic?* Oxford: Oxford University Press, 1999.
Smith, Anthony D. "National Identity and the Idea of European Unity." *International Affairs* 68 (1992): 55-76.
Viehoff, Reinhold, and Rien T. Siegers, eds. *Kultur, Identität, Europa: Über die Schwierigkeiten und Möglichkeiten einer Konstruktion.* Frankfurt: Suhrkamp, 1999.
Wæver, Ole, Barry Buzan, Morten Kelstrup, and Pierre Lemaitre, eds. *Identity, Migration and the New Security Agenda in Europe.* London: Pinter, 1993.
Wallace, Helen. "Whose Europe Is It Anyway?" *European Journal of Political Research* 35 (1999): 287–306.
Wallace, William. *The Transformation of Western Europe.* London: Pinter, 1990.
Weiler, Joseph H. H. *The Constitution of Europe: "Do the New Clothes Have an Emperor?"* Cambridge: Cambridge University Press, 1999.
Wilson, Thomas M. "An Anthropology of the European Community." In Thomas M. Wilson and M. Estellie Smith, eds., *Cultural Change and the New Europe: Perspectives on the European Community.* Boulder, Colo.: Westview, 1993.
Wolf, Klaus Dieter, ed. *Projekt Europa im Übergang? Probleme, Modelle und Strategien des Regierens in der Europäischen Union.* Baden-Baden: Nomos, 1997.

Europe's Cultural Identity

Baras, Jean-Pol. *Gagner l'Europe culturelle.* Brussels: Labor 1989.
De Witte, Bruno. "Cultural Legitimation: Back to the Language Question." In Soledad García, ed., *European Identity and the Search for Legitimacy.* London: Pinter, 1993.
Gerhards, Jürgen. "Westeuropäische Integration und die Schwierigkeiten der Entstehung einer europäischen Öffentlichkeit." *Zeitschrift für Soziologie* 22 (1993): 96–110.
Goddard, Victoria A., Josep R. Llobera, and Cris Shore. "Introduction: The Anthropology of Europe." In Victoria A. Goddard, Josep R. Llobera, and Cris Shore, eds., *The Anthropology of Europe: Identities and Boundaries in Question.* Oxford: Berg, 1994.
Howe, Paul. "Community of Europeans: The Requisite Underpinnings." *Journal of Common Market Studies* 33 (1995): 27–46.
Obradovic, Daniela. "Policy Legitimacy and the European Union." *Journal of Common Market Studies* 34 (1996): 191–221.
Sandell, Terry. "Cultural Issues, Debates and Programmes." In Philippe Barbour, ed., *The European Union Handbook.* Chicago: Fitzroy Dearborn Publishers, 1996.
Schlesinger, Philip R. "Europe's Contradictory Communicative Space." *Dædalus* 123 (1994): 25–52.
———. "Changing Spaces of Political Communication: The Case of the European Union." *Political Communication* 16 (1999): 263–279.
Shore, Cris. "Inventing the 'People's Europe': Critical Approaches to European Community 'Cultural Policy.'" *Man* 28 (1993): 779–799.
Skovmand, Michael, and Kim Christian Schrøder, eds. *Media Cultures: Reappraising Transnational Media.* London: Routledge, 1992.

Theiler, Tobias. "Viewers into Europeans? How the European Union Tried to Europeanize the Audiovisual Sector and Why It Failed." *Canadian Journal of Communication* 24 (1999): 557–578.

Zetterholm, Staffan, ed. *National Cultures and European Integration: Exploratory Essays on Cultural Diversity and Common Policies.* Oxford: Berg, 1994.

Europe's External Political Identity

Bartolini, Stefano. "Exit Options, Boundary Building, Political Structuring." European University Institute Working Paper SPS 98/1, 1998.

Bull, Hedley. "Civilian Power Europe: A Contradiction in Terms." *Journal of Common Market Studies* 21 (1982): 149–170.

Bustelo, Mara, and James Heenan, eds. *The EU and Human Rights.* Oxford: Oxford University Press, 1999.

Katzenstein, Peter J. "Identities, Interests, and Security: American-European Security Relations." *American Studies* 42 (1997): 25–34.

Neumann, Iver B. *Uses of the Other: "The East" in European Identity Formation.* Minneapolis: University of Minnesota Press, 1999.

Neumann, Iver B., and Jennifer M. Welsh. "The Other in European Self-Definition: An Addendum to the Literature on International Society." *Review of International Studies* 17 (1991): 327–348.

Rokkan, Stein. *State Formation, Nation-Building, and Mass Politics in Europe: The Theory of Stein Rokkan.* Edited by Peter Flora. Oxford: Oxford University Press, 1999.

Sedelmeier, Ulrich. "Eastern Enlargement: Risk, Rationality, and Role-Compliance." In Maria Green Cowles and Michael Smith, eds., *Risks, Reforms, Resistance and Revival: The State of the European Union.* Oxford: Oxford University Press, 2000.

Stråth, Bo, ed. *Europe and the Other and Europe as the Other.* Brussels: P.I.E.-Peter Lang, 2000.

Tunander, Ola, Pavel Baev, and Victoria Ingrid Einagel, eds. *Geopolitics in Post-Wall Europe.* London: Sage, 1997.

Wæver, Ole. "European Security Identities." *Journal of Common Market Studies* 34 (1996): 103–132.

Europe's Civic Identity

Anderson, Malcolm, and Monica den Boer, eds. *Policing Across National Boundaries.* London: Pinter, 1994.

Bigo, Didier. *Police en réseaux. L'expérience européenne.* Paris: Presses de Sciences Po, 1996.

Favell, Adrian. "A Politics That Is Shared, Bounded, and Rooted? Rediscovering Civic Political Culture in Western Europe." *Theory and Society* 27 (1998): 209–236.

Geddes, Andrew. "Immigrant and Ethnic Minorities and the EU's 'Democratic Deficit.'" *Journal of Common Market Studies* 33 (1995): 197–217.

Habermas, Jürgen. "Citizenship and National Identity: Some Reflections on the Future of Europe." *Praxis International* 12, 1 (1992): 1–19.

Joppke, Christian, ed. *Challenge to the Nation-State: Immigration in Western Europe and the United States*. Oxford: Oxford University Press, 1998.

Koslowski, Rey. "European Migration Regimes: Emerging, Enlarging, and Deteriorating." *Journal of Ethnic and Migration Studies* 24 (1998): 735–749.

————. "EU Citizenship: Implications for Identity and Legitimacy." In Thomas Banschoff and Mitchell P. Smith, eds., *Legitimacy and the European Union: The Contested Polity*. London: Routledge, 1999.

Miles, Robert, and Dietrich Thränhardt, eds. *Migration and European Integration: The Dynamics of Inclusion and Exclusion*. London: Pinter, 1995.

Schnapper, Dominique. "The European Debate on Citizenship." *Dædalus* 126 (1997): 199–222.

Soysal, Yasemin N. *Limits of Citizenship: Migrants and Postnational Membership in Europe*. Chicago: University of Chicago Press, 1994.

The Contributors

Craig Calhoun is professor of sociology and history at New York University and president of the Social Science Research Council, New York.

Lars-Erik Cederman is assistant professor in the Department of Political Science, University of California at Los Angeles.

Cédric Dupont is assistant professor of political science at the Graduate Institute of International Studies, Geneva.

Vera Gowlland-Debbas is professor of public international law at the Graduate Institute of International Studies, Geneva.

Simon Hug is assistant professor at the Department of Government, University of Texas at Austin.

Jef Huysmans is lecturer at the London Centre of International Relations of the University of Kent at Canterbury.

Iver B. Neumann is senior researcher at the Norwegian Institute of International Affairs, Oslo, Norway. During the academic year 2000–2001, he is senior adviser at the Norwegian Ministry of Defense.

Frank Schimmelfennig is postdoctoral researcher in the Research Project on the Englargment of Western European Organizations (funded by the German Research Association DFG), Institute of Political Science, Darmstadt University of Technology, Germany.

Philip R. Schlesinger is professor of film and media studies and director, Stirling Media Research Institute at the University of Stirling, Scotland. He is also visiting professor of media and communications at the University of Oslo, Norway.

Pascal Sciarini is associate professor of political science at the European Institute, University of Basel, and lecturer in the Department of Political Science, University of Geneva.

Tobias Theiler is assistant lecturer in the Department of Politics at University College, Dublin.

Index

About the Book

Departing from traditional analyses based on internal measures, this book explores the creation of a European identity through the EU's interaction with the external environment. The book concentrates on three broad areas—socioeconomic issues, foreign and security policy, and home affairs—each associated with a Maastricht pillar.

The authors assess not only the benefits but also the costs of attempts to assert a European identity. Referring to debates about the respective merits of deepening and widening, they address the equally important associated trade-offs between exclusion and dilution: They point to the risks on the one hand of a Europe that excludes foreign goods, immigrants, and entire countries, and on the other of an unfocused definition of Europe that may dilute the very values that a "European identity" is intended to protect. Their systematic analysis breaks new ground on which to base future theorizing of European integration.

Lars-Erik Cederman is assistant professor of political science at the University of California at Los Angeles. His publications include *Emergent Actors: How States and Nations Develop and Dissolve.*